EMBRACING
A GAY IDENTITY

EMBRACING
A GAY IDENTITY

Gay Novels as Guides

WILFRID R. KOPONEN

BERGIN & GARVEY
Westport, Connecticut • London

Library of Congress Cataloging-in-Publication Data

Koponen, Wilfrid R.
    Embracing a gay identity : gay novels as guides / by Wilfrid R.
Koponen.
      p. cm.
    Includes bibliographical references and index.
    ISBN 0–89789–336–0 (alk. paper)
    1. American fiction—Men authors—History and criticism. 2. Gays'
writings, American—History and criticism. 3. Homosexuality and
literature—United States. 4. Identity (Psychology) in literature.
5. Gay men in literature. I. Title.
PS374.H63K67   1993
813.009′9206642—dc20   92–42090

British Library Cataloguing in Publication Data is available.

Library of Congress Catalog Card Number: 92–42090
ISBN: 0–89789–336–0

First published in 1993

Bergin & Garvey, 88 Post Road West, Westport, CT 06881
An imprint of Greenwood Publishing Group, Inc.

Printed in the United States of America

The paper used in this book complies with the
Permanent Paper Standard issued by the National
Information Standards Organization (Z39.48–1984).

10 9 8 7 6 5 4 3 2 1

For
Michael Jerman Johnson
and
Michael Arthur Philip

Amor Vincit Omnia

Contents

Tables

Acknowledgments

The following people have made thoughtful comments upon and constructive criticisms of various drafts of this manuscript: Porter Abbott, Robert Barzan, Mark Baum, Arthur Evans, Frank C. Gardiner, Eloise Knapp Hay, Libby Koponen, David Layton, Frank D. McConnell, Stephen Orgel, Jack Pantaleo, Michael Arthur Philip, Tedd Siegel, and Garrett Stewart.

Arthur Evans, Libby Koponen, and Will Roscoe, among others, have provided me with helpful insights into the publishing business.

My thanks are also due to Kenneth E. Bruer, Marsha L. Neilson, Susan Spencer, and others who provided emotional support and encouragement to me during my work on this project.

Financial support from the following helped me to complete the first draft of the manuscript: Saint Michael's Episcopal Church (New York City), the Greater Santa Barbara Community Association, and the Interdisciplinary Humanities Center and a Humanities/Social Sciences Research Grant at the University of California, Santa Barbara.

Finally, I wish to thank my editor, Lynn Flint, of Bergin & Garvey, for her belief in this work, and Margaret Hogan for her help in editing the manuscript.

1

Introduction:
Coming Out and Gay Novels

Gay to me always meant coming out—and out and out, a continuous process of self-realization.
—Mark Thompson, "The Evolution of a Fairie,"
Gay Spirit: Myth and Meaning 297

Coming out means to form and to acknowledge a gay identity. By coming out, gay people accept their sexuality as an intrinsic, and ultimately valuable, part of their self-identity. The struggles, difficulties, and obstacles encountered on this usually long and frequently difficult journey are chronicled in the gay American novels published since World War II. For decades, people have turned to gay novels to understand what it means to be gay, although only recently has gay fiction begun to receive serious literary and critical recognition and analysis. The coming-out stories gay people tell in the narratives of their own lives define and shape their adult identities. Gay novels also help gay people to find a sense of self and a feeling of belonging in the world. Yet none of the full-length studies of gay literature has focused on the crucial process of coming out. This work is the attempt to honor the centrality of coming out both in the lived experience of gay men and in the realistic gay novels that reflect and shape that experience. (This work makes no attempt to cover the journey that lesbians take in coming to accept their sexual orientation. Lesbians are able to speak and write for themselves, and they have done so. The stories they tell, though parallel in some ways to those of gay men, are different in many respects.)

Three categories of male-male sexual desire may be found in literature, as in life: homoerotic, homosexual, and gay. The term "homoerotic" has been used to indicate a person or situation that may elicit male-male sexual desire in the viewer despite the absence of any manifest or overt sexual behavior on the part of the persons being viewed. Such desire may exist only in the eye of the beholder. The persons being viewed either possess no such desire themselves, or if they do, it remains unconscious or subliminal. "Homosexual" indicates conscious awareness of sexual desire between men, whether or not acted upon, that does not necessarily involve reappraising sexual and personal identity or abandoning a heterosexual identity. "Gay" indicates not only a man's self-conscious awareness that his sexual desires are exclusively or predominantly towards other men, but also Acceptance that this sexual orientation is an intrinsic part of self. Men may be homosexual—that is, they may be aware of and act upon same-sex attractions—without ever embracing a gay identity. Such Denial of being gay often accompanies homosexual activity, both in daily life and in literature.

Although the terms "homoerotic," "homosexual," and "gay" are suggested in part by Georges-Michel Sarotte's use, following Ferenczi, of the terms "homoerotic," "homosexual," and "homogenital," the parallels are inexact. Sarotte says that all three involve "desire for physical *contact* with the *body* of another male" (xiii–xiv; emphasis in original). He uses "homoeroticism," as it is used here, to designate authors and/or characters unconscious of such desires. Sarotte's definition of the term "homosexuality," however, contradicts most other definitions and seems difficult to differentiate from his use of the term "homoeroticism." Sarotte says that "obsession with the male body indicates a clear [?] homosexuality, which is never consummated." For cases in which actual sexual contact occurs, Sarotte uses the word "homogenitalism" (xiv). Sarotte's term "homogenitalism" lumps together all sexual activity men have with other men, and thus fails to differentiate between men who embrace a gay identity and those who reject one. Sarotte thus focuses on sexual *behavior* yet ignores sexual *identity*. As recent gay literature and gay theory indicate, gay identity simply is not reducible to the presence or absence of certain sexual acts. A celibate person, for instance, may be gay. A sizeable minority of gay men has become celibate since the outbreak of the AIDS epidemic, without in any way relinquishing a gay identity. Coming to accept being gay typically follows initial experimentation with same-sex sexual encounters and acculturation with the gay subculture. The complexity of this process is overlooked in terminology like Sarotte's.

As new ways of conceiving of gay identity have emerged, the discussion that began with exploration of homoeroticism in literature has given way to the study of homosexuality in literature and, only recently, to what could be termed a distinctly gay literature.

MALE HOMOEROTICISM IN AMERICAN NOVELS

Curiously, the person who has shaken the literary world by proposing that a thinly veiled homoeroticism lies at the heart of the canon of American literature is not gay. In *Love and Death in the American Novel* (1960), Leslie Fiedler identifies homoeroticism as the major tradition within American novels, tracing it through such works as *Moby Dick* and *Adventures of Huckleberry Finn*. Traditional American male quest fiction celebrates male-male relationships. "National prudishness about unabashed heterosexual passion [led to] a glorification of male friendship" in the nineteenth century (Austen 3) through the egalitarian relationships Fiedler terms "manly friendships" and "counter-matrimony" (Fiedler 209). (In American fiction these relationships are essentially egalitarian, whereas in British fiction the hierarchical relationships of master-servant or teacher-pupil were preferred for exploring homoerotic male-male relationships [Boone, *Tradition* 236].) Joseph Boone disagrees with Fiedler over the importance in American novels of male bonding, arguing that "the canonized text of men-without-women represents a minority tradition deviating from a popular one in which women, courtship, and marriage are very much with us" (227). Critics have found these male-male narratives subversive and revolutionary, seeing in Melville and Twain a break from "traditionally masculine terms of domination" and a release from "constricting sexual categories" (272).

Fiedler has postulated that a homoerotic myth recurs throughout American fiction and culture,

> an archetypal relationship which also haunts the American psyche: two lonely men, one dark-skinned, one white, bend over a carefully guarded fire in the virgin heart of the American wilderness; they have forsaken all others for the sake of the austere, almost inarticulate, but unquestioned love which binds them to each other and to the world of nature which they have preferred to civilization. (Fiedler 187)

One example of such a relationship cited by Fiedler is that between Ishmael and Queequeg in Herman Melville's *Moby Dick*. Fiedler insists that such relationships have as their subversive goal nothing less than "to *outwit* woman, that is, to keep her from trapping the male through marriage into civilization and Christianity" (210; emphasis in original).

Fiedler's book appeared more than a decade before the official reversal of homophobic psychiatric and psychological positions by the American Psychiatric Association and the American Psychological Association, and thus it is not very surprising that Fiedler would see in such an avoidance of marriage and male-female bonding a violation of "normal" male development as this was envisioned in the 1950s. Fiedler concluded that "the freedom sought by the male protagonist 'on the run' from society *necessarily* constitutes an arrested adolescent avoidance of adult identity" (Boone, *Tradition* 228; emphasis in original).

Dennis Altman has speculated that precisely because of the importance of male bonding to Americans, "there was a particular revulsion for anything that exposed the sexual nature of such relationships" (*Homosexualization* 70). Even though Fiedler is frequently homophobic, he certainly violates the taboo against such an exposure in *Love and Death in the American Novel*. But can male bonding or even possible homoeroticism be equated with homosexuality? Can the genesis of Paul Monette's *Taking Care of Mrs. Carroll* (which is used here to illustrate Acceptance in Chapter Six) be traced to Mark Twain's *Adventures of Huckleberry Finn?*

Altman upholds the Freudian notion of the polymorphously perverse nature of sexuality and sees homosexuality as part of every man, rather than viewing homosexuals as a distinct class. But is homoeroticism latent in all nineteenth-century fiction that celebrates male friendship? Does it make sense to trace gay novels to the novels of Ernest Hemingway (which Sarotte terms "homoerotic") and those of Jack London (which Sarotte terms "homosexual")? Recent books, such as *Between Men: English Literature and Male Homosocial Desire,* by Eve Kosofsky Sedgwick, and *Double Talk: The Erotics of Male Literary Collaboration,* by Wayne Koestenbaum, have explored homoeroticism in various social arrangements. Sedgwick is concerned with patriarchal systems of power. But her discussion does not concern homosexuality, much less overt sexual encounters between men. Koestenbaum argues that male literary collaboration not only sublimates homoerotic attraction but also creates it. His thesis, though interesting and engagingly argued, seems far afield from the self-consciously gay novels of the past five decades. The literary period he explores ends with T. S. Eliot's *The Wasteland* (1922). (None of the novels being considered in this work is the product of [acknowledged] literary collaboration.) Discussions of homoeroticism (subliminal or unconscious homosexuality) in, say, novels by Hemingway or Melville promise to shed little light directly on the experience of coming out. The novels discussed in this work are explicitly gay (though not pornographic). *City of Night,* for all its calculated effort to shock, for instance, draws a discreet but opaque veil over the physical acts of homosexual intercourse; the explicit sexual acts occur between the lines.

In the case of nineteenth-century gay writers, sublimation was necessary. "With gay men tagged as defective, insane, or criminal as late as 1918, it is little wonder that they were hesitant to write fiction about themselves, even if it could be published in this country" (Austen 3). If classic American novels from *Moby Dick* to *Huckleberry Finn* carry homoerotic content, "Victorian ignorance . . . prevented our grandparents from recognizing what are now regarded as quite obviously gay motifs" (Austen 4). The psychological and sexual sophistication of the contemporary reader has caused a sharper division between gay writing and non-gay writing. There is a greater defensiveness about possib!e homoerotic (mis)reading from those whose writing is not explicitly homosexual. "The natural and unconscious celebration of homoeroticism in traditional quest narrative becomes the ultimate taboo in most contemporary rendering of the form, unless, as in some beat literature, sex between men becomes a mode of consolidating their power and mobility at the expense of women" (Boone, *Tradition* 274). With lurid sexual detail (heterosexual and homosexual) now permissible in published fiction, the subterfuge of latent homoeroticism is no longer necessary. Homoerotic subtexts of classic American novels offer few insights into gay identity, apart from possible Denial. Even there, in most imputed cases of authorial Denial, for instance, in the works of Melville, James, Twain, and Hemingway, unequivocal proof is lacking that these authors were gay or had homosexual affairs. To those who are struggling with pressing needs of defining and embracing their own sexual identity, exploring old novels in search of the homoerotic is likely to seem moot, except as an intellectual, historic, or literary exercise.

THE EMERGENCE OF GAY NOVELS

Formerly, explicit discussion of homosexuality was taboo in polite society. Literature was no exception. Homosexuals, to the extent they appeared at all in novels, were cast as emotionally immature villains, perverts, deviates, and sinners, or at best as persons suffering from a medical or psychiatric problem who were therefore to be pitied. Such homophobic prejudices have become increasingly difficult to maintain. After the advent of gay liberation (in the wake of the Stonewall Rebellion), psychiatrists and psychologists ceased to categorize homosexuality as a mental illness. In 1973 the American Psychiatric Association declassified homosexuality as a mental illness. In 1975 the American Psychological Association followed suit.

In the face of societal pressures to keep gays and gay culture invisible or "in the closet," the emergence of a body of serious gay literature in the decades since World War II has been remarkable. Formerly, many publishers simply refused to accept such works for publication, and in the years before the Stonewall Riots, critics' reactions to the few gay novels that were published by major presses were generally grossly homophobic. Gore Vidal's novel *The City and the Pillar* (1948) is widely acknowledged as the first openly gay novel written by an author with an established literary reputation to be published by a mainstream publisher in the United States. Many said that its publication would ruin Vidal's literary reputation and career. Vidal's writing openly about a gay theme tarnished his masculine credentials earned from his two tough and "manly" war novels. In the controversy that its publication unleashed, *The City and the Pillar* was said by some to be an affront to all the men connected with the war effort. Vidal was attacked in the press for failing to replicate in *The City and the Pillar* "the masculine ethos and wartime atmosphere of *Williwaw* (1946) and *In a Yellow Wood* (1947)," his previous novels, which had been well received (Adams 15). The *New York Times* "refused to print advertisements for it" (Sarotte 23).

Despite the hostility with which it was received in some quarters, *The City and the Pillar* "was a best-seller in America [and] opened the door for the overtly homosexual novel" (Sarotte 23). Its form, the Bildungsroman, "is a genre particularly well suited to capture the complexities of the coming-out process. Not surprisingly, the Bildungsroman that culminates in the protagonist's acceptance of his homosexual identity is the most popular novelistic form of gay fiction" (Summers 23). Nevertheless, although minor presses released gay novels in the wake of *The City and the Pillar*, such as James Barr's *Quatrefoil* (1950), the difficulties of publishing such works are suggested by the fact that "James Barr" is a pseudonym. It was eight years before another major press published another explicitly gay novel, James Baldwin's *Giovanni's Room* (1956). Prior to its acceptance for publication, Baldwin was advised in all seriousness by one publisher to burn the manuscript (Weatherby 119), and many prospective publishers rejected the manuscript. Baldwin, like Vidal, encountered opposition from critics who had praised his earlier work, *Go Tell It on the Mountain* (1953). Yet *Giovanni's Room*, here the subject of Chapter Three, has endured and become one of the most widely read gay novels. In 1956, the year in which it was published, an obscenity case erupted over the publication of Allen Ginsberg's graphically homosexual poem "Howl." The outcome was greater freedom to publish sexually explicit literature, although critics continued to object to frankly gay literature. Critics attacked John Rechy's best-selling *City of Night* (1963), which is discussed here in Chapter Two.

Given the almost complete absence of gay role models in film, television, magazines, and newspapers, the gay novels published in the first two decades after World War II provided one of the few public and readily available sources of information about gay experience. These novels were invaluable for men questioning their own sexuality who were unable or unwilling to travel to the enclaves of the gay underground in the country's largest cities, which had flourished (despite being ignored) since the emergence of large cities in America following the Civil War (Greenberg 355). The unnamed protagonist of *The Beautiful Room Is Empty*, which is set in the mid-1950s through the late 1960s, reads both *Giovanni's Room* and *City of Night*.

Although gay men devoured novels such as these, they may not always have found in them the comfort they sought. Until recently it was a truism that most homosexuals in literature were pathetic and contemptible, or at least sad and lonely. Early gay novels frequently depict anguished gay characters, probably accurately mirroring the internalized homophobia of most homosexuals of the time. Homosexuality was pushed underground.

At least in the pages of those novels, though, the existence of gays, however troubled, was frankly acknowledged, whereas "mainstream" society ignored homosexuality and underestimated its prevalence. Hence the shock that jolted the American public with the publication of the Kinsey Report in 1948. The researchers found that

> ten per cent of the males [in the sample] are more or less exclusively homosexual . . . for at least three years between the ages of 16 and 55. This is one male in ten in the white male population. . . . [The researchers also found that] four per cent of the white males are exclusively homosexual throughout their lives, after the onset of adolescence. [Furthermore,] thirty-seven per cent of the total [American] male population has at least some overt homosexual experience to the point of orgasm between adolescence and old age. (Kinsey 650–51)

These findings have led to a widespread assertion that one in ten Americans is gay. Yet a subsequent Kinsey Institute survey, conducted in 1970, the results of which were not released for almost two decades, casts doubt on the earlier findings. It found the proportion of men with at least some adult gay experience leading to orgasm to be 20.3 percent, rather than the previously reported 37 percent, and found no men in their sample who reported being exclusively gay throughout their adult lives (Freiberg 15). " 'The one-in-ten figure is really a media creation,' said John D'Emilio, assistant professor of history at the University of North Carolina at Greensboro. 'When Kinsey's [1948] study came out . . . the media latched onto it as a big news story. . . . Gay activists picked up on it later' " (Freiberg 15). After the publication of the Kinsey Report in 1948, Sarotte notes, "it became difficult to stereotype the invert without the risk of being regarded as backward [or] ill-informed" (22). Despite Sarotte's ostensible claim that criticism of homosexuals became more difficult, Sarotte uses the pejorative term "invert." The use of this term colors Sarotte's statement and makes it seem more a lament that moral condemnation of homosexuality has become less acceptable.

Since the Stonewall Riots in 1969, social attitudes towards homosexuality have become somewhat more liberal and gay novels have flourished and received critical acclaim from the "mainstream" press. Much of this has no doubt been a result of the changes launched by the civil rights movement and the women's liberation movement in the 1960s. Since the outbreak of the AIDS epidemic in the early 1980s, much more media attention has been devoted to gay concerns (particularly to the devastating AIDS health crisis facing gay men and others) than ever before. A more frank acknowledgment of homosexuality has resulted, though not a wholesale abandonment of homophobic attitudes, as is evident in the seemingly endless pronouncements of various politicians such as Senator Jesse Helms and religious figures such as Jerry Falwell and Jimmy Swaggert. Television evangelists are not the only opponents of gay rights in the Christian religious community; within the Roman Catholic Church, Cardinals Joseph Ratzinger and John O'Connor, among others, have been consistent and vocal opponents of gay rights. Despite continued homophobia in society, gay literature flourished in the late 1970s and throughout the 1980s. This has continued in the 1990s: "Four hundred gay and lesbian books were scheduled for publication in the first three months of 1990 alone" (Frankel n.p.). Yet "some gay observers have ambivalent feelings about the arrival of gay writers in mainstream publishing [because] only 'polite' writers are acceptable . . . [and] grittier, more experimental talents . . . have a much tougher time getting heard" (Clemons et al. 73–74). David Leavitt is cited as an example of a gay author experiencing "mainstream success," whereas Robert Glück and Dennis Cooper are cited as examples of "more experimental talents." Despite the crumbling of the walls of silence surrounding gay literature, many homosexuals continue to live closeted lives, and gay role models are only beginning to emerge from obscurity through the newly visible gay community.

In the absence of readily available gay role models, many men have had to "reinvent the wheel" in coming out and forging a sense of gay identity. The coming-out stories of gay men are thus quite varied, and much of this variety is evident in recent gay fiction. Some recognize they are gay early in life, some late; some accept it swiftly and readily, some only after great struggle, while others deny their homosexuality throughout their lives. In one way or another, however, men who have come to accept being gay regard coming out as the crucible in which their sense of identity as gay men was formed, and it is thus central to the understanding of gay men and gay male culture. The increased willingness of gay men to come out may be the single greatest legacy of the gay liberation movement. But with gay studies and gay scholarship having only recently become a "legitimate" undertaking, much of the coming-out process remains to be studied.

As Herbert Blau notes, "whatever the identity now being claimed or seized, no homosexual is raised *as* a homosexual" (119; emphasis in original). Parents expect their children to be heterosexual. Unlike gay men and lesbians, heterosexuals have many well-established, institutionalized initiation rituals as well as numerous guides for periods of personal transition. Their legally recognized, and socially and religiously sanctioned, sexual unions (namely marriages) are celebrated in elaborate public wedding ceremonies, with entire etiquette books devoted to the minutiae surrounding them. By contrast, same-sex unions are frequently reduced, in effect, to the status of "the love that dare not speak its name" and no clear models exist for the ideal gay relationship. Should it ape heterosexual marriage? Should gay unions be monogamous? Gay activists disagree over such things as whether the fight for legal and religious recognition of gay unions and/or marriages should be undertaken at this time. Despite lack of consensus within and outside the gay community, some municipalities have enacted policies that would extend such things as bereavement leave to gay employees and health benefits to the domestic partners of gay employees comparable to those offered to spouses of married employees. Certain churches, such as the Metropolitan Community Church, are not waiting for the state to grant marriage licenses to gay couples to bless these unions in "holy union" ceremonies. Within some other churches, such as the Episcopal Church, holy union ceremonies are now permitted in some dioceses and parishes but not in others. Gay men have had to forge a sense of sexual identity in comparative isolation, particularly in the early stages of the coming-out process before they have built support networks with other gays. What exactly does it mean to come out, to accept one's homosexual inclinations and to form a sense of identity as a gay man?

COMING OUT: THE GAY HERO'S JOURNEY

> A blunder—apparently the merest chance—reveals an unsuspected world, and the individual is drawn into a relationship with forces that are not rightly understood. As Freud has shown, blunders are not the merest chance. They are the result of suppressed desires and conflicts. They are ripples on the surface of life, produced by unsuspected springs. And these may be very deep—as deep as the soul itself. The blunder may amount to the opening of a destiny.
>
> —Campbell 51

Coming out, the process through which a gay man comes to accept his sexual orientation, may be triggered by a seemingly trivial occurrence, although leading to a momentous outcome. This unfolding of sexual identity is similar in some ways to the three stages of the hero's journey, as discussed by Joseph Campbell, of Departure, Initiation, and Return, although, like the hero's journey, this paradigm allows for almost infinite variations.

The hero of myths and legends is often a youth, that is, a person on the threshold between childhood or adolescence and adulthood, whose choices and actions in his quest will influence his adult life. The coming-out process also typically, though not invariably, begins at a young age, as adult identity begins to take shape. Most gay men report that they were aware of their sexual difference by the age of seventeen (Troiden 363; Bell 80). Although self-labeling as homosexual usually begins in the late teens or early twenties, sometimes it will not occur until the late thirties or forties (Weinberg 164). Some men may not admit to having same-sex attractions or may not express them until much later in life, if at all. (The heroes of both novels discussed in Chapter Two, *Falconer* and *City of Night*, equivocate about their homosexual desires and behavior, and Farragut, the hero of *Falconer*, does not engage in homosexual behavior until he is middle-aged.)

As a young man's awareness grows of feelings that are different from those expected of him by parents, authority figures, and peers, there is an internal call to violate sexual taboos against same-sex encounters. This may lead to a departure from the familiar and the exploration of forbidden desires and behaviors. While a sense of sexual identity remains tentative and confused, there is often an initiation into an "unsuspected world," the gay subculture, which at first may seem alien and frightening to the newcomer, though later it may seem more supportive and consoling. Completing the coming-out process may lead a gay man to a return, a reintegration into a larger society as a transformed person who has integrated being gay with the rest of his roles and activities.

A man who has come out no longer feels any internal need to hide his sexual orientation from others; he has transcended his largely self-imposed sense of social isolation. Potential discrimination from others may cause a prudent individual to be selective about self-disclosure, but this is very different from a nondisclosure motivated by shame, guilt, or self-loathing. The crucial characteristic that distinguishes someone who has come out from someone who has not done so is self-acceptance as a gay person. The hero of American fiction, whether gay or straight, differs from the hero of classical quest romances in that he "strives not so much for reintegration into society as for reintegration of his often fragmented identity" (Boone, *Tradition* 229). The society into which the gay hero becomes assimilated may be the society of those accepting of gay people, rather than society at large. Joining this society may involve leaving behind many who embody homophobic attitudes, including (in many cases) families of origin, which explains why the relatives of gay characters are absent from much gay fiction.

Campbell's model and the theoretical models of the coming-out process discussed below may suggest an invariable progression from beginning to end, an automatic sequence of events. These step-by-step schemas may lend to a narrative framework a sense of inevitability. This is common in retrospective personal accounts of the coming-out process, in which the end result has already been reached, and hence seems certain. Yet usually there is nothing neat and orderly for boys and men discovering their homosexual desires for the first time. Becoming sexually aroused in the presence of others of the same sex may happen without warning. Catching oneself fantasizing about a same-sex sexual encounter may unleash chaotic feelings. Such a "blunder" may occur at a most inconvenient time, when one's thoughts are on other things, and one's self-image as heterosexual has hardly prepared one for such an occurrence. Although disturbing in and of itself, upon closer scrutiny the "chance event" may turn out to have been merely the tip of the iceberg, most of whose mass lies hidden in the dark ocean of the unconscious. Like a ship's collision with an iceberg, the encounter may upset everything. A young man's initial homosexual experiences may precipitate a personal crisis. A complete reassessment of self, identity, life plans, and social values may ensue, leading to a death of the old identity, initiation into a new world, and rebirth as a gay man.

Reappraisal of self may not occur automatically once initial homosexual responses, feelings, or actions become manifest. Such experiences may be repressed and compartmentalized so that the old sense of self can remain "uncontaminated." Much is at stake in preserving a conventional sexual identity. The potential losses (real or imagined) involved in admitting "I may be homosexual" are enormous. Panic may set in. Fears and anxieties multiply. One may lose (or fear losing) the esteem and respect of family, peers, and colleagues. Social standing and prestige may be forfeited, while job security and legal rights may be jeopardized. (In most parts of the country, homosexuals have no legal protection against discrimination in employment and housing.) One may fear becoming cast out of the larger, predominantly heterosexual, society. If one wants to have children and raise a family, this may now seem impossible, or at least enormously complicated. (Even so, a "baby boom" began among lesbian couples during the 1980s, and gay fathers' groups have been organized in many places.) Trying to hold on to a heterosexual identity is akin to the hero's refusal to follow his call away from the familiar, across the threshold symbolically represented by the wall surrounding the city and into the wilderness. (The city represents civilization, consciousness, and the superego, whereas the wilderness represents nature, the subconscious, and the id.) Those who cling to a "safe" heterosexual identity, like the hero who turns his back on his call, are afraid to face the chaos beyond the city wall, the chaos of primal desires.

What can be gained by coming out, like what the hero gains from venturing into the primal chaos beyond the city wall, may become evident only in retrospect: an improved self-image, a sense of integrity and forthrightness, greater confidence, an improved ability to relate to others emotionally, proof that one can live through and prosper in the face of adversity, and respect from others. Deriving such benefits may help instill a sense of purpose into the struggle to come out, as well as making it seem more coherent after it has been completed. But order and an internally consistent logic to the progression of events in coming out may be evident only in hindsight. This process frequently is painful and usually is lengthy. It has been estimated that, on average, ten to fourteen years elapse between the initial awareness of same-sex feelings and Acceptance and integration of them (Coleman, "Stages" 41). "Many people avoid identifying themselves as homosexuals [for] as long as possible" (Fisher 11). Many wait several years before doing anything to reduce the cognitive dissonance surrounding issues of homosexuality and identity (Weinberg 140). Yet coming out may indeed lead to a happy ending. To those in the midst of coming out, however, who have not yet come to accept being gay, the road ahead often seems anything but clear-cut or inviting. The hero's path is often into dark, uncharted places.

The feeling of being the only gay person in the world, of suffering from a unique problem, is common among people who are beginning to suspect they may be homosexual. This feeling of isolation has been reinforced by American postwar novels, which show homosexuals as isolated outsiders on the fringe of mainstream society. The invisibility of most gay people to those struggling with this feeling of aloneness heightens their sense of alienation. The causal link between homosexuals' invisibility and the oppression they suffer makes homosexuals unique among minorities (Altman, *Homosexualization* 136). Most gay people have difficulty finding gay role models and peers, especially at first. The existence of most homosexuals is hidden. Compounding the problem is the furtiveness of typical initial attempts to locate and contact them. Most men who have engaged in homosexual behavior do not consider themselves to be gay and do not publicly identify themselves as gay. The homosexual population thus seems smaller than it actually is (if it is defined simply by sexual behavior) and is hard to find. Most parents, siblings, and other relatives of gays and lesbians are heterosexual, forcing gay people to search outside their family context for gay people to identify with and to emulate, whereas most heterosexuals' parents serve virtually automatically as role models. Just as the hero needs to find helpers to assist him in his perilous journey, the person coming out fares better if he can find supportive peers and role models, guides familiar with what is to the new initiate unfamiliar territory.

The difficulties in finding one's way through the coming-out process have been compounded in American society by the systematic suppression of knowledge about gay people in movies, television, and periodicals. Until recently, gays simply were not mentioned much at all in polite society other than as the butt of homophobic jokes or in other derogatory ways. The Motion Picture Association of America virtually ensured that gay characters did not appear in movies from 1930 until the Motion Picture Production Code was changed in 1966 (Manvell 124). Prior to 1970 all mention of homosexuality on television was effectively prohibited. Gay characters and topics were absent from television situation comedies until the early 1970s, when they began appearing in a few episodes of such popular television series as *All in the Family* and *Maude* (Leo 36).

The *New York Times* all but ignored the riots at the Stonewall Inn that began on the night of June 27, 1969, despite their symbolic and historical importance to the contemporary gay community. That eruption of pent-up anger at what began as a routine raid by New York City police on a gay bar in Greenwich Village has since then come to mark the birth of the gay liberation movement, which quickly replaced the more accommodationist homophile movement of the 1950s and 1960s, and which in turn was superseded by the gay rights movement. Joseph C. Goulden chronicles in *Fit to Print: A. M. Rosenthal and His Times* that the *New York Times* continued its policy of "benign neglect" of gay issues under the leadership of former editor and publisher Arthur Sulzberger. In the mid-1980s, "AIDS activists liked to talk about the occasion when the *New York Times* devoted front-page space to a disease that felled seventeen Lippizaner stallions in Europe, when no story about AIDS had ever appeared on page one" (Monette, *Borrowed Time* 227). The paper refused until 1987 to print the word "gay" (Labonte, "Giving Credit" 60). It was not only the word that was avoided: the *New York Times* "generally avoided mentioning homosexuality except in its science columns, where it was invariably referred to and discussed as an illness" (Brown 29). Only recently has this homophobic tradition of the *New York Times* been altered, as evident in "Richard Hall's five-thousand-word survey of gay literature ["Gay Fiction Comes Home"] in the June 19 [1988] *New York Times Book Review*—an openly gay writer writing with knowledgeable enthusiasm about openly gay writing" (Labonte, "Giving Credit" 60). Hall notes, "Gay writing has changed since World War II from a literature of guilt and apology to one of political defiance and celebration of sexual difference" (1). Gay writing has been characterized by a "progression toward self-acceptance and socialization" (Hall 1).

Despite some progress, historical events involving thousands of gays, such as the Nazi persecution and extermination of homosexuals, continue to be ignored. Gays are seldom mentioned in discussions of the Holocaust, despite the thousands of homosexuals who died in Nazi concentration camps. (Robert Peterson estimates that between one quarter of a million and half a million homosexuals perished in Nazi concentration camps; Richard Plant gives a more conservative estimate: "We may reasonably estimate the number of males convicted of homosexuality from 1933 to 1944 [in Nazi Germany] at between fifty thousand and sixty-three thousand. . . . Altogether, somewhere between five thousand and fifteen thousand homosexuals perished behind barbed wire fences" [149, 154]. Himmler was staunchly homophobic, and after the 1934 murder of Roehm, the chief of the SA, under orders from Hitler, the plight of homosexuals in Germany clearly was bleak. "Gays were often shipped to high-mortality tasks in [concentration camp] factories and quarries. . . . The mortality rate of the homosexuals was higher" than for other groups [Plant 180].)

The homosexuality of individual figures, from kings and presidents to artists, often has been ignored in historical and biographical accounts, just as events affecting large numbers of gay people have been ignored. Acknowledgments of gay contributions to mainstream culture continue to be few and far between. Even now, only a few years after Andy Warhol's death, as the story of his life and career is being told by those in the mainstream, Warhol's homosexuality is seldom even mentioned. The crucial influence of gay culture and gay sensibility on pop culture of the 1960s—ranging from "camp" to Warhol's pop art—is being left out of the official versions of Warhol's life and the catalogues of the retrospective exhibits of his work, which are "stripping away Warhol's identity as a gay man. His image is rapidly being sanitized for public consumption" (Hardy 59).

The difficulties of coming out are compounded by the systematic suppression of gay culture. The quest for gay identity can at times seem as elusive as the Knights of the Round Table's quest for the Holy Grail. Gay identity itself may be hard to define. The two major current theoretical approaches to gay identity, essentialism versus constructionism (which are discussed here in Chapter Seven) seem as irreconcilable as the wave versus the particle theories of light.

DENIAL, ANGER, BARGAINING, DEPRESSION, AND ACCEPTANCE AS STAGES OF COMING OUT

No consensus has yet emerged regarding the process known as coming out. Although several theories exist about how sexual orientation is formed, little empirical research has been conducted on this subject. The names used here of identifiable stages men pass through in the coming-out process are derived from the research of Dr. Elisabeth Kübler-Ross, who used them to describe the individual reconciliation with imminent death.

Discovering that one is homosexual, like learning that death is approaching, may come as a shock, but the coming-out process leads not to annihilation of being but to a rebirth as a gay person after mourning the death of the inauthentic sense of self as heterosexual. Using Kübler-Ross's Denial, Anger, Bargaining, Depression, and Acceptance model is not intended to suggest an intrinsic connection between love and death or homosexuality and mortality, even though, due to the AIDS crisis, " 'making love,' one of the sweetest phrases in the English language, now suggests a cause of death" (Sheppard 68). Indeed, AIDS-phobia in some cases stems from homophobia and its "equation of homosexuality with the unnatural, the irrational, and the diseased" (Edelman 308–9). (All but one of the six novels discussed in depth in this work were written prior to the outbreak of the AIDS crisis. The most recent of the six, *The Beautiful Room Is Empty*, though published in 1988, is set in the years between the mid-1950s and 1969. Thus the impact of AIDS upon gay novels is beyond the scope of this work.) Homosexuality, unlike a disease, is neither "catching" nor a "contagion." Rather, the structure of Kübler-Ross's model charts the stages of reacting to an initially shocking discovery and adjusting to the irrevocable changes such knowledge brings in its wake. Kübler-Ross's model is not meant as a definitive model of the lengthy and complex process of coming out. Yet each phase does correspond with significant milestones in the lived experience, the feelings and perceptions, of gay men in America after World War II. Novels by gay and bisexual male authors reveal this. Crucial differences between the terms as used by Kübler-Ross and the terms as used here should be noted.

Kübler-Ross discusses the stages as follows. Denial is the first reaction most people have to ideas they do not want to consider: "No, not me, it cannot be true" (Kübler-Ross 34). Denial is used to gain time to "mobilize other, less radical defenses" and "is usually . . . temporary" (35). Anger follows when people ask, "Why me?" Feelings of rage, envy, and resentment may be directed or projected virtually at random (44). The third phase, Bargaining, is the attempt, usually successful "only for brief periods of time," to enter "into some sort of agreement which may postpone the inevitable" (72–74). "Most bargains are made with God," usually for a reprieve in return for a promise of some sort of good behavior (74). Soon, "numbness or stoicism, . . . anger and rage [are] replaced by a sense of great loss" (75). So begins the stage of Depression. Finally may come a stage during which Depression and Anger abate and Acceptance grows (99). In the mortality process, Kübler-Ross cautions, "Acceptance should not be mistaken for a happy stage. It is almost void of feelings. It is as if the pain had gone, the struggle is over, and there comes a time for 'the final rest before the long journey' " (100).

In the individual's confrontation with mortality, the end result is the loss of everything one has held dear, including life itself, whereas in coming out, the end result is the creation of a new and positive sense of self, in which one's homosexuality is accepted as an intrinsic part of self. In the coming-out process, Denial, as its name suggests, is the refusal to admit the obvious. It typically involves self-deception as well as deceiving others. Just as Denial of impending death may flourish in the face of manifest physical symptoms of deterioration, Denial of homosexuality often exists concurrently with homosexual behaviors.

Anger in the coming-out process, as in the mortality process, contains an element of rage over the question "Why me?" Homosexuality, like death, is often regarded as an uninvited intruder that complicates and ruins all of one's carefully laid plans. In the case of coming out, however, there is the added burden that those gay men struggling with Anger feel the full brunt of the discrimination and bigotry gay people face. A gay couple faces obstacles and impediments that a heterosexual couple does not encounter.

Bargaining, in the coming-out process, as in the approach of death, is a less well understood phenomenon, and it is probably the phase most frequently bypassed in its entirety in coming out. A homosexual with a weak ego may Bargain to change his sexual orientation in order to recapture the respect and status he feels that gay men are denied. Typical Bargaining strategies fall into the religious (as in the dying process) as well as the psychological (unlike the dying process). Some churches insist that through faith healing or some other intervention, sexual orientation can be changed. Some psychiatrists still claim that through psychoanalysis, homosexuality can be cured, while others make similar claims about aversion therapy. Neither religious nor psychological claims regarding change in sexual orientation are validated by empirical evidence (see Chapter Four).

Depression, in the mortality process as well as in the coming-out process, involves a sense of resignation or reluctant toleration of things that are perceived as regrettable but unchangeable. The dominant feeling is of loss, a process of mourning for what once was and is no more, or what might have been but never shall be. In coming out, this involves feeling alienated from mainstream culture, yet not at peace with the gay subculture, which is seen as an inferior substitute. Feelings of hopelessness and despondency may be accompanied by self-destructive behaviors, such as drug and alcohol abuse and compulsive (and unfulfilling) impersonal sexual encounters.

Acceptance is the stage that differs the most between the process of dying and the process of coming out. In dying, this is the entrance into an emotionless, virtually numb state of readiness to die. In coming out, this is the stage in which one leaves behind the turmoil of soul-searching, rearranging of life plans, experimenting, and trial and error, all of which stem from confronting a homosexual orientation. Changes in self-perception and sexual attitudes continue, though in more subtle, less wrenching ways. It is a rebirth in which joy and other emotions may be felt more acutely now that the defense mechanism of psychic numbing, typical of the preceding stages of the coming-out process, is no longer necessary. In the coming-out process, Acceptance indicates the achievement of a stable sense of gay identity in which being gay is viewed as a positive element of self. Of course, this does not mean that the gay man in the stage of Acceptance has reached some promised land free from the homophobia of others. Rather, it means that the boundaries between self and others have been clarified. The homophobia of others is seen as a reflection of their lack of emotional maturity, tolerance, and understanding, not as an indication that one lacks self-worth. "To come out is to refuse to oppress oneself, to refuse to play the game. . . . It is the only real form of self-respect" (Fisher 250).

Kübler-Ross's five-stage model is parallel to theoretical models of the coming-out process, namely: Richard Troiden's four-stage model of Gay Identity Acquisition, Vivienne Cass's six-stage model of Homosexual Identity Formation, and Eli Coleman's model of the five developmental stages of the coming-out process. Although for purposes of discussion it is useful to differentiate four, five, or six discrete stages of the coming-out process, "It is not uncommon for individuals to work on developmental tasks of several different stages simultaneously" (Coleman, "Stages" 32). The stages in any given model are thus not necessarily mutually exclusive or sequential.

Richard Troiden's Model of Gay Identity Acquisition

Richard Troiden has proposed a model of "gay identity acquisition" with four stages: Sensitization, Dissociation and Signification, Coming Out, and Commitment. Troiden bases his model on gay men's retrospective accounts of the coming-out process (Brady 16) and draws on previous research.

The first stage, "Sensitization," involves feeling alienated from one's peers with little awareness of homosexuality as the cause. This sense of difference emerges in childhood, during the pre-teen years and crystallizes during high school "into a distinct sense of *sexual* dissimilarity" that often leads to homosexual experiences (Troiden 363; emphasis in original). During this stage, past events are reinterpreted and come to be seen as potentially homosexual. Such a reinterpretation "appears to be a necessary condition for the eventual adoption of a gay identity" (363). The alienation felt in this stage resembles that experienced during Kübler-Ross's stage of Anger.

"Dissociation and Signification," the second stage of Troiden's model, involves keeping sexual activity and sexual desires separated from one's conscious awareness of sexual identity. "The suspicion that one 'might' be homosexual . . . mark[s] the outset of the stage" (363). Rationalizations are rife. Homosexuality may be seen at this time as something that, in time, will be outgrown. Others deceive themselves by seeing their homosexuality as resulting from "loneliness and the lack of female companionship" or dismiss it as mere "sexual experimentation and curiosity" (363). Significantly, homosexual feelings and behavior may be acknowledged during this stage without any necessary belief that these are permanent. In fact, for most, this is the case, with such sensations being regarded as temporary (363). This allows a person to perform and acknowledge homosexual acts while simultaneously hedging about being a homosexual. This stage parallels Denial.

Troiden uses the term "Coming Out' for the third stage, the onset of which is marked by "the decision to label one's sexual feelings as definitely homosexual" (366). Of course, others have used the term "coming out" differently (as Troiden acknowledges), to refer to the public disclosure of this shift in identity to other gay people and/or to the public at large. Still others, as in the present work, define "coming out" as the entire process ranging from the first awareness of homosexual feelings and attractions to the full Acceptance of them and integration of them into the sense of self-identity. In any case, resistance to self-labeling as homosexual is indicated by Troiden's discovery that about two out of three of the men he interviewed "*did not* designate themselves as homosexual . . . at the time they designated their feelings as such" (366; emphasis in original). Often these attractions are seen to indicate bisexuality. Confusion, lack of knowledge, and ambivalence eventually prove very taxing. Many men decide at this stage that any clear sexual identity, whether "heterosexual, bisexual, or homosexual[,] would be preferable to the sexual ambiguity and confusion they [are] experiencing" (368). As a clearer sense of sexual identity emerges, men feel happier (370). Self-labeling as homosexual often happens at about the same time as the individual's first participation in the gay subculture, typically long after same-sex sexual expression has become routine (368, 366). Consequently, what is crucial to this stage is not homosexual behavior in itself but rather "changes in the conception of one's identity and of one's view of homosexuality and homosexuals" (366). Becoming involved in and attuned to the gay subculture often leads one to see being gay as a "legitimate life-style alternative," a radical shift in attitude. Troiden reports that almost all of the participants in his study "recalled having viewed homosexuality as a form of mental illness" prior to coming to see themselves as being homosexual (370, 369). Troiden's findings, published in 1979, may be dated, as his sample of respondents was drawn from men who went through their childhoods and teen years prior to the declassification of homosexuality as a mental illness by the American Psychiatric Association and the American Psychological Association. This view of homosexuality as illness has diminished since the 1970s, and has become rare within the gay community. Contact with openly gay people helps individuals to shed the notion of homosexuality as illness. This in turn enables men to accept being gay. Troiden's "Coming Out" stage matches Depression and the transcendence of it.

Troiden terms the final phase of gay identity acquisition "Commitment" and defines this as "the fusion of gay sexuality and emotionality into a meaningful whole," manifested by the taking of a lover or the emotional readiness to do so (369). "The taking of a lover *confirms* gay identity" (369; emphasis in original). " 'You first *know* you are a homosexual,' Christopher Isherwood has said, 'when you discover you can fall in love with another man' " (Altman, *Oppression* 20; emphasis in original). Mere same-sex sexual activity would constitute a homosexual identity, but romantic and social involvement with other gays are seen as essential to a *gay* identity (Troiden 369). This closely matches the stage of Acceptance described in Chapter Six. Troiden defines the terms "homosexual" and "gay" somewhat differently from the ways in which they are defined herein: the term "gay" is used to designate self-acknowledgment and acknowledgment to others of same-sex attractions and behavior, whereas the term "homosexual" is used to designate the presence of same-sex attraction and behavior that may not fully be accepted by the practitioner, who has not integrated these feelings and behaviors into his sense of self in a positive and forthright manner. In any case, most gay people do not use the two terms interchangeably. Being gay involves acknowledging same-sex sexual orientation as a basic part of one's identity, while homosexuality does not.

A significant and controversial conclusion of Troiden's is that "gay identities are not . . . acquired in an absolute, fixed, or final sense" (371). Troiden believes that the vast majority of men in America who engage in homosexual behavior never embrace a gay identity; the proportion of such men who do embrace a gay identity is "tiny" (372). This may account for why so few of the novels chronicling male homosexuals' experiences depict gay men who have fully accepted being gay and who have formed stable long-term relationships. As Troiden notes, "the route to gay identity [is] fraught with ambiguity, confusion, and uncertainty. For only a small minority [is] the gay identity taken on rapidly" (372).

Vivienne Cass's Model of Homosexual Identity Formation

Vivienne Cass developed a theoretical model of how homosexual identity is acquired based on interpersonal congruency theory and on "several years of clinical work" with male and female homosexuals (Cass 219). Unlike Troiden, Cass does not derive her model from retrospective accounts (Brady 17). The six stages in her Homosexual Identity Formation model are: Identity Confusion, Identity Comparison, Identity Tolerance, Identity Acceptance, Identity Pride, and Identity Synthesis. Cass assumes that acquiring a homosexual identity is an active process and that there is nothing inevitable about progressing from one stage to the next; the individual may refuse to go on to the next stage. Cass refers to this as "identity foreclosure" (Cass 220).

Cass calls the first stage "Identity Confusion." This begins when the person can say, " 'My behavior may be called homosexual' " (222). This behavior contradicts the person's self-image as a heterosexual and others' beliefs that the person is heterosexual (222). The person begins to wonder "Who am I?" and "Am I homosexual?" Doubts and "personal alienation are paramount" (223). If the person thinks that he or she is homosexual and that this is basically acceptable, one approach is to gather more information and proceed with the unfolding of a homosexual identity.

If the person in the Identity Confusion stage admits, "Yes, I may be homosexual," but this is perceived to be unacceptable, an attempted suppression of homosexual feelings and behavior may result, accompanied by the denial that such things apply to oneself. The person then refuses to admit that he or she may be homosexual, a close parallel with Denial (223). (The Denial that the homosexual label has personal relevance is a strategy employed by the protagonists of both the novels discussed in Chapter Two: Farragut, the hero of John Cheever's *Falconer* and the unnamed protagonist of John Rechy's *City of Night*.) Such Denial may be reinforced by proclaiming vehemently anti-homosexual opinions. This strategy is reflected in the cliché that some of the most stridently homophobic people are, in fact, those attempting to deny their own homosexuality. If the person cannot inhibit homosexual behavior, he or she may seek out a therapist known to view homosexuality as an illness for help in doing so (224). (This corresponds to the Bargaining strategy employed by the unnamed protagonist in Edmund White's novel *The Beautiful Room Is Empty*, who enters therapy to change his sexual orientation, as discussed in Chapter Four.) Another form of Denial, less drastic than complete suppression of homosexual behavior, is to engage in homosexual behavior while refusing to label it or the people who engage in it homosexual. Cass cites prisons, in which many inmates have sex with others of their gender without labeling this behavior as homosexual or "seeing themselves as potentially homosexual" (224). This is precisely the situation of Ezekiel Farragut, the hero of John Cheever's novel *Falconer*. Cass also mentions that hustlers use a similar rationalization. Thus she accounts for a psychology prevalent in the world of male prostitutes, the principal milieu depicted in many of John Rechy's novels, including *City of Night*. When men preserve their sense of themselves as heterosexual while engaging in homosexual behavior, identity foreclosure occurs (225).

If the person does not deny the possibility of being homosexual, he or she comes to think "I *may be* a homosexual" and thus enters the second stage of Cass's model, the "Identity Comparison" (225; emphasis in original), a time of alienation. The person "has a sense of 'not belonging' to society at large as well as to specific subgroups such as family and peers. 'I'm different' " is a common perception that in some cases may result in the feeling " 'I'm the only one in the world like this' " (225). Passing as heterosexual is often continued, and if successful, reduces but does not eliminate anxiety about social and sexual identity (226–27). Rationalizations of bisexuality or of potential heterosexuality may be employed to lessen the anxiety. A more extreme strategy is to adopt an asexual self-image. In some cases of severe alienation, people may attempt to change their sexual orientation, as in Bargaining. Inhibiting all homosexual behavior, devaluing homosexuality, and portraying heterosexuality favorably are means to achieve this. "This permits the rejection of self as homosexual" (229). (This resembles the Bargaining strategy discussed in Chapter Four.)

Although still reluctant to admit to being homosexual, many reach the "Identity Tolerance" stage, which resembles Depression, deciding, "I probably am a homosexual." The homosexual subculture is sought to reduce feelings of alienation (Cass 229), as happens among the principal characters of *Dancer from the Dance*, as discussed in Chapter Five. Negative experiences can reinforce low self-esteem and confirm homophobic stereotypes. Identity foreclosure may follow. Conversely, positive experiences, such as meeting a potential lover and finding role models and support groups, may lead to increased commitment to homosexual self-image. "The concept of [a gay] 'reference group' . . . can sometimes be quite subtle. It does not necessarily require some continuing, long-term relationship with people whom one knows very well" (Weinberg 121).

In "Identity Acceptance," Cass's fourth stage, a homosexual self-image is accepted, rather than merely being tolerated, and social contacts with gays are strengthened. Increasingly, homosexuality is seen as legitimate, either in private only, which may result in continued efforts to "pass" as heterosexual, or publicly as well (Cass 232).

In Cass's fifth stage, "Identity Pride," the person coming out feels that being gay is completely acceptable. This clashes with "society's rejection of this concept" (Cass 233). Tension mounts, and anger and frustration result. Although Cass's "Identity Pride" stage contains anger, it differs from the stage of Anger as discussed in this work in Chapter Three. David, in *Giovanni's Room*, is angry about being gay. His attitude is "Why me? How could this be happening to me?" He resents society's condemnation of homosexuality and its insistence upon heterosexuality (symbolized by David's father's desire that David marry). David nevertheless looks to the patriarchy (David's father and all he represents) to confirm his self-worth, and he believes that this requires passing as heterosexual. David himself is deeply homophobic and upholds negative stereotypes about the gay subculture. He has not yet come to accept being gay. His resentment of society's contempt for homosexuals and homosexuality is shared by many who have come to accept being gay and to identify with the gay subculture. This resentment parallels that discussed by Cass. It may be expressed through belittling the non-gay world, particularly those not supportive of the gay activists' agenda. Pride in gay identity may be expressed through immersion in gay causes, gay culture, and gay political activism. Greater disclosure of sexual orientation also asserts gay pride and helps eradicate previous self-doubts. Gay pride celebrations and annual marches commemorating the anniversary of the Stonewall riots appeal especially to those in the "Identity Pride" stage, Cass says.

The sixth and final stage in Cass's model of homosexual identity formation is "Identity Synthesis." The "us versus them" mentality of homosexual versus heterosexual evident in the "Identity Pride" stage diminishes as contacts with supportive heterosexuals increase. Homosexuals are not automatically viewed positively nor heterosexuals negatively. The sexual orientation of self and others comes to be seen as only one aspect, albeit an important one, of personality and identity. The person's homosexual identity is now integrated with all other aspects of self (Cass 234–35). This is akin to Acceptance, as discussed in Chapter Six. In *Taking Care of Mrs. Carroll*, the gay characters' closest friends and companions include straight women and straight men as well as lesbians and gay men. This novel repudiates the assumption that heterosexuals are necessarily homophobic; Tony

Carroll, a deeply closeted homosexual, is the novel's most homophobic character. Many of the straight characters are very supportive of gay men.

Cass's model of coming out has been tested by Stephen Brady. He surveyed 225 men in Southern California "who reported homosexual thoughts, feelings, or behavior," and assigned 196 of them to six cells based on Cass's model. He found that those in the third stage, Identity Tolerance, were significantly less well-adjusted psychologically than those in later stages of homosexual identity formation. Brady was unable, however, to find any significant differences on any measure between those in the final three stages (Brady 115–16). Furthermore, Brady found an inconsistent response by those who fit Cass's description of the fifth stage, Identity Pride, and so concluded that this stage was not a useful analytic category. These findings suggest that the later three stages of Cass's model may not be as distinct as her model implies. Perhaps there is only one distinct stage after Depression, namely Acceptance.

Eli Coleman's Model of the Coming-Out Process

Like Troiden, Eli Coleman based his model of the stages of the coming-out process on retrospective accounts. He proposed a five-stage model of coming out, consisting of "Pre–Coming Out," "Coming Out," "Exploration," "First Relationships," and "Integration." Anxiety marks Pre–Coming Out, which resembles Denial: no connection is made between homosexual identity and issues surrounding same-sex attraction. "Denial, repression, reaction formation, sublimation, and rationalization" occur (Coleman, "Stages" 33). During Coming Out, "individuals not only recognize that homosexuality has personal meaning but they also disclose same-sex feelings to others" (Brady 14), which facilitates self-acceptance. Exploration, stage three, consists of experimentation. The First Relationships phase is marked by tentative relationships, typically of short duration. "First relationships can be disastrous" as they "often begin before basic tasks of coming out and exploration are completed" (Coleman, "Stages" 38–39). The final stage, Integration, like Acceptance, is "an open-ended, ongoing process of development lasting for the remainder of the individual's life" (Brady 15).

The stages of coming out derived from Kübler-Ross's model are compared with the stages discussed by Troiden, Cass, and Coleman in Table 1.

THE SIX NOVELS EXAMINED IN THIS WORK

No six novels could capture all the diversity within contemporary gay fiction. In form, gay novels cover a wide range, from realistic to decidedly nonrealistic, and from traditional to experimental in form, style, and content. Charles Nelson revives the rarely used form of the epistolary novel in *The Boy Who Picked the Bullets Up,* which concerns a gay American

Table 1
A Comparison of the Stages in Models of Coming Out

Elisabeth Kübler-Ross	Richard Troiden: Gay Identity Acquisition	Vivienne Cass: Homosexual Identity Formation	Eli Coleman: Coming-Out Process
1. Denial	2. Dissociation & Signification	1. Confusion	1. Pre–Coming Out
2. Anger	1. Sensitization	2. Comparison	
3. Bargaining		1. Confusion 2. Comparison	
4. Depression	3. Coming Out	3. Tolerance	
5. Acceptance	4. Commitment	4. Acceptance	5. Integration 6. Synthesis
{no exact parallels with:}		{5. Pride}	{2. Coming Out} {3. Exploration} {4. First Relationship}

soldier's tour of duty in Vietnam. This form was popular in the eighteenth century. (Samuel Richardson's *Pamela* and *Clarissa* are both epistolary novels.) Although perhaps not shedding as much light on the coming-out process as do more realistic gay novels, surrealistic gay novels such as William Burroughs' *Naked Lunch*, and allegorical gay novels such as Edmund White's *Nocturnes for the King of Naples* and *Forgetting Elena* have won widespread critical acclaim. (*Caracole*, written by White in a similarly allegorical vein, has been called his most ambitious novel. Overwritten, in an attempt to mirror a decadent fictional society in an ornate prose style, the novel collapses under the sheer weight of its bombast. It lacks the evocative beauty, grace, and lightness of White's other novels.) The astonishing merit of much contemporary gay fiction is not limited to realistic novels. Recent gay novels have crossed many literary boundaries. In addition to realistic novels and "highbrow" literary/allegorical works, gay science fiction and gay detective novels have been appearing within genres traditionally notorious for their sexism and homophobia. The hard-boiled detective novel, for instance, was originally largely homophobic. Yet Joseph Hansen has written a noteworthy series of frankly gay novels within that genre, the Dave Brandstetter mysteries, at least nine of which have been published. Surprisingly, Hansen has won high praise from William Buckley's conservative news magazine *National Review*, which has consistently ridiculed gay people, gay rights activists, and the gay rights movement. It said of the sixth Dave Brandstetter mystery, "There's no one more promising on the detective story scene today, and *Gravedigger* is Hansen's best book yet." Yet there seems little reason to provide another general survey of gay fiction, as several already exist, such as *The Homosexual as Hero in Contemporary Fiction,* by Stephen Adams; *Like a Brother, Like a Lover,* by George-Michel Sarotte; *Playing the Game: The Homosexual Novel in America,* by Roger Austen; *Gay Fictions: Wilde to Stonewall,* by Claude Summers; and *Gaiety Transfigured,* by David Bergman. None of these works takes as its point of departure the coming-out process and what light can be shed on it by gay fiction, which is the focus of this work.

The six realistic novels discussed in this work (*Falconer,* by John Cheever; *City of Night,* by John Rechy; *Giovanni's Room,* by James Baldwin; *The Beautiful Room Is Empty,* by Edmund White; *Dancer from the Dance,* by Andrew Holleran; and *Taking Care of Mrs. Carroll,* by Paul Monette) capture many intricacies of the coming-out process as experienced by gay men in contemporary America, illustrating the five phases of the coming-out process described above. These six novels were chosen also for their literary merit and their influence on gay readers, evident in such things as high sales and continued readership.

Although John Cheever denied his homosexuality during his lifetime, he broke his silence, albeit obliquely, in his Pulitzer Prize-winning novel *Falconer* (1977). This novel depicts full-fledged Denial. The homosexual behavior of the protagonist, Ezekiel Farragut, does not match his claimed sexual identity as a heterosexual. The setting of the novel, Falconer Prison, suggests that Farragut imprisons himself within his own homophobia. He falls in love with another prisoner, Jody, but despite their homosexual intercourse, both deny that they are homosexual. It is remarkable that Cheever, an author who was himself in Denial, candidly embodied in this published fiction those homosexual feelings and longings that he kept secret during his lifetime. His private correspondence, published posthumously, reveals the extent to which art (Cheever's novel) is the mirror of nature (his life). Farragut arranges to be smuggled out of prison in a body bag, mistaken for a corpse, a symbolic or ritual death. His escape suggests a spiritual rebirth. Cheever, however, suggests no transformation of Farragut's sexual identity, nor does he hint that Farragut might come out.

John Rechy's *City of Night* (1963) depicts Denial among homosexuals living within the gay urban underground before Stonewall. This novel has been called "the prototype of the gay urban novel . . . a gay *On the Road,* with the unassimilable gay hero becoming the modern world's Wandering Jew" (Frontain 15). Its unnamed protagonist's travels in and through the world of gay bars and cruising areas from New York to Los Angeles, and from Chicago to New Orleans, afford a glimpse into the secrecy and self-hatred that marked gay life in the early 1960s. The critics' response to *City of Night* was hostile and homophobic. The novel was panned in the *New York Review of Books* in a review with the homophobic title "Fruit Salad";

the *New Republic* and the *New Yorker* also attacked the book. Nonetheless, *City of Night* quickly topped the best-seller charts in New York and California and has continued to attract a large readership. As John Rechy notes in an introduction to *City of Night* written twenty-one years after the book's original publication, "Some excellent reviews began appearing, and eventually the book would be translated into about a dozen languages" (xvi). It was recently called "an essential gay read, honest to the core in its depiction of what life is like without pride, self-worth, or liberation" (Labonte, "Bad News" 72). Toward the end of the novel, its protagonist gets a glimpse of what a stable gay relationship might offer him.

The publication of James Baldwin's novel *Giovanni's Room* in 1956 generated enormous controversy. Yet perhaps no other book better captures the Anger and anguish of a man who falls passionately in love with another man prior to coming to accept that his sexual orientation is homosexual. Filled with homophobia, yet offering a scathing indictment of it, this novel has not lost its raw emotional power in the three and a half decades since its publication. It shows as does no other novel how heavy can be the damage caused to loved ones through internalized homophobia. It continues to be read widely within and outside the gay community, even though literary critics have paid scant attention to it relative to Baldwin's other novels (Adams 37).

Edmund White has received extraordinary praise for his novels, including *The Beautiful Room Is Empty* (1988). *Newsweek* proclaims, "White is unquestionably the foremost American gay novelist" (Clemons et al. 72). Writers ranging from Vladimir Nabokov to Gore Vidal have sung White's praises. *The Beautiful Room Is Empty* won the first annual Lambda Literary Award. The *New York Times Book Review* says of this novel, "Here is another coming-up-and-out story, . . . but the tale is told with wit, humor and aphoristic elegance. . . . Mr. White gives us plenty of surface sunshine to neutralize the familiar and melancholy core of the story" (Hall 27). This novel is unique in chronicling the now almost universally abandoned Bargaining strategy of using psychoanalysis in the attempt to make a homosexual into a heterosexual. It thus serves as a reminder of the painful experiences many would like to forget, and a warning of why such psychological brutality against gay people should not be tolerated.

Andrew Holleran's prose style is stunningly beautiful, and his novel *Dancer from the Dance* (1978), which epitomizes the stage of Depression, has been called by *Harper's* "the best gay novel written by anyone of our generation." The *New York Times Book Review* recently labeled it "the brilliant doomed queen novel of a decade ago" (Hall 26). *Newsweek* says it is "witty" and that although it "is now a pre-AIDS period piece, . . . it retains its power to dazzle" (Clemons et al. 73). Like Edmund White, Andrew Holleran receives critical accolades for his prose style. *Dancer from the Dance* has been described as "sensuous," "astonishingly beautiful," "magic," "lyrical," "brilliant," and "superb" (by *Harper's,* the *Library Journal, Newsday,* the *Boston Globe,* the *Los Angeles Times Book Review,* and the *New York Times Book Review*). Set in the gay ghettos of Manhattan and Fire Island of the 1970s—that is, after Stonewall and before the outbreak of the AIDS epidemic—it chronicles gay "life in the fast lane" of those times. Written as an elegiac romance, the unnamed narrator reflects on a deceased hero, Malone. Although initially portraying Malone as glamorous, the narrator eventually rejects the self-destructive, homophobic, promiscuous, substance-abusing "doomed queen" Malone as a role model for gay identity.

Paul Monette's novel *Taking Care of Mrs. Carroll* has been called "marvelously funny" and "refreshing" (by *Library Journal* and the *Advocate,* respectively). It contains a rarity in gay fiction of real literary merit: a realistic and plausible depiction of a successful long-term gay romance between two men in Acceptance that entails neither promiscuity nor codependency. The *Washington Post* called this novel "a moving celebration of gay love." It depicts gay people at peace with themselves and able to function in friendships with a wide variety of straight and gay people. Although published in the same year as *Dancer from the Dance, Taking Care of Mrs. Carroll* is not set in a gay ghetto and its characters are not "doomed queens."

Newsweek, Time, and even the previously homophobic *New York Times Book Review* all published major favorable articles on gay fiction during 1988. Similar attention has been given to gay literature since then by other major periodicals. "The evidence is ample . . . that serious gay and lesbian fiction is being taken seriously" (Labonte, "Giving Credit" 60). At long last, mainstream critics have begun to recognize the literary merit of much gay fiction. Gay people, though, have long recognized the value of these novels, turning to them for practical insights about coming out and developing a gay identity.

2

Denial: *Falconer* and *City of Night*

This year's trade is next year's competition.

—Gay Saying

Denial, most basically, is the response, "No, not me, this cannot be true" (Kübler-Ross 34). Usually it is temporary. "Denial functions as a buffer after unexpected shocking news, allows the [person] to collect himself, and with time, mobilize other, less radical defenses" (Kübler-Ross 35). This is as true of the coming-out process as it is of the individual confrontation with mortality that Kübler-Ross charts. Most people react with shock and disbelief upon first experiencing homosexual longings and resist concluding "I am homosexual" even while having homosexual sex. Such is the case for the protagonists of John Cheever's *Falconer* and John Rechy's *City of Night*. In *Falconer*, the protagonist, Ezekiel Farragut, enters Falconer Prison. In flashbacks, he reminisces about his married life and his childhood. Farragut falls in love with another inmate, Jody. The two have an affair, all the while explicitly denying that they are homosexual. Farragut and many of the other married prisoners rationalize that they are engaging merely in "situational homosexuality," as women are not available sexually. *City of Night* follows its unnamed protagonist, a male hustler, through various urban gay undergrounds coast to coast. The protagonist rationalizes that because he hustles for money and does not reciprocate sexually, he is not homosexual. Finally he is confronted with a client who tries to force him to admit that he is really looking for love from another man and who offers to give it to him. But Rechy's hustler bolts, unable to handle the prospect of true intimacy rather than impersonal sex.

From the earliest stages of life, sex roles are defined for children by their parents, teachers, and popular culture. Parents expect their children to be heterosexual and punish them if they deviate from these expectations. Homophobia is absorbed by those who later identify themselves as lesbian and gay long before they begin to suspect that they may be homosexual. Gays and lesbians are raised as heterosexuals and the first awareness of their same-sex attractions, fantasies, and behavior disrupts and challenges their assumption that they are heterosexual. At least until the Stonewall Rebellion of 1969, shame and guilt overshadowed gays and lesbians, who readily internalized society's homophobia. Most chose to conceal their sexual orientation.

Homosexuality to some extent remains "the love that dare not speak its name." In almost all parts of the country, people fired from jobs or denied housing or public accommodations simply because they are homosexual have no legal recourse. Until recently, there were no statewide gay rights laws. In 1982 Wisconsin became the first state in the country with a law forbidding discrimination on the basis of sexual orientation in employment, housing, and public accommodations. Other states that, as of early 1993, had gay rights laws were Massachusetts (1989), Hawaii (covering employment only, 1991), Connecticut (1991), New Jersey (1992), Vermont (1992), and California (covering employment by legislation and housing by court interpretation, 1992). Scores of cities have similar legislation. No state and only a very few municipalities recognize gay unions by granting such things as spousal benefits and bereavement leave to gay lovers. The penalties for "coming out" can be high: loss of job, loss of family, physical assaults, myriad forms of discrimination and persecution. Some forms of discrimination, such as racism and anti-Semitism, have become less socially acceptable and thus are no longer expressed as openly as they once were, but many people feel no such restraint in expressing their homophobia.

Given the stigma that traditionally has been attached to homosexuals and homosexuality, most people who begin to suspect that they are homosexual are hesitant to acknowledge this. There are powerful disincentives for acknowledging to oneself and to others, "Yes, I am a homosexual." This may stem as much from self-hatred (internalized homophobia) as from fear of discrimination by others. People at this initial stage in the coming-out process are riddled by doubts and alienation about their identity. " 'Who am I?' is the burning question" (Cass 223). Cass thus terms the first stage in the process of homosexual identity formation the "Identity Confusion" stage. Most gay people become aware of their sexual orientation only gradually, often with great resistance. In a study of gay men, Thomas Weinberg found that it takes people from " 'a few months' to ten years" to go from a tentative and vacillating sense of possibly being gay to the certainty that this is so (150).

Each step of awareness may entail mourning the loss of the former sense of self. Deeply held beliefs about one's sexual identity and masculinity or femininity may come to seem inaccurate. Most children and adolescents realize only too keenly that their parents' expectations—and those of authority figures and peers—might be shattered by a disclosure of homoerotic feelings. In short, in the first stages of awareness of homosexual inclinations, there is typically an enormous gap between what one is feeling and what one believes one should be feeling. To many people, intense guilt, shame, and confusion result, feelings not easy to resolve, particularly as homosexual longings persist despite attempts to ignore or repress them. The defense and coping mechanisms used to patch over this conflict between "is" and "ought" may become extremely elaborate and highly self-destructive, involving self-deception and alienation from one's feelings. "If acknowledged, same-sex feelings would mean rejection and ridicule. Consequently, individuals protect themselves from awareness through defenses, such as denial, repression, reaction formation, sublimation, and rationalization. . . . The consequences of this concealment can be enormously destructive" (Coleman, "Stages" 33). Identity and self-acceptance are at stake. Coming out involves struggling for a coherent sense of self while passionately held beliefs about different parts of one's identity clash. In many cases, people opt to escape from the conflict between self-identity and "unacceptable" feelings and behavior through the abuse of alcohol and other drugs. Such abuse is more prevalent among homosexuals, particularly among those who have not completed the coming-out process, than among the population at large.

Complete repression of homosexual desire cannot work for long. As Jung notes, repression inevitably leads to the return of the repressed, usually in uncontrollable ways, with the very energy used to repress "undesirable" feelings fueling the energy of the repressed content. The Shadow (the disowned part of the self) carries what has been repressed from the ego or conscious sense of self. The Shadow can come to seem autonomous, powerful, and mighty. Most of those with strong homosexual feelings who deny "I am homosexual" nevertheless manage to express their homosexual desires in their sexual behavior to some extent. For most people, same-sex behavior "does not necessarily lead to . . . definition . . . of self as homosexual; . . . most have homosexual behavior before labelling themselves as homosexual" (Weinberg 6, 162). This contradiction between sexual behavior and sexual identity can be sustained by defining a "homosexual" not by behavior or by sexual attraction towards others of one's sex, but by upholding stereotypical images of homosexuals. These stereotypes often seem irreconcilable with self-image. In *Falconer*, Ezekiel Farragut and his lover Jody deny being homosexual in that way. They refuse to admit that the homosexual label applies to them and their own sexual behavior. When a homosexual "succeeds in applying this strategy, conflict and confusion are removed, and identity foreclosure takes place," particularly if past homosexual behavior is denied and elements of heterosexual identity are reaffirmed (Cass 223).

Many who later come to accept their homosexuality try for a time to put on a heterosexual facade. A high proportion of gay male activists in the years right after Stonewall were married or had been married. "Many of them had been deluded into believing they were straight and marrying to prove it," in part because they could not identify with the outrageous stereotypes of gay men "that were regarded as scientific fact" (Brown 109). Attempts to reassert a heterosexual identity usually prove unsuccessful. "If an individual is 'doing' homosexual acts but does not consider himself to 'be' a homosexual, the immediate question is, 'How does he perceive his behavior?' " (Weinberg 7).

After the pretense of being heterosexual wears thin, a reluctant acknowledgment of being homosexual may emerge. "This marks the beginning of what may become a negative or self-hating identity" (Cass 224). When the thought arises, "I may be homosexual," the initial emotional reactions of most people "are overwhelmingly negative, such as fear, guilt, hatred, repulsion, frustration, hurt, anxiety, and the refusal to think about the possibility of being homosexual" (Weinberg 92). In short, in the stage of Denial, self-doubt, confusion, dishonesty, rationalization, and equivocation are rife. Hiding in the closet, at least at first, seems easier than coming out. The status quo can be maintained because "you become your own jailor, your own cop" (Fisher 246). Melodramatic, sudden strains can be kept at bay by such an arrangement, which may seem more appealing than facing the explosiveness that can erupt, for instance, from telling a parent that one is gay. Yet the cost of coming out may be likened to the sacrifice of making a big payment up front that pays off a debt in full, while staying in the closet can be likened to making weekly payments, each in itself manageable, to a loan shark year after year. After years, one has paid a lot without ever having paid off the debt. Such are the constant emotional costs of repressing feelings and lying to others. "Over the years, these tiny denials have a cumulative effect" (Fisher 249).

John Cheever, both in his novel *Falconer,* written late in life, and in his posthumously published correspondence, provides a textbook case of Denial. Unequivocal evidence exists of Cheever's homosexual affairs, coupled with his persistent and absolute Denial of being homosexual. Denial, though absolute at first, usually recedes. Cheever, however, remained in what Cass calls the "Identity Confusion" stage by adamantly rejecting the notion of himself as "potentially homosexual." Thus "Identity Foreclosure" occurred, to use Cass's phrase. Cheever never "came out"; he remained in Denial. As Cheever's son Benjamin notes in *The Letters of John Cheever,* his father denied having any homosexual experiences during his adulthood. When his daughter interviewed him for *Newsweek,* John Cheever said, " 'I've had many . . ., all tremendously gratifying, and all between the ages of nine and eleven' " (Cheever, *Letters* 326). Although explicit references to his own homosexual experiences do not appear in his letters until late in life, Benjamin Cheever says he knows that his father had been sexually active with men since the 1950s and may have "been bisexual almost from day one . . . [even though] in public he was an ardent heterosexual" (Cheever, *Letters* 300).

Cheever upholds a traditional belief that simply by being homosexual, a man betrays the dominant sex and thus forfeits his right to enjoy its privileges. The homosexuals in Cheever's short stories live on the fringe of society. They have sex in public, work as prostitutes, get fired for pedophilia, and work in distinctly non-butch indoor occupations. A homosexual gropes another man in public to proposition him in "The Fourth Alarm." A male prostitute known as "Doris" services men in "The Jewels of the Cabots." In "The Ocean," the narrator says that when his mother-in-law's "only son was fired out of secondary school for improper conduct and went to live with an older man, [the narrator's mother-in-law] said, 'I know it's revolting, but it seems to be *terribly* fashionable' " (Cheever, *Stories* 569). A homosexual poet is mentioned in passing in "Artemis, the Honest Well Digger," presumably to serve as a foil to the tough, working-class heterosexual hero; the poet complains that the noise from the rig "was ruining his meter" (650). Mr. Rowantree, another effeminate homosexual character, in "Clancy in the Tower of Babel" is a hysterical, aging antique dealer who is abandoned by his lover and then tries to take his own life. The story is peppered with words like "pervert" and "Sodom." In "A Miscellany of Characters That Will Not Appear," Cheever writes, "Out go all those homosexuals who have taken such a dominating position in recent fiction. Isn't it time that we embraced the indiscretion and inconstancy of the flesh and moved on?" (469). In that essay, he portrays the typical fictional homosexual figure as a beautiful, sensitive, sixteen-year-old boy who is smothered by his mother's love and "timid about competitive sports" (479).

Cheever's remarks about homosexuality were invariably negative. He claimed "homosexuality made men vain, ungenerous, and ultimately ridiculous" (Cheever, *Letters* 300). His son states that Cheever told him "over and over again that he hoped I would not have his 'difficult propensities' " (328). Looking back now, with the knowledge of Cheever's homosexual love letters, we can conclude that Cheever was projecting his self-loathing onto others. He wrote to his Russian translator, Tanya, that he wished he could live in a world that was free from homosexuals (264). Perhaps it would have been closer to the mark for him to have written that he wished he were free from homosexual desires. If he had had none, chances are he simply would have ignored homosexuals, rather than wishing to rid the planet of them. As Ronald Alexander notes, "a certain tension exists when one (A) sees value in oneself, yet (B) devalues homosexuality as inferior, sinful, etc., and (C) identifies oneself as homosexual" (Alexander 94).

Cheever's blanket Denial of his homosexuality is contradicted by his letters. One of his male lovers and protégés allowed Cheever's love letters to him to be printed, upon condition of anonymity. Cheever waxed eloquent in a letter of April 1977 to his lover about the large size of his lover's cock and of his delight in his lover's company (Cheever, *Letters* 334). Cheever wrote to this same male lover a few months later of their love: "*Neither of us is homosexual* and yet neither of us are [sic] foolish enough to worry about the matter. If I want your cock or your mouth I know I have only to ask. . . . I can find nothing false in my love for you. . . . It's terribly simple. I love you and love to be near you" (Cheever, *Letters* 341; emphasis added). Cheever did worry about the matter, though. How could a man engaged in a homosexual love affair who simultaneously denied being homosexual not worry about this discrepancy between behavior and self-image? To this same lover, Cheever wrote,

> Both your short life and my long life have been . . . singular adventures and to hold your nice ass in my hands and to feel your cock against mine seems to be a part of this astonishing pilgrimage. I want your soft balls, I want to take off your glasses, I want your ass, your laughter and your loving mouth. (Cheever, *Letters* 356)

Despite this frank private acknowledgment of his own homosexual desires, Cheever's public stance remained homophobic, even as Cheever dealt more explicitly with homosexuality in his later fiction, particularly *Falconer*.

At first glance *Falconer* seems a tacit admission of the importance of homosexuality to Cheever, but his treatment of homosexuality is hedged with Denial. It is not an admission of his own homosexuality. The title of the novel underscores the importance of the setting, Falconer Prison, which holds the novel's protagonist, Ezekiel Farragut. Farragut is constrained by his inability or unwillingness to admit his sexual desires forthrightly. As Oscar Wilde says in *The Picture of Dorian Gray*: "It was the passions about whose origin we deceive ourselves that tyrannized most strongly over us" (53). Cheever depicts not a single character in Falconer Prison as exclusively homosexual. Homosexuals are dismissed as "fruits," "pansies," and "queers." Those who engage in homosexual acts within the prison walls are portrayed either as bisexual or as resorting to sex with men simply because female sexual partners are unobtainable. Cheever depicts the characters' homosexuality as a situational, rather than an invariable, inherent, permanent sexual orientation. But as Peter Fisher concludes, "Situational homosexuality is no different from any other sort, except that society is willing to look the other way" (20). The term "situational homosexuality" itself "is fallacious if it implies that there is some 'true' homosexuality which is not situated. All homosexuality is situational, influenced and given meaning and character by its location in time and social space" (Katz 7). The pose of bisexuality all too often manifests a Denial of homosexuality, as some men have sex with women once in a while to prove to themselves that they are not "really" homosexual. This does not always work: "Some men find themselves, while having sex with women, thinking about men; some can only perform if this is the case" (Weinberg 111). The inmates of Falconer Prison are spared these psychosexual acrobatics by the unavailability of women within the prison walls. Farragut has difficulty imagining his love for Jody surviving outside the walls of Falconer Prison. Perhaps Cheever wondered if he could bring off in his fiction a homosexual love affair without recourse to the dodge of "situational homosexuality." Could Cheever have portrayed gay lovers in a favorable light who could not use the excuse that sexual contact with women was not available for extended periods of time?

There are many reasons for supposing that Cheever identified closely with Ezekiel Farragut, the novel's main character, apparent bisexuality being one clue, loathing for his brother another, and substance abuse a third. Furthermore, Farragut's self-referential language matches language Cheever uses to describe himself in his letters. Even Farragut's physical appearance resembles Cheever's: Farragut feels like "a runt" (Cheever, *Falconer* 7); Cheever himself was small and wiry. Farragut, like Cheever himself, and like most of the other inmates, is married, though this does not stop him from having sex with men. (See Table 2.) Farragut is imprisoned for the crime of "fratricide," which is used in the novel as a legal term, although the law does not differentiate between fratricide and other forms of murder. This suggests that the novel should be read more as a mythic night journey—a descent into a psychic hell—than as a realistic narrative.

Conflict and hatred between brothers appears not only between Ezekiel and Eben Farragut, but also as a major theme in Cheever's stories "Goodbye, My Brother" and "The Lowboy," suggesting a nagging persistence of brotherly ill will in Cheever's own psyche. Farragut enters Falconer Prison as a drug addict on methadone maintenance. This parallels Cheever's alcoholism, which nearly killed him. Cheever himself had to be hospitalized to break his pattern of alcohol abuse. Many gay men who have not achieved full Acceptance of their homosexuality seek to escape through alcohol and drug abuse, and in the case of Cheever and Farragut, the problem of Denial and substance abuse may well be causally linked. Alcoholism and drug abuse are higher in the gay community than in the population at large, which probably reflects the difficulties of coming out.

Perhaps Cheever's identification with Farragut accounts for the curiously restrained descriptions of Farragut's prison affair with Jody, which make Cheever's letters to his unnamed male lover quoted above seem bold indeed. In third-person narration, Cheever introduces Jody, Farragut's lover, by calling him Farragut's best friend. Calling someone with whom one has a passionate affair a best friend seems odd; Denial surfaces in language not

Table 2
Similarities Between Ezekiel Farragut and John Cheever

	Farragut	Cheever
Marital status	Married	Married
Sexual orientation	Denied being homosexual	Denied being homosexual
Sexual partners	Men and women (mainly Jody)	Men and women (mainly men?)
Brother	Killed his brother	Hated his brother
Substance abuse/ detoxification	Drug addict (detoxified in prison)	Alcoholic (hospitalized)
Size	"a very small man, a runt"	small and wiry
Language (example)	"You can put on my headstone: 'Here lies Ezekiel Farragut, who never took it up the ass' " (Falconer 128)	Cheever "said his epitaph should read: 'Here lies John Cheever. He never . . . took it up the ass' " (Letters 18)

only through direct lies but also through evasion and understatement. Cheever continues by mentioning that they met in the shower, where the young black-haired Jody smiles at Farragut. Cheever does not mention that both men would of course have had the chance to examine each other's naked bodies in that setting. Jody's homophobic and hypocritical stance is evident from the outset. In the first conversation between Jody and Farragut, Jody says, "I know you're Farragut but so long as you ain't homosexual I don't care" (Cheever, *Falconer* 91). It is as important for Jody to establish as it is for Cheever to assert in his letter to his male lover, "Neither of us is homosexual" (Cheever, *Letters* 341). Presumably men may have sex with each other without stigma only if neither is homosexual. (One might wonder then why either would be interested in having sex with the other, but Denial often lacks logical rigor.)

Jody's Denial of homosexuality preexists his incarceration. He takes Farragut to his "hideout" in the water tower and tells of the unsuccessful scheme with his friend Howie that resulted in Jody's own conviction. Jody says that Howie planned to rob an old stationery store owner of tickets worth thousands of dollars that the man kept in his bedside drawer. Jody explains that Howie knew this fact because he allowed the old man to perform oral sex on him for money. Jody has already indicated his preoccupation and discomfort with self-avowed homosexuals by telling Farragut "as long as you ain't homosexual I don't care." Similarly, he denies his friend Howie's homosexuality by depicting Howie as "trade," a nonreciprocating sexual partner. To establish Howie's heterosexual credentials, Jody immediately mentions Howie's wife and children. Like Cheever himself, Jody refuses to associate with homosexual men who have come out. Homosexual acts seem permissible to Jody, as to Cheever, only if one plays the game of posing as heterosexual. Yet like many men in the stage of Denial, Jody can't get the topic of homosexuality off his mind or keep it out of his conversation. Thus even while carefully denying his own homosexuality, Jody continually raises the topic of homosexuality with Farragut, thereby hinting at the possibility of a homosexual encounter between them. No doubt Jody mentions homosexuality to Farragut while they are alone together in a secluded spot in order to facilitate such an encounter.

The meetings between Farragut and Jody continue. Cheever tersely notes that they became lovers after having known each other for a month. In the next sentence, Jody, in words that echo Cheever's words to his lover, repeatedly asserts his homophobic Denial: " 'I'm so glad you ain't homosexual,' Jody *kept saying*. . . . Then . . . [Jody] unfastened Farragut's trousers . . . *with every assistance from Farragut*" (Cheever, *Falconer* 96; emphasis added). Cheever indicates that Farragut, who is forty-eight years old, enthusiastically enters into a sexual liaison with this attractive, slender man sixteen years his junior, but then coyly suggests that such male-male sexual encounters are somehow a peculiarity of prison life (as one might, in different circumstances, say of English public schools or any other all-male environment). Cheever mentions that Farragut "expected" something like this might occur, based on what he had read about prison inmates. (More forthrightly, he might have said he "hoped" or "wanted" this to happen.) Yet nothing he had read or thought prepared him for such depth of love to grow out of "this grotesque bonding of their relationship" (Cheever, *Falconer* 96). The sentiments behind the choice of the words "grotesque bonding" parallel those of Cheever himself in his letter to a male lover, in which he admits that although he used to think "such love must be perverse, cruel and inverted" that Cheever could "find no trace of this" in his love for his male lover (Cheever, *Letters* 356).

Cheever's prose about Farragut's sexual encounters with Jody lacks the graphic language of Cheever's letters to his male lovers. Cheever conveys Farragut's sexual desire obliquely through detailed descriptions of his anticipation, couched in the language of romance. But the sexual acts between Farragut and Jody occur off-stage, between the lines; we are told how often they meet (twice or three times each week) and of Farragut straining his ears as he waits for the sound of the squeak of Jody's sneakers. Due to Cheever's reticence, we do not see the sex acts between Farragut and Jody, but we do discover Jody's hypocrisy. Jody's Denial and his aversion to homosexuals conflict not only with his encounters with Farragut, but also with his other behavior in the prison. Tiny tells Farragut that Jody has "blown half the population [of the prison] and he's hardly begun." According to Tiny, Jody's fine scruples about homosexuals are a sham. Tiny gives a graphic description of a fan dance Jody performed with a newspaper he had folded to resemble a fan in which he danced and repeatedly switched the newspaper "from his cock to his asshole" (Cheever, *Falconer* 101). Tiny adds that he was revolted by Jody's performance. Farragut learns from one of Jody's other male lovers, DiMatteo, after Jody's escape, that Jody has married, betraying a promise to wait for DiMatteo. Jody's numerous homosexual encounters within prison walls are thus presumably left behind him as he puts on the respectable facade of heterosexual married life.

Farragut's entire affair with Jody is covered concisely between pages 91 and 103; Jody is completely offstage from pages 104–28, only to reappear briefly on pages 129–30 to kiss Farragut goodbye before making his escape from the prison. But Farragut's affair with Jody is not the only sexual encounter in the novel, and it is instructive to compare it with the much more explicit narration provided by the inmate nicknamed "the Cuckold" of an encounter he had prior to his imprisonment. This story is told on pages 116–24, and is thus framed by Farragut's affair with Jody and Jody's escape. As we might expect from Cheever, the Cuckold, as his name suggests, is not exclusively homosexual. (Apparently, in Cheever's fictional world, the only men who are exclusively homosexual are antique dealers, poets, teachers, or others in "effeminate" occupations.) The Cuckold admits to "scoring" with a man while on a sales trip outside Kansas City. In the Cuckold's unromantic narration, he strives to create a matter-of-fact aura around his experience, as if to say, "I'm not queer; this could have happened to any man." He describes the man he meets in a Chinese restaurant as attractive merely because of his youth, adding that this man's good looks would vanish as soon as he aged another ten years. The Cuckold exhibits homophobia even while describing his sexual arousal during his encounter with the young man in the motel room. He tells Farragut that the youth made drinks and began kissing him. He says he does not feel comfortable with the thought of men kissing other men, but admits that when this young man kissed him, " 'It gave me no pain' " (Cheever, *Falconer* 118). The litotes reflects the Cuckold's reluctance to admit his sexual excitement. He continues, " 'A man kissing a man except maybe in France is a very worthless two of a kind" (Cheever, *Falconer* 118). People often project despised aspects of themselves onto others. Frequently, illicit sexualities are projected onto people of other races or nationalities. The Cuckold denies his own homosexuality by "exporting" it to France, a device James Baldwin resorted to in *Giovanni's Room* after his publisher rejected the original homosexual ending of his previous novel, which is set in America. It is as if the Cuckold and Baldwin were both saying, "No, this can't happen here in America." The Cuckold's homophobia heightens his self-consciousness, saying, "If someone took a picture of this fellow kissing me it would be [an] unnatural picture, but why should my cock have begun to put on weight if it was all so . . . unnatural?" (Cheever, *Falconer* 118). The Cuckold, after describing his increasing sexual excitement and the unfolding of sex on the couch, adds that no one had ever performed oral sex on him before. Should we believe him? The Cuckold has previously indicated his ex-wife's nymphomania and promiscuity, a willingness to do almost anything sexual with almost any man, so it is odd that the Cuckold has never had oral sex before. Can one infer that his ex-wife's extramarital escapades resulted from her dissatisfaction with her sex life with her husband? The Cuckold again betrays his concern for appearances and self-image, being preoccupied with how his actions would look in a newsreel or in a newspaper, but, as he says, " 'Evidently my cock hadn't ever seen a newspaper because it was going crazy' " (Cheever, *Falconer* 118). The two men then go to bed with each other.

This speech reveals much about the Cuckold's sexual attitudes, sexual history, and sexual identity. As with the other supposedly bisexual characters in this story (and as with Cheever himself), the Cuckold's self-image rests on the shaky foundation of Denial. His view of his sexuality is largely determined by his belief about how it should appear to others (and to himself). Thus he refers repeatedly to how what he was doing would look in a photograph or a newsreel. What he did does not fit with his image of himself, but he struggles nonetheless to embrace both his self-image and his life experience. He never tells of a passionate encounter with a woman, so the importance of this encounter with the man may well be far greater than he lets on through his matter-of-fact tone. Appearances and self-image, however, are contrasted with the unequivocal physiological response of sexual arousal in this male-male encounter, which the Cuckold acknowledges straightforwardly, despite some rhetorical hedging, as in the litotes "it gave me no pain."

The Cuckold says things that Cheever does not permit Farragut to say in this novel. Given Farragut's role as protagonist, not to mention Cheever's identification with him, Cheever delicately veils the sexual encounters between Farragut and Jody. But the veil is lifted in the Cuckold's case. Why? The Cuckold is portrayed unsympathetically, as a boring windbag who has murdered his wife, so less is at stake in allowing him to narrate his homosexual experiences explicitly. We are not supposed to like him, anyway; certainly Farragut does not, as is evident in his description of the Cuckold, in which he indicates that the Cuckold deliberately has his prison garments cut too tight, although this does not make the Cuckold any more appealing to Farragut, who concludes that although the pants are revealing, "there was nothing appetizing to be seen" (Cheever, *Falconer* 193). The Cuckold fits Cheever's view of homosexuals as vain, pathetic, and contemptible.

Given not only the position of the Cuckold's story, sandwiched between Farragut's affair with Jody and their leave-taking, but also the parallels between the Cuckold's case and Farragut's, the Cuckold's story provides an oblique commentary upon Farragut's affair with Jody. There are many parallels between Farragut's affair and the Cuckold's fling. Neither Farragut nor the Cuckold admits to prior homosexual experience in adult life. Each understates the extent of his homosexual longings.

Farragut, we are told, "had not loved a man, *he thought,* since he had left the Boy Scouts" (Cheever, *Falconer* 22; emphasis added). Yet we see Farragut's wife Marcia, in one of Farragut's flashbacks, necking with a woman, and Farragut asks himself, "But if she loved Sally Midland, didn't he love Chucky Drew?" (22). Establishing Marcia's previous homosexual forays lessens the outrageousness of Farragut's lapse from marital fidelity and heterosexuality; after all, Farragut could claim that his wife "did it first." Perhaps because her own bisexuality has led her to recognize the homosexual potential in others, Marcia expresses concern about her husband as the possible object of homosexual advances. On her first visit to Falconer Prison, she asks Farragut if the man who gives him his methadone, whom Farragut has just called a "pansy," has made a pass at him. Farragut says to his wife, " 'He asked me if I liked opera.' " She is relieved when Farragut tells her he said no: " 'That's good. I wouldn't want to be married to a homosexual' " (23). "Opera" is a code word, based on the stereotype of gays as artistically inclined and drawn to florid displays of emotion; the subtext is homosexuality. "Do you like opera?" means "Are you gay?" while "You don't, of course," means "You mustn't encourage him to make advances. You didn't, did you?" Marcia accepts Farragut's Denial of homosexuality because this is what she wants to hear; she, too, is in Denial, as are many women married to gay men. Marcia's sarcastic concluding line unwittingly reveals her deep-seated suspicion that she has married a homosexual after all. Farragut's Denial is equally ineffective. Farragut responds to his wife's comment about marrying a homicidal drug addict, "I did not kill my brother." Marcia, a true codependent, scripts Farragut's Denial of homosexuality, but finds it impossible to accept his denial of fratricide and reminds him that it was his blow with a fire iron that caused his brother's death. As Farragut's denial of murder is exposed unequivocally as a lie, his Denial of homosexuality (not liking opera) should seem suspect as well.

By the time of her second visit Marcia evidently has confronted her own Denial and has allowed her suspicions about her husband's sexual orientation to surface. Farragut, however, relies on the age-old distinction between the active and passive male partners in anal intercourse to deny that he himself is homosexual, even while admitting to a homosexual affair. Marcia states, rather than asks (despite the question mark): " 'I suppose you have boyfriends in here?' " Farragut responds, " 'I've had one, but I didn't take it up the ass' " (128). As we have seen above, this matches Cheever's jocular description to his son of his own possible epitaph. The phrase or concept of "taking it up the ass" recurs throughout *Falconer*, indicating its importance to Cheever (69, 77, 121, 128, 159). For thousands of years, the passive or receptive partner in anal intercourse has been seen as taking on the feminine (inferior) role. Doing so has been equated with a loss of masculinity. The active partner has been viewed as dominant and therefore still able to identify himself as masculine (superior). The stigma attached to the "female" role reflects misogyny, which tends to rise and fall with homophobia. This double standard has led some to conclude that only those who take on the passive (feminine) role are homosexual, while the active partner's masculinity and heterosexuality supposedly remain intact. (The historical emergence and persistence of such attitudes is explored in John Boswell's *Christianity, Social Tolerance, and Homosexuality* as well as in Arthur Evans's *The God of Ecstasy: Sex-Roles and the Madness of Dionysos.*)

Those in Denial of their homosexuality are quick to search for a loophole in society's convoluted definitions of masculine and feminine behavior. A man's supposed masculinity or effeminacy is a complex social construction that has never rested solely on the presence or absence of homosexual behavior per se. According to Michel Foucault, for the Greeks in ancient times

> the opposition between activity and passivity . . . was essential . . .; thus, . . . a man might prefer males without anyone even suspecting him of effeminacy, providing he was active in the sexual relation and active in the moral mastering of himself. On the other hand, a man who was not sufficiently in control of his pleasures—whatever the choice of object—was regarded as "feminine." The dividing line between a virile man and an effeminate man did not coincide with our opposition between hetero- and homosexuality; nor was it confined to the opposition between active and passive homosexuality. (Foucault, II 85)

The Cuckold admits to cheating on his wife, but cagily leaves the gender of his partner in adultery unspecified when admitting to feeling guilty about a sexual encounter with "a stranger" in South Dakota (Cheever, *Falconer* 33). Given his homophobia (what he terms his "strong prejudice against fairies"), wouldn't he have specified the stranger's gender had she been female, to prove his own supposed heterosexuality? Had the stranger been a woman, would he have felt guilty? One wonders about the Cuckold's other sexual adventures during his other long sales trips.

In any event, in both Farragut's affair with Jody and the Cuckold's fling with the hustler, an older man encounters an attractive and sexually more experienced younger man who seduces him. In both cases, the older man is led on and deceived by the younger man. Farragut learns that Jody has been extraordinarily active sexually; the Cuckold discovers that the youth, who acknowledges being a hustler, has slipped him a Mickey Finn and stolen his money. The Cuckold's case is different from Farragut's, however, in that Farragut learns of Jody's antics only after the fact. The Cuckold, however, knows he has been robbed the first night, yet nevertheless asks the hustler back the next night, during which the hustler admits to having taken the money, which the Cuckold already knows. Inviting back a sexual partner who has drugged and robbed him, the Cuckold shows that such abuse counts for little compared with his own sexual desperation. Lacking physical or personal charm, the Cuckold knows full well that to obtain desirable sexual partners he must pay. Farragut also feels physically unattractive. The white-haired Farragut feels Jody's compliments on Farragut's appearance are mere flattery of the type whores use on older men. Nevertheless, Farragut feels "helplessly susceptible" (Cheever, *Falconer* 109).

The Cuckold's narrative depicts events fairly explicitly. But the homophobic Cuckold denies the depth of his sexual feelings for other men. Only by piecing together his failure to satisfy his wife sexually with the absence of any mention of sexual encounters with other women can we see that this motel room fling exposes a much-denied part of his nature. The Cuckold remains homophobic, despite his frankness. He says he expected the hustler " 'to sound like a fairy, but he never did. . . . I have this very strong prejudice against fairies. I've always thought they were silly and feeble-minded' " (122). One might think that Cheever is ironically undercutting the Cuckold's homophobic prejudices, but the Cuckold's sentiment resembles a comment Cheever made about his one-time sexual partner, John Gurganus. Cheever wrote in a letter: "Gurganus is brilliant but he suffers acutely from the loss of gravity that seems to follow having a cock up your ass or down your throat once too often" (Cheever, *Letters* 339). Silliness and feeble-mindedness are similar to "loss of gravity." Note, too, the contempt reserved once again for the passive partner. Significantly, neither Cheever nor the Cuckold defines a homosexual simply as a person who engages in same-sex sexual acts. To form such a definition would be equivalent to admitting "I am a homosexual." Each, rather, seeks to distance himself from the taint of his own homosexuality by embracing a stereotype of homosexuals with which he cannot identify. Each characterizes homosexuals as somehow distinct in speech, manner, occupation, or role, rather than by sexual behavior.

Perhaps the most homophobic or reactionary aspect of the Cuckold's tale is its ending: while waiting for the hustler to return on the third night, the Cuckold receives a phone call from the police, is asked to go to the county courthouse, and there is led to the morgue, where he is shown the hustler's corpse. Apparently the victim of a drug-related vendetta, the hustler has been stabbed thirty-two times; his murderer stabbed him repeatedly after killing him. This ending colors and comments upon the entire encounter. Neither the frank narrative of a man's sexual arousal by another

man nor the straightforward description of their sexual encounters celebrates the sexual freedom of gay life. On the contrary, the narrator is un-
sympathetic and his young sexual partner dies violently. Homosexuality is
cast in a negative light. This story within the larger story suggests that
leading an openly homosexual life leads to disaster. Conventional morality
dictates that homosexual narratives end unhappily. The Cuckold's tale upholds this homophobic convention.

The Cuckold's story is not the only device used to comment upon and
denigrate Farragut's love for Jody; Farragut does this in his own reflection
upon homosexuality and its causes. Farragut thinks, in third-person narration, "If love [is] a chain of resemblances, there [is], since Jody [is] a man,
the danger that Farragut might be in love with himself" (Cheever, *Falconer* 108). Farragut then recollects a certain narcissistic man preoccupied
with his own appearance: that his eyes are not the same size, that he might
look better if he grew a mustache or beard, whether his shoulders are too
narrow and his hips too wide, whether his biceps are overdeveloped. Farragut then thinks, in third-person narration, that "in loving Jody he loved
himself, there was that chance that he might . . . have become infatuated
with his lost youth" (110). Farragut's speculation becomes increasingly
morbid; as in the Cuckold's story, homosexual desire is linked ultimately
with death, although this association seems to rest upon the old homophobic premise that homosexuality is unnatural: "In covering Jody's body he
willingly embraced decay and corruption. To kiss a man . . . was as unnatural as the rites and procedures in a funeral parlor" (110). The coupling
of homosexual desire with death stems from Farragut's guilt and self-loathing, rather than from any intrinsic connection. Farragut's uninformed theories about homosexuality reveal his homophobia. Such speculation as to
the cause of homosexuality and the nature of homosexuality would seem
patently absurd if applied to heterosexuality. Does anyone ever agonize,
"What caused my heterosexuality?" Asking "Why am I homosexual?" carries the subtext, "What went wrong?"

John Rechy's protagonist also speculates unconvincingly about the causes
of homosexuality in *City of Night*. This search for "what went wrong" extends even further than Farragut's, to "Whose fault is it?" Apparently Rechy attributes homosexuality to fathers' sexual abuse of their sons. In *City
of Night*, the narrator recalls that when he was eight he was fondled repeatedly by his father and his father's friends. The narrator was given nick-
els for letting these men fondle him. The implication is that his later life
as a hustler was established by this pattern of his selling his sexual favors
to men at an early age. Dennis Altman labels Rechy's special pleading "a
maudlin invocation of early childhood experience to 'explain' his homosexuality" (*Oppression* 15). Rechy suggests not merely an individual case but
a general theory by examining other gay characters' childhood fixations with
their fathers. Neil traces his fetish for leather as a symbol of power and

male dominance to his father's boots and his leather belt, with which he was whipped. Such theorizing stems from the need to displace guilt, as if to cry out, "It's not my fault I turned out this way!" Rechy refers to the hustler's "scorching, horrendous guilt" and "churning unfocused guilt" (Rechy, *City* 83, 305). George-Michel Sarotte lists Rechy among many authors who advance the cliché of a boy's attachment to a smothering, clinging, possessive mother as "a principle cause of homosexuality," citing that the narrator of *City of Night* refers to his mother's " 'ferocious love' from which he has had to escape in order to discover his identity" (Sarotte 170, 169). Sarotte also mentions that some other authors find an opposite pattern leading to male homosexuality: a son whose mother is "hostile or indifferent" (Sarotte 170). Sarotte provides no explanation of this discrepancy. The flourishing of such contradictory theories brings to light not the actual causes of homosexuality, which remain mysterious, but rather the lack of logical rigor in the desperate attempt to assign blame for something—homosexuality—that supposedly is wrong. In a non-homophobic society, the supposed "cause" of homosexuality would be a moot point.

Like *Falconer*, *City of Night* depicts homosexual men in a state of Denial, although some of Rechy's characters have worked through this stage. The protagonist makes strides towards overcoming his Denial and embracing his sexuality towards the end of the novel. Yet "the way in which hustling becomes a means of denying one's homosexual impulses is the underlying theme of John Rechy's first two books, *City of Night* and *Numbers*" (Altman, *Oppression* 15); the hustler's behavior, self-image, and rationalizations are based on his unwillingness to consider himself homosexual. People typically overcome Denial only after contact with openly gay people. Farragut never has any such encounters in *Falconer*. Even such exposure does not lead overnight to Acceptance, however. Whereas *Falconer* depicts "situational" homosexual activity among men who claim a heterosexual (or possibly bisexual) identity, *City of Night* illustrates how Denial can exist even in a gay milieu, the very setting most conducive to overcoming Denial. People who engage in same-sex sexual behavior "do not come to suspect themselves of being homosexual until they have acquired from people who are 'significant others' the notion of classifying people in this way, the language for doing it, and a set of 'reasons' for assigning oneself to that category" (Weinberg 11). Rechy's hero immerses himself in the gay world, and Rechy shows the gay world in greater detail than that provided by Gore Vidal or James Baldwin, but even though the hero is *in* the gay milieu, he denies that he is *of* it. Rechy never resolves the "deep and unacknowledged conflict between the hero's progressive involvement in homosexuality and his frantic determination to contain this within a traditional male identity" (Adams 84).

The protagonist of *City of Night* lives in and travels through the heart of many of the nation's largest gay ghettos in New York, Los Angeles, Hollywood, San Francisco, Chicago, and New Orleans. He hustles the streets, parks, and "tea rooms"; visits gay bars, gay X-rated movie houses, and gay beaches; and interacts with distinct minorities within the gay world, from hustlers to transvestites to leathermen. Rechy masterfully "depicts big cities as hellish neon jungles" (Austen 206) in which hustlers cannot mask their alienation and melancholy. Despite all their banter and bravado, the hustlers are starved for love and affection. The queens they encounter in the sordid gay ghettos use camp to acknowledge their longing for love, but the hustlers, who feel the same longing, are paralyzed beneath their butch facades and cannot express their true desires directly.

John Rechy patterned his character's journey upon his own experiences, and many readers and reviewers have forgotten they are reading a work of fiction in their haste to condemn Rechy for his alleged personal adventures from Times Square to Pershing Square. "Rechy's fiction deals in romanticized versions of himself," Adams declares (83). Sarotte concurs that Rechy's hero, "the hustler, the character who must fend for himself, who lives outside the law and struggles along in the jungle of cities, is the final embodiment of the pioneer, the lone man against the elements, against adversity" (189). John Rechy "has cast the homosexual male in the role of the new frontiersman, glorifying in his outlaw existence" (Adams 83).

Cheever uses third-person narration and names his protagonist to differentiate his protagonist from himself, despite all the similarities the two share. Rechy lacks Cheever's reluctance to be identified with his character's homosexual activities. Rechy uses the first person, and does not name his hero. (The convention of leaving the central character nameless in an autobiographical work of gay fiction is also followed by Edmund White in his two autobiographical novels, *A Boy's Own Story* and its sequel, *The Beautiful Room Is Empty*.) Near the end of the novel, the protagonist is asked, " 'What is your name?' " (Rechy, *City* 345), and he tells us, "I told him my first name" and then "I told Jeremy Adams my own last name" (345). These correspond to similar questions and narrative responses in Ralph Ellison's novel *Invisible Man*. In both cases, they remind us that we never learn the protagonist's name. Although leaving the narrator nameless may cast him in the generic role of a gay Everyman, an "I" with whom the gay reader can identify, the use of a nameless first-person narrator may also make it difficult to differentiate the narrator from the author. Many of the book's early reviewers utterly failed to make this distinction. As Rechy says in an introduction to the novel written twenty years after the original publication of *City of Night*:

> Only the book's subject seemed to be receiving outraged attention; its careful structure, whether successful or not, was virtually ignored. I was being viewed

and written about as a hustler who had somehow managed to write, rather than as a writer who was writing intimately about hustling—and many other subjects. (xv–xvi)

The title of the review in the *New York Review of Books,* "Fruit Salad," screams its homophobia. This review refers to "queer parties," "faggot social life," " 'Sodom on Five Dollars a Day,' " and Rechy's "determination to boil every last drop of poetry out of pederasty." In one of many sarcastic moments, the author of this review says "you just wish like mad that sodomy wasn't against the laws of heaven and earth so this sweet little whore could make it for life with some nice guy" (Chester 80, 83). The review does, however, comment on the two-part structure of the novel (despite Rechy's remark), but concludes that it is "two books of short stories" masquerading as a novel (Chester 79). Nevertheless, it seems fair to characterize the tone of the article as shrill if not hysterical on the subject of homosexuality, as the above quotations illustrate.

Curiously, no such outrage from critics greeted the deeply entrenched homosexual Denial evident in *Falconer.* The Denial of *City of Night's* unnamed protagonist, by contrast, is not monolithic. He takes steps towards coming out not taken by Farragut and the other inmates in *Falconer,* who remain imprisoned within their refusal to enter into or even to acknowledge the existence of a distinct gay subculture. Nevertheless, the protagonist of *City of Night,* though less closeted than Ezekiel Farragut, seems unable to develop an intimate relationship with a man. Like many hustlers, he equivocates about his sexual activities, hiding, quite implausibly, behind the facade of heterosexuality or bisexuality. Hustlers move in circles in which the label "homosexual" can be avoided, however unconvincingly. *City of Night* provides a glimpse of another of the many faces of Denial. As in *Falconer,* the sex takes place offstage or between the lines in *City of Night.* The outrage that greeted Rechy's first novel in many quarters was not elicited by graphic descriptions of sexual acts, which Rechy avoids. The narrator matter-of-factly but discreetly chronicles his actions. In view of the increased permissiveness in more recent years, in society and in gay and straight novels, *City of Night* now seems tame. Its hero fails to admit he desires other men sexually and romantically. Impersonal sex does not frighten him the way intimacy does; the narrator denies his emotional need for intimacy with another man and runs away whenever a situation threatens to become intimate. A potential score says to the narrator, carefully avoiding mention of the gender of the "people" he might go to bed with: " 'I can't see just going to bed with a lot of people—different ones every night.' " The potential score then goes on say that everyone needs companionship and that a "lonely fairy" epitomizes all that is most pitiable. The narrator tells us, "I liked him right away" (Rechy, *City* 216). Yet once in his score's apartment, the narrator flees as soon as he is touched. This panic is caused by the conversation, which reveals the score's desire for intimacy—and perhaps the protagonist's as well, though he cannot face it directly—rather than by imminent sexual contact. The narrator engineers his life so that he remains alone most of the time. His peers, male hustlers, never form close or long-lasting friendships with each other. Although Kerouac is a probable influence upon Rechy, "the only thing that these male prostitutes share with the Kerouac gang is the reassuring thought that in spite of conspicuous lapses, they are all fundamentally heterosexual" (Austen 206).

The narrator, like many of Rechy's characters, pretends to be heterosexual, a facade he could not maintain were he to admit that his romantic desires as well as his sexual desires are for men, not women. The narrator occasionally has sex with one of the vagrant girls in order to prove that there is nothing wrong with him. Rechy says that "in any hustling bar," the hustler feels "the necessity . . . to assert his masculinity with . . . any woman" (Rechy, *City* 297). When Pete is told about Flip, a drag queen he mistakes for a nymphomaniac, he asks the protagonist that the three of them have sex because, " 'It's Sexier that way" (45) because to him sex with a man is more stimulating than sex with a woman, though he refuses to admit this directly.

Even while earning their livelihood by having sex with men, many of the hustlers deny having any desire for the marks who hire them. In his novel *Myron*, Gore Vidal hints at the flimsiness of the heterosexual pose used by those men willing to have sex with other men in exchange for money. In this novel, the title character suddenly finds himself sent twenty-five years back in time, from 1973 to 1948, and he hears the slang term "jam," used in 1948 "to describe those males so addicted to heterosexuality that they will not drop their drawers for another male no matter how high the price—under $20, that is" (Vidal, *Myron* 75). The hustlers' Denials in *City of Night* also frequently seem farfetched, as in the case of one hustler, who claims that usually he does not get excited by sex with men. In fact, he insists, he is so bored by it that usually he falls asleep. This makes things easier for him, because he usually sleeps with an erection. Clearly, we are not meant to believe him. Jeremy asks the narrator how much of the appeal of being a hustler " 'is being a part of this alluring defiant world without really joining it?— . . . so you can say, "I do it only for the money involved"; or "I don't do anything back in bed myself; my masculinity is still intact—and in the meantime I can go with as many men as I— . . . *need* . . . to"?' " (Rechy, *City* 349; emphasis in original).

Pete foregrounds the economic transaction to deny actual homosexual desire. He says that any sexual act a man performs with a man for money is strictly business and does not mean he is homosexual. " 'It's when you start doing it for free . . . that you start growing wings' " (Rechy, *City* 40), that is, becoming a "fairy." Although the hustlers' pretense of heterosexuality was an absolutely necessary part of maintaining their masculine sexual appeal to their clients, this still leaves the sexual orientation of Rechy's hustler somewhat ambiguous. Is he gay? "*City of Night* and the other dark, brooding, lost novels of the sixties contained an out that allowed them, if necessary, to be interpreted as more than merely gay novels. . . . The authors were depicting queerness as a rather heavy burden which they were not quite ready to claim as their own" (Austen 206–7).

Awareness of their homosexuality alters and, at least initially, undermines men's sense of masculinity to the extent that this is defined by heterosexual norms. Rechy was writing during the early 1960s, before the Stonewall Inn riots. In those times, homosexuals sometimes overreacted in an attempt to hide their sense of alarm over not fitting into heterosexual roles. Thus in *City of Night* gay men frequently adopt hypermasculine poses, such as that of the tough, pseudo-heterosexual hustler or that of the leatherman (such as Neil), with his obsession with power and dominance (traditionally masculine traits). The roles of hustler and leatherman, in Rechy's vision, however, represent anything but a celebration of masculinity. Instead, these poses develop out of a sense of guilt, inadequacy, and self-hatred. The hustler feels that to lust frankly after men would destroy his illusory masculinity and hence his desirability to "scores." As for the leatherman, Altman thinks that for writers like John Rechy, self-hatred and guilt produce the belief that one deserves to be punished for being homosexual. This punishment is enacted through the rituals of sadomasochism, in which "men dress as the cops who persecute them and punish themselves, either directly or through others, for their homosexuality" (Altman, *Homosexualization* 193).

Occasionally these hypermasculine roles are spurned, and the role of transvestite or queen is adopted, as by Miss Destiny and other drag queens in *City of Night*. This role playing reflects the tendency within the pre-Stonewall gay world to allow straight society to define gender roles. *Falconer* illustrates that such stereotyping of homosexual men has persisted since Stonewall in the inmates' fears of being identified as homosexual, a fear not powerful enough to prevent them from indulging in homosexual behavior. (Cheever, in his late fifties at the time of the Stonewall riots, carried his pre-Stonewall homophobia with him to his grave.) In general, drag queens and other exaggeratedly effeminate gay men are products of societies that attach severe stigma to homosexuality. In a society that denies that gay men are real men, that is, in a society in which gay men are seen automatically as unmasculine, a drag queen is less threatening to the status quo than an openly gay man who is as masculine as a typical heterosexual man. But as sexual roles become more fluid, gay men themselves no longer see any need to act effeminate simply because they are gay, as they no longer equate homosexuality with effeminacy, and no longer fear asserting their own masculinity. Drag queens and other flagrantly effeminate gay men (such as those Rechy depicts in *City of Night*) are becoming less common in the gay world.

Since the publication of *City of Night*, there have been great efforts to develop new ways of conceiving of gender roles, masculinity and femininity, heterosexuality and homosexuality. Myra Breckinridge (in Gore Vidal's eponymous novel, published in 1968) announces her "mission: the destruction of the last vestigial traces of traditional manhood in the race in order to realign the sexes thus reducing population while increasing human happiness and preparing humanity for its next stage" (Vidal, *Myra* 41). Such a statement, even in this camp novel, shows the extent to which sex roles shifted in the five years following the publication of *City of Night*. Some of the masculine/feminine role-playing among Rechy's characters appears dated today. Unfortunately, many gay men still find that their initial awareness of their homosexuality threatens their sense of masculinity, a powerful incentive for denying their homosexuality.

Some of the characters in *City of Night* are confronted with the flimsiness of their own Denial when a woman questions their rationalizations that they have sex with other men only for the money, and that even when they have sex with other men, they do not reciprocate, at least supposedly. " 'Sure, maybe it's true—Now! . . . Why dont you split the scene, man— *if you really want to!'* " (Rechy, *City* 146; emphasis in original). Significantly, Rechy's hero hustles by choice, not out of any inability to secure conventional "respectable" employment elsewhere. Each time he leaves the hustling scene for a regular job, he soon returns.

Just as the woman points out the implausibility of the "trade's" pose, the saying "This year's trade is next year's competition" pithily and pitilessly lampoons the bogus macho pose of the male hustler as straight. People discuss Glen, a hustler in Santa Monica. One score says, " 'At first, Glen was strictly trade. Now—well— . . . He'll do everything!' [A]nother man told me, 'Glen will . . . have a . . . boyfriend' " soon (Rechy, *City* 213). The protagonist adheres to his pose of sexual indifference to men. He never develops the ability to form an intimate relationship with a steady boyfriend. Indeed, one homophobic cliché concerns "the pathos of the aging gay who has not managed to settle into a long-term relationship" (Blau 111). Hence *City of Night* chronicles loneliness. The words "loneliness," "lonely," "lonesome," and "lonesomeness" recur throughout this novel, to excess, according to Adams, who says Rechy "turns repetition into a stylistic device, with tiresome results" (91). In any event, the narrator's loneliness is a direct and predictable result of his deliberate attempt to seem aloof (Adams 86).

In the final section of the book, during Mardi Gras in New Orleans, the protagonist meets Jeremy, who offers him the possibility of an end to loneliness via a steady, loving relationship. The hustler attracts Jeremy not because of any bogus tough masculine pose, but because he has glimpsed the narrator in a unique unguarded moment in public, in which he blurts to two Johns: " 'Im not like you want me to be, the way I tried to look and act for you: not unconcerned, nor easygoing—not tough; no not at all. . . . No, . . . Im Scared' " (Rechy, *City* 341). Unsurprisingly, the scores lose interest as soon as the hustler breaks the rules of the game, spoiling the sexual fantasy. Mardi Gras, the time of wearing masks, becomes the only occasion in which the narrator unmasks himself. The gypsy tells him that Mardi Gras is the only time of the year when rather than wearing masks, people " 'wear their own faces! What you think is masks is really— . . . *Themselves!* ' " (291; emphasis in original). Sarotte claims that all of Rechy's "stories end when the masks are removed and the protagonists finally admit that they prefer men" (Sarotte 184). But when the narrator removes his mask, resists the commodification of his sexuality, and tentatively seeks to integrate his sexuality into the rest of his being, the scores abandon him in an apparent confirmation of his obsessive fear of being viewed as undesirable. Yet, unlike the scores, Jeremy wants a deep relationship, not an impersonal sexual encounter or a masturbatory sexual fantasy. He sees the individual beneath the hustler's mask and finds his vulnerability charming. The prospect of a sexual relationship that transcends the physical marks a possible milestone in the hustler's surmounting of his own Denial. Such a relationship would require overcoming self-hatred and internalized homophobia. Jeremy analyzes the hustler's loneliness, narcissism, and chronic avoidance of intimacy: " 'Some people tell themselves they want to be . . . wanted . . . when, actually, they wish . . . they could want someone back. . . .' Suddenly I heard myself saying: 'If I ever felt that I had begun to need anyone, I would— . . .' I stopped. 'Run away,' he finished" (Rechy, *City* 351). Jeremy touches upon the narcissism of the hustler, his frenetic and ceaseless struggle to prove his desirability. The vanity and narcissism of *City of Night*'s protagonist superficially resemble those Farragut recalls in the man who was obsessed with his appearance. The hustler's ability to function as a hustler depends upon youthful good looks, hence the hustler's narcissism and fear of aging. Yet Rechy suggests a psychological motivation that may outweigh any such practical consideration. Farragut terms narcissism self-love, but Rechy portrays it as a lack of self-love, an inner emptiness that one tries to fill by hustling an endless stream of men who not only find one attractive but also tangibly demonstrate this by paying one for sex. Only someone incapable of loving himself would feel impelled to prove himself in this way. No amount of success in cruising and scoring can compensate for this emotional emptiness. The narrator's insecurity, rather than his vanity, surfaces when he stares in the mirror and confronts his narcissistic obsession with himself.

Our hero is strongly attracted to Jeremy, who lets him be himself; around Jeremy the narrator drops his pose of indifference. Jeremy says that in a relationship love doesn't have to "send rockets into the sky"; he cautions the narrator against jettisoning the pose of indifference for an equally spurious romanticism. Love is " 'just the absence of loneliness. Thats love enough. . . . When you don't believe it's even possible, then you substitute sex' " (Rechy, *City* 352).

Denial exists so long as no admission is made that homosexual longing extends beyond the sexual act to one's identity and one's desire to share love with someone of the same gender. Being gay is more than mere sexual activity—a frightening prospect for those who engage in homosexual acts without acknowledging the implications of such behavior. The political implications of this are enormous. Altman concludes that from 1972 to 1982 the gay movement's greatest victory was to recast the terms of the debate over homosexuality "from behavior to identity." Opponents of gay rights came to be seen as people "attacking the civil rights of homosexual citizens" rather than as crusaders against isolated immoral or antisocial acts (Altman, *Homosexualization* 9). In acknowledging even to oneself that this desire for same-sex love is integral to one's identity, one becomes aware, as does David in *Giovanni's Room*, of myriad forms of discrimination against gays. Coming out is difficult. Particularly in questing to forge a stable gay union in a homophobic society, rather than in settling for furtive sexual encounters, one realizes that gay couples are denied many things taken for granted by heterosexual married couples, ranging from the encouragement and understanding of colleagues and parents to income tax breaks and legal rights. Feeling the brunt of the pervasive and insidious social, religious, legal, and economic obstacles facing gay people can lead one to Anger. No novelist expresses this stage of the coming-out process better than James Baldwin does in *Giovanni's Room*.

EXERCISE: IDENTIFYING DENIAL

We have seen many strategies of Denial in exploring *Falconer* and *City of Night*. Think back on those that struck you the most forcefully. Do they reflect emotions you have felt or experiences you have gone through? Does either Farragut or the protagonist of *City of Night* tell part of your own life story?

Each statement of Denial could be summed up by a logical argument something like this:

Homosexuals are effeminate.

I am not effeminate.

Therefore, I am not a homosexual.

Of course, in this as in many other logical arguments, key premises are often assumed to be true, and thus are left unstated. A man in Denial might think: "I couldn't be a homosexual; I'm not effeminate." The most basic strategy of Denial is to define homosexuality or homosexuals in a particular way that allows the person in Denial to say, "I am not that, therefore I couldn't be gay."

The forms of Denial are endless. Most broadly, they might be grouped around appearance, behavior, and miscellaneous traits, such as likes, interests, and occupation. Several of each type follow. Do any sound familiar? What is the unstated premise in each? What stereotypes about homosexuals does each embody? How accurate is each such generalization about homosexuality?

See if you recognize yourself (or your former self) or someone you know in any of the following statements. Can you think of other statements of Denial? You might wish to discuss these with a friend with whom you can be frank.

I am not gay [or] I could not be homosexual (because) . . .

APPEARANCE

I do not look effeminate.

I am muscular.

I do not wear tight pants.

I never dress in loud colors.

BEHAVIOR

I sleep (or have slept) with women.

I have no trouble "performing" sexually with women.

I've never had sex with a man.

I've had sex with men, but . . .

   it was just sex; it wasn't anything romantic.

   I prefer sex with women.

   it won't happen again.

   I was only experimenting (or going through a phase).

   I only do it (or did it) for the money.

   not in the past (week/month/year).

   not much [or not more than x times in the past (week/month/year)].

   only when there were no women around.

   only when I was drunk or high.

I take only the active role when I have sex with other men.

I never let a man kiss me.

I've never even set foot in a gay bar.

PERSONALITY TRAITS/MISCELLANEOUS

I don't even know anyone who is gay.

I don't like opera [or ballet].

My father was not distant and my mother didn't smother me with her love.

I enjoy playing/watching sports.

I'm not an interior decorator [or dancer or florist or antique dealer or . . .].

I am married.

I have children.

3

Anger: *Giovanni's Room*

I could have cried, cried for shame and terror, cried for not understanding how this could have happened to me, how this could have
happened *in* me.
—James Baldwin, *Giovanni's Room* 15

Anger seethes in David, the first-person fictional narrator of James Baldwin's novel *Giovanni's Room*. He narrates the entire story retrospectively
in the course of the night before his ex-lover, Giovanni, is executed. David, an impoverished American in Paris, had met a beautiful Italian youth,
Giovanni, and moved in with him to a tiny squalid room. But when David's
fiancée returns from Spain, he abandons Giovanni. David's homophobia,
reinforced by pressure from his father, is to blame. Giovanni falls into desperate straits, and in a fit of rage kills his former employer, Guillaume, a
rich homosexual who, like David, has refused to help him. Giovanni, in a
sensational case, has been convicted of murder.

The novel is David's anguished confession of his guilt for Giovanni's doom.
David's narration of his story—and Giovanni's—may be his way to purge
his guilt and to keep others from accusing him. As Oscar Wilde notes in
The Picture of Dorian Gray, "There is a luxury in self-reproach. When we
blame ourselves we feel that no one else has a right to blame us" (84).
Foucault says that "Western man has become a confessing animal" and that
Western literature is becoming increasingly confessional (I 59). The literary
form of the confession, Foucault says, appeals to the modern taste for self-
analysis and offers the promise that truth can be glimpsed between the
lines.

David's anguish and Anger over being homosexual separate him from others. He is still trying, unsuccessfully, to please his father, all the while resenting that this futile effort keeps him from what he wants. David has been characterized as a "self-hating latent homosexual" who cannot fully accept himself and who is thus a "tortured creature" (Sarotte 294). He initially characterizes his own homosexuality as vileness and equates it with the loss of his manhood. To distance himself from this "vileness," he projects a contrived self-image to win the love and approval of his manipulative father, whose presence is felt, though an ocean separates father and son. As David cynically notes that his rapport with his father was possible because "the vision I gave my father was exactly the vision in which I myself most desperately needed to believe" (Baldwin, *Giovanni* 30). This remark reveals the anger David carries towards his father. David's failure to break away from the patriarchal attitudes his father embodies cripples his ability to love and honor Giovanni. David is still bound, by his anger, to his father, and thus any true and lasting union with another man remains impossible. During his time with Giovanni, David had not yet come into an independent sense of self. David lets his father act like a dictator. As he looks back on his time with Giovanni, David comes to regret his former Denial bitterly. In the process of narrating his story, David finally answers the question "Who am I?" and leaves his Denial and "Identity Confusion" behind. He enters the second stage of the coming-out process, which Vivienne Cass terms "Identity Comparison." In this stage, one must cope with social alienation. David's homophobia, a self-hatred he projects upon others, alienates him from both gay and straight. He still uses the derogatory word "fairy," for instance, which "was considered to be in bad taste. It was fashionable to say a person was 'gay' " (Vidal, *City* 246). (In an ironic reversal, a quarter-century after the publication of *Giovanni's Room*, the term "fairy" was reclaimed with pride in the formation in October 1975 of the Faery Circle in San Francisco.)

David is not alone among homosexual men in being angry, either in fiction or in fact. Men coming to awareness of their homosexuality have many reasons for developing Anger over the way homosexuals have been treated in America and elsewhere, and this is reflected in many gay novels. If John Rechy's novel *City of Night* exemplifies Denial, his book *The Sexual Outlaw: A Documentary*, like *Giovanni's Room*, epitomizes Anger. In *The Sexual Outlaw*, John Rechy rails against the oppression of gay people in America. Its hero, Jim, seems as preoccupied with preserving his masculinity as David is. Unlike David, though, Jim claims to have had over seven thousand sexual partners! Yet Rechy notes that "Jim has never been fucked" (264), and Jim is proud of this sexual nonreciprocity. In flimsy special pleading, Anger is used to justify promiscuity of Casanovan proportions: "Imagine being forbidden by law to seek out a sexual partner. Imagine that—and you begin to understand the promiscuous rage of the sexual outlaw" (102). Like the unnamed protagonist of *City of Night*, and like Johnny Rio, the hero of Rechy's novel *Numbers*, Jim seems to learn little or nothing from his numerous impersonal sexual encounters. By contrast, David's Anger fuels the alchemical fire in which his sexual identity is transformed. In more recent novels, gay characters express anger over the way in which society has responded to the AIDS crisis. The character Dell Espinoza in Paul Monette's novel *Afterlife* murders a television evangelist, Mother Evangeline, who proclaims that AIDS represents the judgment of God upon homosexuals. But Dell has already come out; his anger does not stem, as does David's in *Giovanni's Room*, from unresolved issues surrounding his homosexuality.

Reasons for gay men's Anger are not merely to be found in works of fiction, however. From the mid-sixteenth century to the mid-twentieth century, American homosexuals were variously

> condemned to death by choking, burning, and drowning; they were executed, jailed, pilloried, fined, court-martialed, prostituted, fired, framed, blackmailed, disinherited, declared insane, driven to insanity, to suicide, murder, and self-hate, witch-hunted, entrapped. ,tereotyped, mocked, insulted, isolated, pitied, castigated, and despised. They were also castrated, lobotomized, shock-treated, and psychoanalyzed. (Katz 11)

Elisabeth Kübler-Ross observes that "when the first stage of denial cannot be maintained any longer, it is replaced by feelings of anger, rage, fury, and resentment. The logical next question becomes: 'Why me?' " (Kübler-Ross 44). In the coming-out process, some say "every gay man is filled with . . . rage. . . . We're forced—starting in childhood—to undergo anti-gayness. Our rage is the child of our impotence and suffering, of our fear. Unless we deal with it directly and usefully, it serves anti-gayness and fuels our self-destruction" (Walker 32). In letting go of the false security of Denial, one admits that Denial entails endless lies. With great and often sudden bursts of Anger, one becomes aware of the staggering psychic and emotional costs of maintaining elaborate schemes of deception and self-deception in attempting to be accepted by other people on their terms. In striving for authenticity and integrity, rather than trying to fit others' standards by living a lie, one is aware of how much one is up against and how insidious are the forces that impose conformity, at great cost in repression and oppression of gay people. Such awareness leads to Anger. "This anger is displaced in all directions and projected onto the environment at times, almost at random," frequently over trifles (Kübler-Ross 44–45).

Giovanni's act of murder stems from his Anger and desperation. Yet the Anger in this novel is not Giovanni's alone. This story primarily concerns the narrator's Anger. David relives his experiences as he discusses them, and eventually comes to reject his previous convictions. David's long period of vacillation about his sexual identity seems typical. Thomas Weinberg's recent study of gay men shows that it can take anywhere from " 'a few months' to ten years" for people to stop equivocating and to become certain that they are homosexual (150). In vacillating between men and women, David has an impersonal sexual encounter with Sue. David, like Rechy's hustler in *City of Night*, feels he must have sex with women in order to keep himself from having to confront being homosexual. But he must force himself to have sex with women; such acts do not spring from any natural desire he feels. David's sexual torment is suggested by the name of his girlfriend, to whom he proposes. The name "Hella" suggests that being with a woman rather than with a man is hell for David or, more generally, that for a homosexual to force himself to pose as heterosexual and to be sexually involved with a woman is hellish. David's pattern of sheltering himself behind a supposedly heterosexual identity is evident from the beginning, in his flashback to his first male-male sexual encounter. David runs away from his first adolescent sexual partner, Joey, and ignores him. David eventually runs into Joey and tells him an elaborate story of the heterosexual relationship he is in, although it is all a lie.

In chronicling his former Denial, David transcends it. He sees that those (like himself) driven by internalized homophobia to create a false heterosexual facade become experts in an intricate form of self-deception. "Baldwin's acute consciousness of the power of homophobia to shape character and destroy lives helps make David's self-deception and betrayals comprehensible if not altogether forgivable" (Summers 177). Brooding upon Giovanni's doom, David can look back on his first homosexual encounter and admit how much it had upset him, and how it had damaged his personality, making him "secretive and cruel. I could not discuss what had happened to me with anyone, I could not even admit it to myself" (Baldwin, *Giovanni* 24). David no longer denies what happened. He now bitterly regrets mistreating the men who made love to him. His Anger, in part, stems from his guilt over the ways in which his own internalized homophobia and corresponding Denial of being homosexual led to his betrayal of Giovanni and hence may be to blame for Giovanni's impending death. David is tormented by guilt. He cannot blame Giovanni's death on Jacques' failure to lend him money; David realizes that he is as much to blame as Jacques is. Giovanni's death leads to the possibility of David's redemption from a life of lies. David recalls that he used to lie in bed at night, listening to Giovanni's breathing and dreaming of his hands "or anybody's hands, which would have the power to crush me and make me whole again" (117). "Giovanni's death is the ritual sacrifice which saves David from the 'male prison,' the tragic source of his self-knowledge and ultimately the catharsis from which a real spiritual purification can be hoped for" (Adams 44).

When he first meets Giovanni, though, David's Denial seems unshakeable. Jacques suggests to David that he buy a drink for Giovanni, the new bartender in Guillaume's gay bar. David protests that he is attracted to women, not men: " 'If that was his sister looking so good, I'd invite *her* to have a drink with us' " (Baldwin, *Giovanni* 43; emphasis in original). David says he does not buy drinks for men. But his own body, via a tightening in his chest, belies his supposed indifference. Later, when Hella is due back in Paris, David tells Giovanni that he does not want Hella to find out. " 'People have very dirty words for—for this situation' " (107). At first David tells Hella that Giovanni is only his roommate. Eventually, however, David admits even to Hella, " 'I was lying to myself' " (216), but only after she has spotted him with a sailor in a gay bar. He simply cannot sustain his lies.

As David starts to admit to himself, "I may be homosexual," rather than maintaining, "I am not homosexual," he begins to alter his self-image. He has left what Vivienne Cass terms the "Identity Confusion" stage of the coming-out process and has entered the "Identity Comparison" stage. Rather than seeing his homosexual behavior as an occasional lapse from his supposedly heterosexual nature, as do Farragut and Jody in *Falconer*, he begins to admit that he is different from others. " 'I'm different' . . . is a [concise] expression of these feelings of alienation" (Cass 225).

Baldwin hints at the essentially homosexual nature of David and Giovanni in the names he gives to the male lovers. *Giovanni's Room* follows Baldwin's religiously charged *Go Tell It on the Mountain*, and Baldwin, who had been a preacher, was influenced by the Bible (Weatherby 28). The name David possibly suggests the Biblical King David, while the name Giovanni may allude to Jonathan. (The names Giovanni and Jonathan are both variants of the name John.) In the Bible, David says of Jonathan, "Your love for me was wonderful, surpassing the love of women" (II Samuel 1:26, New English Bible). Giovanni, like Jonathan, is killed in his youth, leaving a man behind to reflect on his wonderful love. In so naming his characters, Baldwin suggests that the homosexuality of David and Giovanni is part of their destiny, just as it was for David and Jonathan. "Giovanni" may also allude to John, the Beloved Disciple. Some gay scholars have speculated about a possible homoerotic bond between Jesus and the Beloved Disciple (John). Surviving second-century references to the apocryphal manuscript *The Secret Gospel of Mark* link Jesus sexually with Lazarus, indicating that speculation about the possible homosexuality of Jesus is not merely a recent phenomenon. The interpretation given by Claude Summers that "the name David means 'loving' and the name Giovanni means 'God has given' " (192) suggests that David spurns the gift of God (Giovanni) out of his failure to be as loving as he should be.

David recognizes the depth of his love for Giovanni. In doing so, he senses the futility of playing the game of passing as heterosexual. Nevertheless, he knows that abandoning the pretense will be costly. He fears a severe loss of status and privilege in coming out as a homosexual man. In most contemporary Western cultures, such a fear would be justified, even though Walter Williams' research among the Native American berdaches and Arthur Evans's historical research on prepatriarchal Western religions indicate that not all cultures have stripped gay men of power and prestige.

David sees himself as an outsider. He refrains from revealing his new self-image to others. He knows his love affairs with other men will never be praised, protected, rewarded, or encouraged by his father or his society. David recalls overhearing his father say he wants his son to grow up to be a man, a stereotypically masculine man, not " 'a Sunday school teacher' " (Baldwin, *Giovanni* 24). David's father seems like a fairly typical American man in that he projects his self-doubts about his own masculinity upon his son and seeks to confirm his own manhood through him. David feels heavy-handed pressure from his father and tries to appease him. When he can do so no longer, he becomes bitter, as he has crossed the line of respectability and cut himself off from his father's approval. Gay people "are closely watched to see what constitutes the limits of a thing. . . . One of the strongest measures heterosexual culture has is how close each of its members comes to being 'like a faggot' or 'like a dyke.' We are essential to them knowing who they are" (Grahn 5). David is angry as he realizes that he will dwell on the fringe of society, apart from the heterosexual majority, a position to which he has not yet reconciled himself. David's neurosis stems from his "desperate attempt to adhere to the American virile ideal" (Sarotte 27). David wants the security that he thinks the role of fatherhood can offer. He imagines having his "manhood unquestioned, watching my woman put my children to bed" (Baldwin, *Giovanni* 137). Now David knows this will never happen. Like others in what Cass defines as the second stage of the coming-out process, the "Identity Comparison" stage, David no longer feels he belongs "to society at large as well as to specific subgroups such as family and peers" (Cass 225). David's new self-image entails resentment, anger, self-loathing, and ambivalence, rather than Acceptance of his homosexuality.

Coming to realize "I may be homosexual" is no easy task in the world Baldwin depicts, in which homosexuality carries a strong stigma, forcing concealment and duplicity. "The gay world—then called 'queer'—was mainly underground" (Weatherby 46). Strong incentives exist for passing as heterosexual, even at the cost of self-deception. Baldwin himself had experienced this first-hand; in his teens, he "carr[ied] on a double life, a life of deception—sinner during the week and saintly Young Minister on Sundays" (Weatherby 29). David, likewise, remains between the gay and straight worlds, not feeling he belongs to either. Sarotte sees David's conflict between his powerful yearning for sexual contact with other men and his fear and loathing of homosexuality as far from unique, as the protagonists in several of Baldwin's other novels and the protagonists in many of Gore Vidal's novels face the same struggle. David, like these other protagonists, must wrestle with his "fear and guilt" in "a desperate attempt to preserve mental health" (Sarotte 58).

Baldwin himself, unlike John Cheever, publicly acknowledged his sexual orientation, at some cost to his literary and political reputation. Yet upon its emergence, Baldwin ridiculed the new gay liberation movement: "gay liberation . . . I feel very dubious about all that. . . . If you happen to be homosexual or whatever, you don't have to form a club in order to learn to live with yourself" (Weatherby 344). As his biographer notes, Baldwin "seemed at times to feel there would be some terrible judgment on his sexuality. That theme seemed to obsess him. He seemed to have come out of the closet so many times" (Weatherby 338).

The climate in America was charged with homophobia at the time Baldwin was writing *Giovanni's Room*. A conservative reaction had set in following the liberalization of gender roles that had occurred during World War II. The backlash against homosexuals was fierce. Alfred Knopf, whose firm had published Baldwin's first novel, *Go Tell It on the Mountain,* "found the homosexual theme [of *Giovanni's Room*] 'repugnant' " (Weatherby 119). Many felt that Gore Vidal had thrown away a promising career in 1948 by allowing the publication of *The City and the Pillar,* which is considered to be the first novel issued by a major American publishing house that portrays homosexuality frankly. At the time Baldwin sought a publisher eight years later, no similar novel had been published by a major American publisher since Vidal's. "Baldwin said he was told the novel would ruin his reputation as a leading young black writer and he was advised to burn the manuscript" (Weatherby 119). Roger Austen notes that had *Giovanni's Room* been Baldwin's first novel, it probably would have remained unpublished. Its publication was made possible by the success of *Go Tell It on the Mountain* (1953), which had established Baldwin as a major black writer of great potential in the United States (Austen 149).

To disguise autobiographical influences and to blunt criticism, given the political climate in America, Baldwin chose to set the novel elsewhere. In doing so, Baldwin followed a long-standing convention of depicting unconventional love (which includes any type of homosexual love) and explicit lust of any kind (whether homosexual or heterosexual) in a foreign country. Thomas Mann, for instance, had done so in "Death in Venice," as had André Gide in *The Immoralist,* though the latter used northern Africa rather than southern Europe for a setting. Similarly, "fluid movement across sexual boundaries" occurs in Egypt in Durrell's *Alexandria Quartet* (Boone, "Mappings" 83). Although Gore Vidal's *The City and the Pillar* takes place in the United States, *Giovanni's Room* takes place (apart from a few flashbacks) in France. In 1791 homosexuality had been made completely legal in France. This continued under the Napoleonic Code, although homosexuality has never enjoyed widespread social approval in France. But the United States had no such legal protection for homosexuals in the 1950s (and still lacks them in all but seven states and scattered municipalities). Discrimination against gay men and lesbians actually increased during the 1950s. For instance, "In April 1953, just weeks after Eisenhower was inaugurated, the new president issued an executive order banning gay men and lesbians from federal jobs" (D'Emilio and Freedman 293). Giovanni is reminded by David that homosexuality is a crime in America, where he grew up.

Perhaps to lessen the possibility of the novel being read as autobiographical, Baldwin also chose to portray all the characters in this story as white. There is not a single black character in *Giovanni's Room*. Baldwin's own anger, of course, stemmed not only from the oppression he felt as a gay man but also from the discrimination he faced as a black man. Early in his adulthood, long before the civil rights movement, Baldwin was refused service in a diner, and, he later explained, "a seething anger took over: this fever has recurred in me, and does, and will until the day I die" (Weatherby 38). Some of this double-edged anger seems evident in *Giovanni's Room*, even though Baldwin's hero is white and "adrift in the Old World decadence of Paris. . . . By keeping his persona both white and just bisexually confused and by setting him in the midst of foreign rather than domestic depravity," Baldwin could keep his critics at bay (Austen 150). Nevertheless, some have ignored the many differences between David and Baldwin and have viewed David merely as a psychological case study in Baldwin's personal sexual problems even though "the confessional style is the necessary expression of David's character and situation" (Adams 37).

Baldwin's difficulties in coming out were compounded by his role as black spokesperson, which he probably wished to keep separate from the public reaction to the autobiographical elements in *Giovanni's Room*. This may be why Baldwin made his characters in *Giovanni's Room* white and set the novel entirely in France. Some critics feel that *Giovanni's Room* lacks the immediacy of Baldwin's work about American blacks. Although most critics accept the ability of heterosexual upper-middle-class white males to write credibly about any kind of people (or did so until quite recently), people from racial and sexual minorities have often been viewed as incapable of writing about anything beyond the experience of their own minority. Although some critics faulted Baldwin for eschewing writing about American blacks from a black perspective in *Giovanni's Room*, the novel is among the best-known and best-read American gay novels (Austen 152). *Giovanni's Room* created a sensation in the gay underground almost immediately after its publication, as so little then in print addressed gay issues. Gay readers quickly identified the novel as gay:

> Gay readers were, after all, old hands at recognizing pertinent fiction disguised by multiple-choice interpretations. These readers could completely identify with the central struggle of the novel, as it was basically a description

of coming out, which was much the same for young American men in Peoria as for those in Paris. (Austen 150)

Apart from the gay underground's eager reception of *Giovanni's Room* and some critical acclaim, the book was criticized. It was not only white literary critics who found fault with Baldwin's decision to forgo writing about blacks in *Giovanni's Room*. Baldwin could not escape criticism from black militants. The counterculture of the 1960s was often just as homophobic as was the dominant culture (Altman, *Homosexualization* 2); "there was some opposition to gay rights even within the New Left" (Greenberg 459n). At times, under pressure from black militants, Baldwin mirrored their homophobia. In response to savage homophobic attacks in print from Eldridge Cleaver, "for whom homosexuality is a 'sickness' on a level with 'baby-rape' " (Adams 36), Baldwin made some homophobic remarks of his own. Speaking of Cleaver, Baldwin said, "All that toy soldier has done is call me gay. . . . I also felt I was confused in his mind with the unutterable debasement of the male—with all those faggots, punks, and sissies, the sight and sound of whom, in prison, must have made him vomit more than once" (Weatherby 292).

Baldwin's novels betray ambivalence about homosexuality, as did Baldwin himself. Baldwin avoided the gay label: "I love a few people; some are women and some are men" (Weatherby 340). Baldwin seems to concur with Sigmund Freud's notion that all people are basically bisexual; Freud referred to the "polymorphously perverse" nature of sexuality and denied the existence of homosexuals as a separate category of people. Freud's conception can be employed to avoid dealing with homosexuality or homosexuals as such. A common strategy, and one that reduces anxiety and alienation is to perceive oneself as "both homosexual and heterosexual. . . . Strategies that focus on perceiving others as ambisexual allow further reduction of these feelings by minimizing the perceived differences between [oneself] and others" (Cass 227). In his novel *Another Country*, Baldwin deliberately blurs distinctions between black and white as well as those between gay and straight characters. In a contrived symmetry, Vivaldo, a (mostly) straight white man, has an affair with Ida, a straight black woman, whose late (mostly straight) brother Rufus has had an affair with the (essentially) gay white Eric; later, after Eric returns from France, Vivaldo goes to bed with him, while Eric and the straight, white Cass have a fling. "The role Eric . . . plays in the lives of Cass and Vivaldo is what critics commonly identify as the novel's major weakness" (Adams 51). Far from subordinating gayness to blackness in this novel, though, it has been argued that "Baldwin ultimately produces the reverse effect by having everyone go to bed with nearly everyone else" (Austen 202). Yet *Giovanni's Room*, unlike *Another Country*, shows the anguish that such sexual ambivalence can produce. After meeting Giovanni, David suddenly longs to leave the bar and find Hella and to play the role of her protector. Jacques preaches to David: " 'Confusion is a luxury which only the very, very young can possibly afford and you are not that young anymore' " (Baldwin, *Giovanni* 57).

Baldwin nevertheless avoids depicting any of his heroes as exclusively homosexual. Sarotte concludes, in what seems an accurate assessment, that in Baldwin's novels a woman always threatens to come between male lovers because in Baldwin's novels, some trace of heterosexuality must exist in a man for him "to remain the Beloved" (Sarotte 57). Apparently, for whatever reason, Baldwin shied away from presenting a thoroughly homosexual character as desirable. But Sarotte goes much further than this, insisting that Elisha, the protagonist of *Another Country*, and David "are both *primarily* heterosexual" (Sarotte 57; emphasis in original), mistaking David's former pretense of heterosexuality for David's present narrative stance, in which he admits that his supposed heterosexuality was a sham. Although we do not glimpse Giovanni until page 39, David acknowledges his own homosexuality on the novel's second page: he imagines that on the train the following morning, after Giovanni's death, a woman will expect him to flirt with her and will be puzzled when he does not do so. David thus indicates that as a result of his vigil of introspection preceding Giovanni's execution, he has admitted much that he refused to face while he and Giovanni were together. Henceforth, he will drop the pretense of sexual interest in women. He will not flirt with women because they do not sexually attract him; he has merely used them to convince himself and others that he is heterosexual. He is no longer in Denial, and this present stance of narrative consciousness must be contrasted with that which he held during his affair with Giovanni, when he was still in Denial. Why would a "primarily heterosexual" David imagine in advance of boarding the train that he will not flirt with the woman sitting across from him? As Sarotte himself notes, though Hella competes with Giovanni for David's sexual and social favors, she is only "momentarily successful" (Sarotte 58); to the extent that David may be considered bisexual, his homosexual yearnings clearly outweigh his heterosexual ones. Baldwin may be drawing from his own experience in noting that in hesitating and vacillating, in holding on to two mutually exclusive options, one loses both. At sixteen, Baldwin, "torn between [his first love] affair [with a man] and the pulpit, . . . eventually gave up both" (Weatherby 30). Procrastination and ambivalence produce loss.

Like Baldwin himself, David, the narrator of *Giovanni's Room*, discloses ambivalence and homophobia, and he suffers as a result. His past attitudes are transformed as he acknowledges the consequences of his dishonesty. In *Giovanni's Room*, exclusively gay characters, such as Jacques and Guillaume, are effeminate and repulsive, but David comes to realize that he has only been projecting his self-contempt onto Jacques. David thus sees his former projection of self-hatred for what it was, unlike *Falconer*'s Ezekiel Farragut who never realizes that he projects his self-hatred onto the Cuckold. When David tells Jacques that he finds much of Jacques' life despicable, Jacques replies, " 'The way to be really despicable is to be contemptuous of other people's pain' " (Baldwin, *Giovanni* 75), words that come back to haunt David after he realizes that he has caused Giovanni excruciating pain. Even though David has grown, however, the novel itself seems ambivalent about homosexuality.

It is moot to calculate how much of David's ambivalence may stem from Baldwin's own ambivalence, and how much may derive from pressures upon Baldwin to produce a novel that upholds traditional sexual morality, according to which homosexuals are "deviants" who must be made to suffer for their "perversion." That Baldwin chose to depict David as ambivalent does not necessarily mean that Baldwin himself was ambivalent. In any case, the negative outcome of the novel is ambiguous, and certainly can be read as a condemnation of homosexuality, which may be why this novel could be published in 1956, during the notoriously homophobic, conservative Eisenhower years. Such apparent condemnation of homosexuality was virtually obligatory then, for without it, gay writers would despair of getting their works published or reviewed favorably in America (Austen 152). Baldwin had been forced, in order to get Knopf to publish *Go Tell It on the Mountain*, to delete its original ending, in which "John, the young Baldwin character, reveal[s] his homosexuality, saying, in effect, 'I want a man' " (Weatherby 96). Baldwin's homosexuality was not public knowledge prior to the publication of *Giovanni's Room* (Weatherby 82). Due to its homosexual theme, considered shocking at the time, *Giovanni's Room* was rejected by many publishers in the United States, and was first published in England (Weatherby 122). Predictably, despite favorable reviews, "the novel did officially identify [Baldwin] as a homosexual writer, which limited his image in the literary community" (Weatherby 129).

For all the controversy surrounding the manuscript, it does anything but glamorize the gay subculture of its time. "The ending of *Giovanni's Room*—like that of *The City and the Pillar*—is brutal and fatal" (Sarotte 27). On the surface, this novel thus adheres to the time-honored literary convention evident in Cheever's *Falconer* in the Cuckold's tale (see Chapter Two), in Gore Vidal's *The City and the Pillar*, and in other gay novels, of portraying homosexual expression as leading to violent death. Historically in the West, a violent death for homosexuals was not merely fictional. For centuries, the Church, in league with secular authorities, tried homosexuals for heresy and condemned them to death. Under the Inquisition, "homosexuality came to be viewed as a form of heresy" and thus the existence of homosexuality, or the mere accusation of it, "confirmed" by confessions extracted via torture, was considered in and of itself proof of heresy. The Roman Catholic Church continued to sanction the execution of homosexual "heretics" until the seventeenth century (Evans, *Witchcraft* 99). Executions of homosexuals continued under Protestant authorities after the Reformation. Secular rulers also executed gay men. In 1290, for example, King Edward I of England passed a law calling "for death by burning in the case of sodomites" (Evans, *Witchcraft* 92). The number of gays and lesbians put to death in this fashion is incalculable: five thousand Knights Templar alone were accused of homosexuality and other trumped-up charges and arrested in France in 1307 under orders from the King of France. They and their brethren in other countries were exiled, imprisoned, or executed, and all their property confiscated (Evans, *Witchcraft* 92–93). "It is impossible to determine how many people were killed by Christian witch-hunters. Estimates vary between several hundred thousand to almost ten million. But if anything, most estimates are probably low" (Evans, *Witchcraft* 99).

Secular authorities continued executing men for homosexuality long after Catholic and Protestant churches ceased doing so. During the nineteenth century, approximately eighty men were hanged in England by the state between 1800 and 1835 for practicing homosexuality (Crompton 55). The killing of homosexuals by government order has taken place within living memory. Under Hitler, there were "massive deportations of homosexuals to Nazi extermination camps"; after 1937, "any SS member convicted of homosexuality was executed," and, to compound an already massive injury, the Federal Republic of Germany kept the anti-homosexual Nazi statutes on the books, "sending survivors of the concentration camps to prison with sentences as long as six years" (Greenberg 436, 438, 456). It is said that Fidel Castro's brother Raoul was much impressed with the People's Republic of China's crackdown on homosexuals in the parks of Shanghai, in which homosexuals were clubbed to death by the police. Under Castro, gays in Cuba have been imprisoned and fired from their jobs; in 1968, "men suspected of homosexuality on the basis of their style of clothing and haircut were arrested indiscriminately on the streets and induced into special militarized work units" (Greenberg 441). In short, state-instigated violence against homosexuals has had a long history, which has led to the deaths of countless homosexuals.

The fictional narrative device of linking homosexuality with death obliquely suggests that Denial and repression are preferable to giving homosexuality free rein. The message seems to be that homosexual passions can lead only to a bad end. But *Giovanni's Room* can be read as a criticism not of homosexuality but of homophobia. Giovanni's demise is caused not by his homosexuality but by David's inability or unwillingness to deal forthrightly with his own homosexuality.

David's unsuccessful strategy of Denial throughout most of his story is to avoid feeling responsible for his choices by denying that they are his to make. When Hella writes of her impending return, David feels relief, as this spares him from having to make a decision. He admits he had believed all along that his relationship with Giovanni could not endure. Similarly, after Guillaume fires Giovanni, David feels that fate is settling things, so that he does not have to make the tough decisions himself. But a magic transformation of his sexual orientation does not occur upon his reunion with Hella, despite his wish that this meeting would lead to instant clarity about his identity. David thus tries to escape from being held morally responsible for his actions. He wishes to drift along passively, imagining that persons and forces act upon him without his ability to counteract them. He notes that his sexuality unfolded in France "with no one to watch, no penalties attached" and concludes, "nothing is more unbearable, once one has it, than freedom" (Baldwin, *Giovanni* 9–10). David cannot quite bring himself to admit that he has the freedom to be true to himself. The thought that he must make choices terrifies him. Curiously, the concept of choice is linked etymologically with the word "homosexual": "In medieval times the word for *heresy* and the word for *homosexual* were synonymous in several languages. What *heresy* means literally is 'choice' (from *herite*)" (Grahn 8). David does not admit even to himself that he would rather be with Giovanni than with Hella, his girlfriend who becomes (briefly) his fiancée, until her presence becomes odious to him, as neither party has much genuine desire for the other. Both are motivated by fear and a cold calculation of benefits rather than passion. Even "Hella communicates in clichéd terms which betray her . . . lack of genuine feeling" (Adams 39).

This entire strategy of denying responsibility rests on lies: to his father, to Giovanni and his gay friends, to Hella, and to himself. David confesses his dishonesty while telling his story: "I repent now . . . one particular lie among the many lies I've told, . . . lived, and believed. This is the lie which I told to Giovanni but never succeeded in making him believe, that I had never slept with a boy before. I had. I had decided that I never would again" (Baldwin, *Giovanni* 10–11). This resolve also is a lie. David thus admits at the outset of his story that his homosexual history predates his encounter with Giovanni. Furthermore, David indicates that he is not sexually interested in women and will not flirt with women to camouflage this. Yet even in admitting that he lied to Giovanni, David seeks to deny the conscious choices he made in unfolding and expressing his homosexuality. He says that he and his teenage friend Joey "kissed, as it were, by accident" (13), a transparent lie; one's first kiss in life is a deliberate and bold act, not an accident.

Baldwin insisted that the theme of the novel is lying to oneself. "The bisexual triangle was only the surface concern. . . . To [Baldwin], the real theme was the price of lying to yourself" (Weatherby 118). But in the hysteria surrounding the novel's depiction of homosexuality, most readers lost sight of this: "Very few readers would see the novel the way [Baldwin] did. It would merely be a homosexual novel to most people" (Weatherby 118).

David lies to his father, who may symbolize the entire system of patriarchal authority in society, which dictates behavior by controlling prestige, power, and pursestrings. Homosexuality undermines patriarchy. James Nelson notes, "Unconsciously, the hetero-male seems to fear that an acceptance of male homosexuality in others would open him to the risk of being 'womanized,' losing his power, and becoming the same sort of sex object into which he has made women" (174). This patriarchy rests on male bonding and misogyny without being "primarily or necessarily homosexual"; on the contrary, "homophobia directed by men against men is misogynistic" (Sedgwick 20), given the tradition of equating the passive/receptive role in male homosexuality with effeminacy, a distinction that can be traced to ancient Greek times. Only "one role . . . was intrinsically honorable and valorized without question: the one that consisted in being active, in dominating, in penetrating, in asserting one's superiority" (Foucault, II 215). The connection between homophobia and misogyny is evident in early Christian writers, such as Chrysostom and Augustine, the latter of whom "expressed feelings of disgust similar to Chrysostom's in regard to a man allowing his body to be used 'as that of a woman' since, in Augustine's words, 'the body of a man is as superior to that of a woman as the soul is to the body' " (Boswell 157). It should be remembered that the equation of male homosexuality with effeminacy is an arbitrary social construct. "The virility of the homosexual orientation of male desire seemed as self-evident to the ancient Spartans, and perhaps to Whitman, as its effeminacy seems in contemporary popular culture" (Sedgwick 26–27). However society defines virility, access to money, social standing, and respectability all hinge upon "playing the game" according to the patriarchy's (manipulative father's) rules. Violating those conventions carries the cost of poverty, ostracism, and isolation.

Like David's father, Hella is also "society's representative," and her reaction represents provincial American values (Sarotte 176). (Sarotte's subsequent assertion that "there are few tolerant women in American literature of the homosexual" (176)—Auntie Mame notwithstanding—may have been true of the period preceding publication of his book *Like a Brother, Like a Lover* [1978] but seems inaccurate when applied to gay novels published during and since the late 1970s, such as *Taking Care of Mrs. Carroll*.) Hella grows tired of pretending to a sexual sophistication that, for her, is forced. An American innocent abroad, Hella yearns to return to America, to marry, to become a housewife, and to have babies. David tries to fit into this plan, but once Hella and David recognize that he cannot, they part. Given its explicitly gay theme, Baldwin's novel "stands in ironic relation to that genre perfected by Henry James, where the American innocent is put to the test of experience in the Old World" (Adams 38). In writing to his father, David omits all mention of his homosexuality. He plays up his relationship with Hella, hoping to convince his father to send money. David knows full well that his father would not send money if he knew about David's affair with Giovanni.

David is broke when he meets Giovanni. David moves in with Giovanni partly out of financial desperation, and this burden of financial panic strains their relationship relentlessly. It puts both of them at the mercy of older, unattractive, effeminate homosexuals, such as Jacques and Guillaume, who use money to manipulate younger men and to secure sexual favors from them. David's financial situation mirrors Baldwin's own early circumstances in France. He lived hand to mouth, relying on friends and acquaintances for loans, many of which he never repaid (Weatherby 101).

Giovanni occupies a tiny first-floor maid's room in a squalid section of Paris. As the novel's title suggests, this room that David and Giovanni share for a few months serves as the unifying symbol of this novel. Claustrophobic and chaotic, the room symbolizes the gay subculture of the early postwar pre-Stonewall period of the 1950s and the repression, restriction, and furtiveness of the homosexual life of those times. "Homosexuality in *Giovanni's Room* is not merely a private experience, for the social prohibitions against homosexuality . . . intrude even into Giovanni's closet-like retreat" (Summers 175). Giovanni's odyssey takes him from cramped room to prison cell, yet David imagines that the latter is probably no more cramped and restricting than the former. As in *Falconer,* the prison setting suggests that being homosexual in a homophobic society is akin to being imprisoned. Baldwin had no need to exaggerate the homophobia of the period or the clandestine nature of the homosexual underground. Indeed, to portray the gay world positively in print was at that time virtually unthinkable, and certainly any such positive portrayal was unpublishable in America. Gays shared much of the larger society's homophobia. Thus David refers to the "mutual contempt" of the habitués in Guillaume's bar. As Harry Hay, who founded the Mattachine Society, a pioneering homophile group, in 1950, explains in an interview:

> "At this moment in 1979, it is difficult to project what our position in 1950 was like. Homosexuality was not only immoral but illegal. . . . [Homosexuals had] total fear of being turned over [at] any time to the police. . . . We thought of ourselves as being illegal. The idea of self-respect didn't exist." (Thompson, "Harry Hay" 189, 191)

The Mattachine Society kept a very low profile. Its activities consisted primarily of private discussion groups and social events. The post-Stonewall gay liberation movement criticized the quietism of such early homosexual rights groups, comparing them negatively with the high-visibility political activism of gays in the 1970s and 1980s; the Mattachine Society was "generally regarded by young activists as an Uncle Tom organization" (Brown 24). But it should be remembered that the risks involved in simply attending a meeting of homosexuals during the McCarthy era were enormous. It is hard to imagine the emergence of the gay liberation movement after the Stonewall riots of 1969 without the pioneering work of Harry Hay and the Mattachine Society, which faced enormous obstacles. Society's laws and attitudes were intimidating and homosexuals' internalized homophobia was boundless. Some homophile groups held discussion groups in the 1950s and 1960s to consider seriously "Is homosexuality a mental illness?" (The milieu in which homosexuals could torment themselves with such questioning is re-created in *The Beautiful Room Is Empty*, the subject of Chapter Four.)

Giovanni's room symbolizes a small subculture struggling to come into its own, a place that is not yet all it might be. Giovanni's plans for renovating the room are never realized. His attempts to remodel may suggest the need the gay community had for regeneration from within, a process only just beginning when Baldwin wrote *Giovanni's Room*. Harry Hay sees regeneration from within as crucial for the future of gays: "In a sense, the earlier homophile movement and gay liberation movement were movements reactive to heterosexuals. For the first time, we have to create a movement that doesn't start with them, but within us" (Thompson, "Harry Hay" 198). But Giovanni's remodeling of the room is premature and abortive, symbolizing internal turmoil and chaos that cannot be resolved happily. Despite Giovanni's grandiose plans for renovating the room, the plans result in having to live amidst stacks of bricks and plaster dust everywhere. Much of the relationship between David and Giovanni is evident in the setting of the room as David stares at the walls and sees in their wallpaper "distant, archaic lovers" in a huge rose garden (Baldwin, *Giovanni* 115). The wallpaper pattern of the courtly lovers (male and female) serves as a harsh reminder to David that he and Giovanni have no such public meeting place. Even the ceiling "obscured but failed to soften its malevolence behind the yellow light which hung like a diseased and undefinable sex in its center" (Baldwin, *Giovanni* 115). Rather than being able to parade their romance in the genteel and spacious setting reserved for the lovers in the wallpaper, David and Giovanni are confined to a tiny room and oppressive gay bars. In the latter, David must endure the leers of men who disgust him; in the former, lacking curtains, David smears furniture polish over the windows to gain some privacy, but at the cost of making the room even more isolated and confining.

David feels trapped in Giovanni's room and in the homosexual milieu. The walls themselves seem to close in on him. Given the cramped quarters, coupled with David's homophobia, it is hardly surprising that as soon as they start sharing the same apartment, "their ephemeral happiness begins to deteriorate," for David cannot prevent his fears and psychological conflicts from contaminating his relationship with Giovanni (Sarotte 27). David remembers the anguish and fear beneath the pleasure and excitement he and Giovanni felt at the beginning of their relationship. They face great odds in trying to last as a couple. Indeed, "cohabitation by David and Giovanni is obviously impossible" (Sarotte 177). Sarotte insists that traditionally, in American literature, homosexual couples are unhappy (27). Some have seen the literary convention of unhappiness in romantic love as a given in Western literature, pertaining to all couples, whether gay or straight. Dennis de Rougemont, tracing the literature of romantic love back to the myth of Tristan and Iseult, maintains, "Unless the course of love is being hindered, there is no 'romance' " (43). In any case, a gay couple in which one or both partners hold homophobic attitudes or fail to accept their sexual orientation seems bound for unhappiness. A gay man holding "strong negative prejudices about gay men . . . [probably] would have great difficulties forming intimate, trusting relationship[s] with gay men" (Alexander 90–91). David asks Giovanni, "What kind of life can we have in this room?—this filthy little room. What kind of life can two men have together, anyway?" (Baldwin, *Giovanni* 188). David is infuriated.

Their relationship is doomed, like most of the gay relationships depicted in literature when Baldwin was writing. Baldwin also follows a venerable American literary tradition in pairing David, a man "white, blond, puritanical, stifled by his culture, [with] Giovanni, . . . the virile yet gentle Latin, sensual, warm" (Sarotte 100). Depicting a homoerotic relationship between a white American man of Nordic or Anglo-Saxon descent and a dark man (black, Native American, or Mediterranean) can be traced at least as far back as James Fenimore Cooper. Leslie Fiedler discusses this American literary archetype of homoerotic male-male bonding in his book *Love and Death in the American Novel* (1960). In the case of David and Giovanni, David represents the frigidity of the colder temperament associated with those from colder places, while Giovanni embodies the stereotypical hot-bloodedness and sexual expressiveness of swarthier men. David's sterility contrasts with Giovanni's "sensual, living beauty" (Sarotte 301). The sensuous pagan Italian who expresses his desires openly is the foil of the inhibited and guilt-ridden American puritan. "These differences form part of a cultural dialectic . . . a confrontation between . . . outlooks on life" (Adams 42).

David's sexuality is crippled by the cultural baggage he carries. He has been symbolically castrated by American and Anglo-Saxon homophobia. Homophobia flourishes most virulently in the Anglo-Saxon world, particularly among Americans. Europeans in general are more tolerant than Americans of homosexuality (Altman, *Homosexualization* 217). It is left to Giovanni to heal David's wounds and to thaw out his frozen emotional and sexual energies. Giovanni pays the supreme price for relying on and loving David, who, out of his own woundedness, betrays Giovanni. Giovanni asks David why he has deserted him and begs him, " 'Please don't leave me' " (Baldwin, *Giovanni* 186). David abandons Giovanni because of his unwillingness to make the descent into his own hell and wrestle with the demons of the sexual inhibitions his culture has instilled in him. Hella's "fears of not being a 'real' woman coincide with David's fear of not being a 'real' man" (Adams 39). Although the Americans try to cling to their imagined purity, they are not innocent, as they are guilty of causing Giovanni's suffering. This parallelism between Hella and David indicates that American standards of sexuality thwart the free expression of love, affection, and passion. David refuses to embrace "what Giovanni later describes as the 'stink of love' " (Adams 40). But in rejecting the physical expression of love, David comes to realize, once he can never see Giovanni again, that in attempting to deny his bodily desire for Giovanni, David has only intensified its power over him: "Now, as though I had been branded, his body was burned into my mind" (Baldwin, *Giovanni* 191). David, knowing Giovanni is soon to face his execution, sees that he has forsaken his beloved due to his own homophobia and cowardice. He is left with extreme bitterness and Anger. But he has repented. David's Anger finally serves as the alchemical fire in which his very soul is transmuted. His Denial is behind him. He is determined never to spurn such genuine love again, should it ever be offered to him. David declares that despite any appearances to the contrary, "I must confess: I loved him. I do not think that I will ever love anyone like that again" (148). He will never again underestimate so grossly the value of genuine love from another man, no matter how homophobic those around him might be.

EXERCISE: IDENTIFYING ANGER

In coming out, Anger can erupt when one feels, "It isn't fair that I am gay." The way gay people are treated by society at large can also lead to Anger. David experiences many of the following types of Anger in *Giovanni's Room*. Which of them have you felt?

I am angry about being gay because . . .

homosexuality is vile.

it is unfair that this should happen to me.

it means that I am different.

it makes my choices and decisions in life more complicated.

it places me on the fringes of society.

my parents will not (or do not) approve.

it often leaves me in an ambiguous position.

I have to hide it from other people, sometimes even having to lie to them.

it is hard to face being gay; Denial sometimes seems tempting.

I don't like having to play the game of pretending to be heterosexual.

I don't know what to do about being gay.

the gay subculture seems claustrophobic, confined, pushed indoors and underground.

I am angry over the ways homosexuals are treated; I am angry at . . .

legal penalties against homosexuality.

police brutality against gays.

beatings and murders of gays.

government imprisonment and execution of gays.

the type of social disapproval gays face.

discrimination in jobs, housing, and public accommodations.

governmental/public foot-dragging in response to AIDS because of how many PWAs are homosexual.

EXERCISE: EXPRESSING ANGER

It can seem dangerous to express Anger. Many people are quick to judge and disapprove of all expressions of Anger. Yet some Anger is quite legitimate, and denying its existence and repressing its expression do not help. Consider the following questions:

- What are the situations, circumstances, and people that make me feel angry?
- With whom can I discuss my feelings of Anger safely?
- In what ways do I displace my Anger?
- When I feel Anger, what are constructive ways to express it?

You might think of a situation that has made you or that currently makes you particularly angry. With someone you can trust, recreate that situation, playing roles and rehearsing ways you could conduct yourself that would help preserve your feelings of self-worth and allow you to express your true feelings. Whether this becomes a rehearsal for an actual encounter, or merely an imaginative foray into what might have been or what might be, such as the common fantasy of being able to have the last word (in twenty-twenty hindsight), it may help release you from the stranglehold of Anger and keep you from turning it upon yourself.

4

Bargaining:
The Beautiful Room Is Empty

QUESTION: How many psychiatrists does it take to change a light bulb?
ANSWER: Only one, but the light bulb really has to want to change.

Edmund White's autobiographical novel *The Beautiful Room Is Empty*, a Bildungsroman, takes its unnamed hero from his adolescence at Eton, a mid-Western boarding school, in the mid-1950s through his college years at the University of Michigan and to his job for a magazine in New York City in the 1960s. He falls in with Maria and other bohemian artists during his prep school years and becomes aware of his attraction to men. His homosexuality troubles him and his parents so much that he enters psychoanalysis to change his sexual orientation. During his college years, the protagonist continues in psychoanalysis with Dr. O'Reilly, while leading a lonely life in which sex in the campus men's rooms gives him night after night "of perverse pleasure and excruciating remorse" (White, *Room* 96). In Manhattan, while working in a homophobic environment, he has an abortive affair with a man named Sean, but both decide they need to change their sexual orientation. Both reenter therapy. Finally, he begins to question his attempt to change his sexual orientation. One night in June 1969, he wanders into a small bar on Christopher Street, the Stonewall Inn, and is present when the police raid the bar. The clients riot. The protagonist's rejection of his attempts to change from homosexual to heterosexual are thus linked in this narrative with the birth of the gay liberation movement marked by the resistance at the Stonewall Inn on the night of June 27, 1969. The hero's path, from mid-West origins to his presence at the Stonewall Rebel-

Table 3
Similarities Between the Hero and Edmund White

	Hero	Edmund White
Date of birth	1940	1940
College	University of Michigan	University of Michigan
Date moved to New York	1962	July 19, 1962
Employment in New York	writer for an unnamed magazine	staff writer for Time, Inc. (1962–70)
Stonewall	present at the riot	present at the riot

lion, matches White's life, as shown in Table 3. Anti-homosexual psycho-logical and psychoanalytic dogma were successfully challenged soon after Stonewall. Homosexuality is no longer officially considered a mental ill-ness. Since then, psychological approaches to Bargaining, such as those depicted in *The Beautiful Room Is Empty,* have become increasingly rare.

In the coming-out process Bargaining is the effort to change one's sexual orientation from homosexual to heterosexual. "Bargaining" suggests getting something in exchange for a promise or "bribe," but Bargaining only delays the inevitable. Many bypass this stage altogether. Bargaining, Kübler-Ross says, "is less well known but [as] equally helpful [as the other stages], though only for brief periods of time" (Kübler-Ross 72). In the confronta-tion with mortality, Bargaining represents the attempt to defer dying. "The bargaining is really an attempt to postpone; it has to include a prize offered 'for good behavior' " (Kübler-Ross 74). The "good behavior" promised in Bargaining for prolonging life might be greater piety, while in Bargaining to become heterosexual, it might be entering into psychoanalysis and fol-lowing the psychoanalyst's instructions. The hero of *The Beautiful Room Is Empty* strikes the latter type of Bargain. He pleads with his mother that he is " 'a brilliant person saddled with a terrible disease' " trying earnestly to cure himself. (White, *Room* 127). In an attempt to ward off further wounding criticisms of his homosexuality, he tells her that he has already discussed thoroughly with his therapist any objections she can raise against him. He realizes years later, however, that all he has done through his prolonged therapy is to have prolonged his self-deception and self-loathing.

Vivienne Cass does not use the term "Bargaining" in her discussion of Homosexual Identity Formation but notes that occasionally, "when ex-treme alienation has occurred," a person will perceive both himself and his sexual behavior as undesirable and will wish "to change both" (Cass 229). White's hero displays such alienation, admitting that he does not feel any connection with anyone else. Such inner turmoil can leave its sufferers susceptible to the claims that sexual orientation can be changed. Such claims promise to resolve acute inner conflict. Putting such claims into effect is attempted "by the inhibition of all homosexual behaviors, the devaluation of homosexuality, and positive portrayal of heterosexuality. This permits the rejection of self as homosexual" (Cass 229). Even those who proceed from the "Identity Comparison" to "Identity Tolerance" stage may waver about their sexual identity and therefore may also "Bargain" in hopes of becoming heterosexual. A person experiencing such conflict is "actively engaged in constructing a self that he can live with. The self must be clear-cut and unambiguous" (Weinberg 21). Clarity often emerges only after lengthy struggle. It requires acknowledging the deeply held feelings and tendencies that have been denied and suppressed for a long time. Prior to completing such a change in perception, these repressed feelings often resurface in increasingly disruptive ways, shattering inner harmony. Cognitive dissonance peaks just before a transformation in self-identity:

> Because individuals belonging to stage three (tolerance) are on the brink of changing their identity from non-homosexual to homosexual, it is therefore reasonable to assume they would experience greater dissonance, manifested in less perceived psychological well-being, than [those] who have already made the cognitive shift to a homosexual identity. (Brady 118)

Coming out is a quest to resolve inner conflicts in self-image in order to form a stable identity. One study of gay men's coming-out process showed that "perceived levels of happiness increased with the crystallization of a sense of identity" (Troiden 371), the very thing that eludes those battling their homosexuality through a Bargaining strategy. It is logical that Bargaining would occur when unhappiness and inner conflict are most acute: after Denial can no longer be maintained, but prior to reaching Acceptance. Meanwhile, it becomes more upsetting for some to have their sense of identity remain completely unsettled than it would be to admit being homosexual, despite all the disadvantages of a gay identity. Some men therefore decide "that any form of sexual identity—heterosexual, bisexual, or homosexual—would be preferable to the sexual ambiguity and confusion they [are] experiencing" (Troiden 369). They may then admit that they are homosexual, which leads them into the stage of Depression, a state of resignation and tolerance of being homosexual that precedes Acceptance (see Chapter Five). Others, however, may attempt to bypass the soul-searching and the gradual readjustments of conflicting values and personal attachments. They may thus seek a "quick fix" or a sudden change in sexual orientation in hopes of eliminating the need to work through these painful inner conflicts step by step.

Why is it so difficult for some people to accept their homosexuality that they try to become heterosexual? Bargaining arises from oppressive and pervasive homophobic pressures gays internalize from their families, peers, and colleagues. In *The Beautiful Room Is Empty*, Edmund White depicts the homophobic attitudes most heterosexuals and homosexuals held during the 1950s and the 1960s, the years of his adolescence and early adulthood. During those times, many believed that Communism, heroin addiction, and homosexuality were the most unspeakable abominations. Three institutions (among others) sustained this homophobia: "The law regarded homosexual activity as criminal, the church as immoral, and the medical profession as perverse, if not psychopathic" (Brown 202). White focuses upon the medical profession's contempt for homosexuals, but suggests the power of the law through his mention of police raids upon gay bars during the 1960s. He scarcely mentions the church's homophobia.

In the coming-out process, Bargaining commonly takes religious and psychological forms. The religious approach entails faith in a premise such as, "If I do everything my church tells me to do, God will make me heterosexual." The psychological approach, such as that employed by the protagonist of *The Beautiful Room Is Empty*, rests on the unstated belief or "Secret Bargain," "If I enter psychotherapy and do anything my analyst tells me to do, I'll become heterosexual." A few decades ago, such attitudes were commonly supported. For example, in a 1950 document from the eighty-first Congress entitled "Employment of Homosexuals and Other Sex Perverts in Government," the bald assertion is made that "the authorities agree that most sex deviates respond to psychiatric treatment and can be cured if they have a genuine desire to be cured" (quoted in Duberman, *About Time* 153).

The Beautiful Room Is Empty charts the gay central character and first-person narrator's Bargaining in psychotherapy. This character's desires for men become more pressing even as he struggles to stifle them. He insists that he longed to be heterosexual. Although not drawn into the "born again" path to change his sexual orientation, he grows wistful about his inability to believe in such an escape from his dilemma over his sexual identity. Although he views homosexuals as damned, he has no religious beliefs or rituals through which he can find relief for his secret torment and guilt. He does flirt with a fuzzy sort of Buddhism as a way to avoid acknowledging his sexual orientation. Otherworldly aspects of Buddhism, which stress the impermanence of the things of this world, fit in neatly with his belief and hope that he can change his hated sexual orientation, because Buddhism's rejection of the concept of fixed essences means he "could wake up one morning gay or straight—or as nothing" (White, *Room* 71). But through such beliefs he merely avoids coming to any reckoning with his sexuality. But procrastination in resolving painful issues surrounding sexual identity only prolongs cognitive dissonance and self-doubt. The hero and others in Bargaining typically find more than their sexuality up in the air. Their entire sense of self remains tentative as they repress "suspect" emotions. White's hero speculates that because he thinks that his sexuality, which he despises, can be changed, his identity itself is fluid and life itself has yet to begin.

Those who attempt a Bargaining strategy fear rejection should their homosexuality come to light. The protagonist of *The Beautiful Room Is Empty* fears losing his friends and becoming a pariah should his sexual desires become known. He feels alienated from himself and from others. He is torn between the desire for approval from others and his own troubling instincts and desires—what John Cheever referred to as his "difficult propensities" (Cheever, *Letters* 328). Bargaining rests on ideas, theories, or theologies that promise to impart a sense of order and coherence. It also often rests on an attachment to some group that appears to have the power to convey to the insecure individual a sense of legitimacy or to withhold it from him. Those in Bargaining, in joining such groups, often strike outsiders as "true believers," people who have embraced a belief system ununcritically. The protagonist's friend Maria tells him that his attachment to the dogma of his therapist has made him as bigoted and "smug as a Catholic convert or an American Marxist" (White, *Room* 185). White's hero wants others to like him, but he cannot believe they will do so unless he suppresses his sexual impulses. He feels cut off from his emotions. He tries hard each day to be jovial and to express interest in other people and then lies awake at night plagued "by feelings not of hatred but of unreality" (17). In severing his conscious mind from desires he dares not embrace, he is left with only a tentative sense of relatedness with the world. Although his Bargaining strategy involves psychoanalysis, religion (a word deriving from *religare*, to reconnect) also possesses a compensatory allure to those experiencing such disconnectedness. White's protagonist laments that he does not feel comfortable anywhere. Religion may offer a sense of belonging to a supportive social group. It may provide a sense of connecting with a divine or transcendent order. It may promise a feeling of legitimacy and respectability, a foundation for a coherent, harmonious, and positive self-image.

RELIGIOUS APPROACHES TO BARGAINING

Apparently no novel has as its central character a gay man who undergoes a religious conversion that leads him to attempt to go from gay to straight by means of a Bargain with God. Many gay characters in fiction, however, do experience conflict between their sexuality and their religious beliefs. In *Afterlife* (1990) Paul Monette sends up the homophobia to be found in religious guise, whether within the New Age movement or among television evangelists, the first through the character Sonny Cevathas, who becomes convinced by a channeler that he's not really gay after all, and the second through the character Mother Evangeline, who preaches that AIDS represents God's judgment on homosexuals.

There are novels, such as *The Bell* (1958), by Iris Murdoch, and *The Catholic* (1986), by David Plante, in which gay characters experience religious guilt about their sexuality. In *The Bell*, the character Michael is a member of a lay religious community who has been suppressing his homosexuality for years. He lost his job at a prep school and dashed his hopes for ordination when his love for one of his male students became known. "He had been guilty of that worst of offences, corrupting the young" (Murdoch 107). Dan, the main character of David Plante's novel *The Catholic*, is a gay man and a lapsed Catholic. During his first sexual encounter with Henry, a Protestant who becomes his lover, Henry asks Dan, " 'Aren't you ashamed, a Catholic fucking like this?' " (Plante 36). Dan thinks a lot about sin and the Holy Family, but despite his guilt, he never tries to change his sexual orientation. Richard Hall says of this novel, "Dan's remorse . . . occupies—or rather, pre-empts—the book. . . . Only at the end does he begin to justify his need for another man. . . . But homosexual guilt and expiation are overfamiliar in fiction. Do we really want a long session with a tortured conscience again?" (Hall 27).

Sexual guilt also looms large in Sanford Friedman's novel *Totempole* (1965), in which Stephen Wolfe, the protagonist, briefly attempts complete sexual abstinence. His guilt stems in part from his earlier review of Leviticus with his rabbi. During his period of sexual abstinence, Wolfe reads the Bible as well as "Meister Eckhart, Hopkins, Tagore, Pascal, Cardinal Newman, Swedenborg, and St. John of the Cross" (Friedman 277). Yet Wolfe does not use religion to attempt to change his sexual orientation.

Although the psychological theories and practices of the 1950s and 1960s depicted in *The Beautiful Room Is Empty* largely have been discredited during the past two decades, religious pressures on gays and lesbians to "change" continue to flourish in many quarters. They therefore deserve to be examined in any discussion of homosexuals who try to Bargain to change their sexual orientation.

Among monotheists, Bargains to change from heterosexual to homosexual are sometimes attempted with God in the coming-out process, as is typical among the dying: "Most bargains are made with God. . . . We have been impressed by the number of patients who promise 'a life dedicated to God' or 'a life in the service of the church' in exchange for some additional time" (Kübler-Ross 74). Certainly, while coming out many gay people experience severe conflicts as a result of their religious training. This is virtually inevitable, given the response of Judaism and Christianity to homosexuality in American society. Perhaps all monotheistic religions condemn homosexuality.

Not all religions instill such anxiety over a homosexual orientation, however. Polytheistic religions generally tolerate gays. Rather than being repressed, homosexuality was acknowledged, for instance, in most Native American tribes and incorporated into their social and religious structures. Berdaches (who would now be called "gay") were healers, shamans, medicine men, teachers, and craftsmen. They were seen as spiritually gifted individuals, revered for their special gifts in bridging the human and divine realms. Their spiritual role did not require celibacy. The berdaches took the "passive" or "feminine" role in their sexual relationships with other men. The male sexual partners of the berdaches were not seen as any less masculine than those who preferred women's sexual companionship. Even male chiefs sometimes took male berdaches as wives. (See *The Spirit and the Flesh: Sexual Diversity in American Indian Culture* by Walter L. Williams.)

Those in the midst of the coming-out process, whose sense of identity may be fragmented, may be particularly susceptible to homophobic religious diatribes. While struggling to resolve their own dilemmas surrounding their sexual identities, those who are coming out may find that messages of condemnation resonate with their internalized homophobia, guilt, uncertainty, confusion, and fear. They are ripe for attempting a religious Bargaining strategy. Religious manifestations of Bargaining are probably as numerous as the different theologies held by people who are coming out. Two examples of religious Bargaining that have taken on institutional form are the so-called "ex-gay" ministries and a group that calls itself "Homosexuals Anonymous."

The "ex-gay" ministries use the same "brainwashing" techniques that have been used upon some victims of kidnapping by their abductors and upon some prisoners of war by their captors. The sense of self is undermined through intensifying the feelings of inadequacy already present in the subject, such as guilt, confusion, shame, and cognitive dissonance. (Dr. O'Reilly produces a similar effect upon his patient in *The Beautiful Room Is Empty*.) These feelings are brought to a fever pitch until the subject's ego collapses. Then the subject's sense of self can be reconstructed, based on the values and teachings of those conducting the "reeducation." Some religions use the concept of "sin" to undermine self-worth. Christians who regard homosexuality as a particularly severe sin may heighten the "sinner's" feelings of sinfulness so that he will renounce the "old" self in order to be "born again." For instance, John Sorenson, "a Baptist church deacon and former head of the Miami vice squad," said, apparently voicing a view shared by others, " 'I think the sin of homosexuality is worse than the sin of murder' " (Katz 123–24). Such attitudes assault the homosexual's sense of self-worth. Supposedly, being born again will set the repentant homosexual free from his "sinful" homosexual thoughts, feelings, and behaviors, which had troubled him enough to make him susceptible to the claims of the "ex-gay" ministries. What happens, in fact, is a process of repression: a disavowal of experiences, memories, and feelings, as well as physiological and sexual responses that conflict with the new sense of self as non-gay or "ex-gay." Friendships with gays or those supportive of gay rights are discouraged. Such people may come to be seen as dangerous, if not worse. The ministries claim to love the person (provided he is sufficiently repentant, contrite, and malleable to their designs), while hating his "sin." Yet this practice of "ex-gay" ministries and of many Fundamentalist groups "is both naive and cruel." They tell lesbians and gay men, " 'Your sexual orientation is still unnatural and a perversion, but this is not judgment upon you as a person.' The individual knows otherwise" (James Nelson 169).

The "ex-gay" ministries make extraordinary claims, which are paid much credence in some evangelical circles. *Christianity Today* ran on its cover of February 6, 1981 the headline: "Homosexuals CAN Change." But such claims deserve close scrutiny and melt under it. Dr. Ralph Blair, a practicing psychotherapist and the founder of Evangelicals Concerned, has provided such an examination in his work *Ex-Gay*. His conclusion is clear that there is

> no documented empirical verification of any permanent change from homosexual orientation to heterosexual orientation through the "ex-gay" processes. There is, however, plenty of evidence of diagnostic error, reaction formation, dishonest manipulation of terminology, fraud, self-deception, misunderstanding of the claims of others, and more manifestations that counter the claims of "ex-gays" themselves. (Blair 2)

Some have been candid about the failure of the "ex-gay" efforts. Ernest White, a Christian psychiatrist, concluded after treating fifty homosexuals that not even one of them had rid himself of his homosexual desire " 'by spiritual measures' " (Blair 29). Unfortunately, other ideologues have been less forthright.

What is the evidence used to bolster the claims of the "ex-gay" ministries? Probably the most ambitious study, and the one with the greatest claims to scientific validity, is summarized in an article by E. Mansell Pattison and Myrna Loy Pattison, " 'Ex-Gays': Religiously Mediated Change in Homosexuals." But this report fails to acknowledge the failure of the "ex-gay" movement to produce any permanent change in sexual orientation and the feelings this fosters in those who have been through the harrowing process only to discover it has been for nothing. These people feel an intensification of the guilt that led them to seek to change in the first place and often feel forsaken by God. Usually such disillusionment leads these former "ex-gays" to encounter "despair as the baby (faith) is tossed out with the dirty bath (the homophobic churches and their niggling Pharisees)." Most "ex-gay" groups cannot conceal their failures for long and soon fold (Blair 30). The Pattison article claims that eleven men achieved a sexual reorientation. These eleven "ex-gays" were the remnant of three hundred persons who sought the "ex-gay" experience in order to change their sexual orientation from homosexual to heterosexual. The eleven consented to interviews with the Pattisons out of the thirty who allegedly were "cured" (out of the three hundred who went through the "ex-gay" experience). But "the Pattisons do not tell us why cooperation was not obtained from the presumably grateful remainder of nineteen" of the thirty, nor is any explanation offered as to why by their own admission at least ninety percent failed to be "healed" (Blair 30–31). The testimony of the eleven is suspect in that "former 'ex-gays' . . . say that as part of their testimony they have had to lie and/or withhold information 'for the good of the ex-gay ministry' and in order to 'keep from slipping back into homosexual sin' " (Blair 31). But lying, for whatever reason, does not promote spiritual development. " 'Telling a lie for Christ' has sadly been a requirement that not only killed much of gay spirituality, but [also] maimed any kind of spirituality" (Boyd 83). Although the Pattisons claim that eleven of the three hundred men were "cured," their own data indicate that of the three hundred, only three *"claim to have no current homosexual dreams, fantasies, or impulses and one of these three is listed as being still incidentally homosexual. That reduces the 'ex-gays' to two men out of the original group of three hundred who sought the 'ex-gay' experience"* (Blair 33; emphasis in original).

Even this low rate of "cure" (less than one percent) is subject to slippage over time. "Ex-gay" claims are based on retrospective accounts given within a few months (at most) of the conversion experience, and most of the "ex-gays" simply disappear from the "ex-gay" ministries as they realize that their sexual orientation has not changed. Occasionally, the "ex-gay" ministries in effect admit that their approaches do not always work. Even Pattison admitted that some of the eleven so-called "successes" of the three hundred who tried to become "ex-gays" might well "return to homosexual lifestyles' " (Blair 34). Indeed, among the eleven were counted Gary Cooper and Michael Bussee, cofounders of Exodus, the very "ex-gay" fundamentalist organization whose ministry furnished the basis for the Pattison study. But "the unthinkable happened—they fell in love" and were still together as a gay couple ten years later (Millen 39). " 'If Exodus is the most successful ex-gay group,' says Bussee, 'you can imagine what the others are like' " (Millen 39). So much for the "ex-gay" ministries' empirical evidence.

Unfortunately, many religious groups remain unyielding in their condemnation of homosexuality and their determination to eradicate (or repress) it. "The church has generally been an alien environment for gay people" despite the occasional parish that accepts and warmly welcomes gays (Boyd 83). The Mormons, for instance, have administered aversion therapy to Mormon homosexuals seeking to change and have all those who complete this brutal process of behavior modification sign statements immediately afterwards indicating that they have been "cured." The Mormons, on the basis of these forms, claim a ninety-nine percent success rate for those who complete the aversion therapy. No follow-ups are conducted to measure slippage over time. Many of these "success stories" can be found years later in viable gay relationships, after they have come to accept their sexual orientation. By then they are typically "ex-Mormon" rather than "ex-gay."

Often, people resolve religious conflicts over their homosexuality by distancing themselves from formal religion and declining to continue to participate in its institutional expressions (Weinberg 296). Some gays, however, struggle to remain within the fold while embracing their homosexuality. The group Affirmation has been formed to serve gays and lesbians willing to renounce neither their homosexuality nor their commitment to the Mormon faith. Similar groups have been formed within other churches as well, such as Affirmation (Methodist), Dignity (Roman Catholic), Integrity (Episcopal), Kinship (Seventh-Day Adventist), Lutherans Concerned, and Sovereignty (Jehovah's Witnesses). Gay and lesbian Jews have organized gay/lesbian synagogues.

Under various guises, programs offering some kind of spiritual "recovery" from homosexuality keep cropping up, such as a group called Homosexuals Anonymous, which was founded in 1980. Although it models itself loosely upon the Twelve Step program pioneered by Alcoholics Anonymous, and despite the similarity in names, the resemblances between the two programs are quite superficial. Homosexuals Anonymous (H.A.) has fourteen (not twelve) steps, only "five of which are modified from Alcoholics Anonymous" (Schrader 34). The first step is that " 'We admit that we are powerless over our homosexuality and that our emotional lives are unmanageable' " (Schrader 38). H.A. receives its funding from Seventh-Day Adventists, unlike Alcoholics Anonymous (A.A.), which refuses to accept financial contributions from outside sources. A.A. relies solely on donations from its members. A.A. advocates and exists through self-help and peer support. H.A. pushes a specifically Christian agenda, opening each meeting with "Amazing Grace," for instance, whereas A.A. avoids any theological dogma, allowing each person to call on a higher power as he or she conceives of it. Another discrepancy between H.A. and A.A. is that A.A. is run by and for recovering alcoholics, whereas one journalist at an H.A. weekend in 1988 noted the presence of many heterosexuals there trying to "help" homosexuals. H.A. has not followed the peer-to-peer approach so essential to A.A. One couple in H.A., for instance, had a "34-year-old son recently 'turned gay.' They want to help, though their son does not want them to" (Schrader 34).

H.A. is riddled with homophobia. This is reflected in the theoretical "explanations" of the "causes" of homosexuality offered at H.A. meetings. H.A. imports heterosexual "experts" to condemn homosexuality. If left to their own devices, the participants might draw the "wrong" interpretations of their own experiences. In this, H.A.'s approach differs markedly from

A.A.'s. The effectiveness of A.A. stems largely from its avoidance of hierarchical power structures and authority figures. A.A. focuses upon testimony from peers about their actual real-life experiences, which are narrated but neither analyzed nor interpreted by self-appointed experts. At an H.A. meeting, one imported (thoroughly heterosexual) "expert" testified: " 'A major explanation for homosexuality,' Dr. Fitzgibbons [began], 'is an absence of athletic gifts, resulting in rejection, so that at adolescence a boy's desire to claim a more attractive body is so strong, he becomes homosexual' " (Schrader 40). (Evidently Dr. Fitzgibbons would be at a loss to explain the gay athletes from all over the world who compete in numerous events during the international Gay Games.) Those at H.A. meetings apparently continually disparage homosexuals and perpetuate homophobic stereotypes, calling gays "tense," "selfish," and "compulsive." They maintain that homosexuals lose their attractiveness upon turning thirty and are never in relationships of more than five years' duration (Schrader 38–40). This appears similar to the "ex-gay" ministries' systematic efforts to break down any lingering attachment to a homosexual identity that the participants may have. Testimony emphasizes the most lurid and degrading aspects of homosexual experience, including "pornographic obsession, . . . promiscuity, alcohol and drug abuse, compulsive masturbation, prostitution, tearoom sex, and peep shows" (Schrader 34). The main reason people join the program appears to be "guilt feelings springing from religious beliefs" (Schrader 34).

Of course, guilt and remorse are insufficient to eradicate homosexual desire and replace it with a heterosexual orientation. As with the "ex-gay" ministries, the best that can be hoped for appears to be repression and celibacy, as is suggested by one H.A. member's remark that "she feels spiritually advanced enough to skip heterosexuality and jump to celibacy" (Schrader 40). Obviously, she feels no heterosexual desire and has not become heterosexual. Programs like the "ex-gay" ministries and Homosexuals Anonymous fail to turn homosexuals into heterosexuals or to create heterosexual desire within them. Is it reasonable of such groups to expect homosexuals to abandon their homosexuality even if this means forgoing any and all sexual expression for the rest of their lives?

Not all religious efforts to suppress homosexuality are based on the false premise that sexual orientation can be changed. Some churches, notably the Roman Catholic Church, although its recent pronouncements about homosexuality have become more intolerant, have made a more sophisticated distinction between homosexual orientation (a concept nowhere mentioned in scripture) and homosexual behavior, which is condemned by the Roman Catholic Church. Even this distinction is of little comfort to the person whose behavior—whether actual or potential—is being judged: "When the church presumes to be non-judgmental toward orientation but then draws the line against any genital expression, it is difficult to understand how the sense of guilt—even in the celibate—will be significantly alleviated" (James Nelson 169).

Christian churches are not monolithic in their condemnation of homosexuality, nor has Christianity been homophobic throughout its history. Much recent scholarship on the Bible, as well as on ancient apocryphal Christian manuscripts and church history, has challenged traditional homophobic interpretation of scripture and homophobic claims about the Christian tradition. We have no scriptural evidence whatsoever, canonical or apocryphal, that Jesus ever condemned homosexuality. On the contrary, according to surviving references to the apocryphal *Secret Gospel of Mark*, which probably dates from the early part of the second century, Jesus may have been sexually intimate with Lazarus, whom Jesus raised from the dead, according to the eleventh chapter of the Gospel according to John. The pertinent passage in the *Secret Gospel of Mark* reads:

> But the youth [Lazarus], looking upon him [Jesus], loved him and began to beseech him that he might be with him. And going out of the tomb they came into the house of the youth, for he was rich. And after six days Jesus told him what to do and in the evening the youth comes to him, wearing a linen cloth over his naked body. And he remained with him that night. (quoted in *Secret Gospel* 342)

The surviving fragment of the *Secret Gospel of Mark* is preserved in a letter of Clement of Alexandria, who viewed the *Secret Gospel* as a deliberate falsification of the Gospel according to John. Yet, as Ron Cameron notes, "On form-critical and redaction-critical grounds, the version of the story in the *Secret Gospel of Mark* is to be judged more primitive than the one preserved in John 11" (340). Although "Clement also states that the *Secret Gospel of Mark* is an expansion of the (now canonical) Gospel of Mark, . . . the precise opposite may well be the case: the canonical (or 'public') Gospel of Mark appears to be an abridgment of the *Secret Gospel of Mark*" (Cameron 340). Even in the canonical gospel by John, Lazarus is described by his sisters to Jesus as "he whom you love" (John 11:3, Revised Standard Version). Several books have been published in recent years that challenge traditional homophobic interpretations of the few passing references to homosexual behavior in the canonical scriptures, such as *Is the Homosexual My Neighbor?: Another Christian View*, by Letha Scanzoni and Virginia Ramey Mollenkott and *The Bible and Homosexuality*, by the Reverend Michael E. England.

It is often forgotten that "Christianity's opposition to homosexuality was not original but derived from non-Christian sources. Nor has it been consistent. There were centuries of Christian tolerance" (James Nelson 167), as has been shown by John Boswell in his book *Christianity, Social Tolerance, and Homosexuality*, which indicates that the church was not invariably homophobic during its first twelve centuries. Even in recent times, the Roman Catholic Church has not been uniformly homophobic. Dutch bishops and clergy in particular have been very liberal and held a gay wedding in a Roman Catholic church in the late 1950s. Rome fumed, but the bishops refused to discipline the priest (Brown 185). Even apart from churches that minister primarily to the gay and lesbian community, most notably the Metropolitan Community Church, various Christian churches have shown support and understanding towards gays and lesbians, as borne out by the ordination of gays and lesbians to the priesthood and ministry in several denominations in the United States, including the Episcopal Church and the United Church of Christ. Holy union ceremonies have been performed in various churches. Legal and religious sanctions against homosexuals had been relaxed prior to the Stonewall Rebellion. "Only the medical establishment remained unyielding" (Brown 202). The hero of *The Beautiful Room Is Empty* bears the brunt of unreformed homophobic psychoanalytic practices.

PSYCHOLOGICAL APPROACHES TO BARGAINING

The hero of *The Beautiful Room Is Empty* employs what was until the 1970s probably the most frequently used strategy to change from homosexual to heterosexual: therapy. Although the church had labelled homosexuality as "sin," psychiatry preferred the supposedly scientific label of "sickness." Only after the medical establishment displaced the church as the final authority on sexual matters was the term "homosexuality" coined, as *Homosexualität*, by Dr. Karoly Maria Benkert, a gay Hungarian writer, in 1869 (Greenberg 409). It was first translated into English as "homosexuality" in 1881 (Moritz 139). The notion of sexual orientation emerged as medical doctors began to view sexuality as an intrinsic part of personality, whereas theologians had treated sexual acts as isolated events ("the sin of sodomy"). Yet the "scientific" approach was often equally condemnatory and brutal. The "treatment" of homosexuals has ranged from surgical measures, such as castration and vasectomy, to drug therapies, "including the administration of hormones, LSD, sexual stimulants, and sexual depressants" (Katz 129). Hypnosis still was used even in the late 1960s for "treatment." "Other documented 'cures' are shock treatment, both electric and chemical; aversion therapy, employing nausea-inducing drugs, electric shock, and/or negative verbal suggestion; and . . . 'sensitization,' intended to increase heterosexual arousal [using] pornographic photos" (Katz 129). As one gay man notes, although psychiatry did not use religious grounds to condemn him, psychiatry's terminology "was just as devastating. . . . In the later stages of therapy I was privileged to learn that, as a homosexual, I was narcissistic and incapable of love" (Brown 181).

Long before Stonewall, some writers had suggested that psychiatric attempts to change sexual orientation were futile. They also exposed the arrogance of the psychiatrists attempting to make such changes. In E. M. Forster's novel *Maurice* (finished in 1914 but not published until after Forster's death), its eponymous hero decides he "could undergo any course of treatment on the chance of being cured" of his homosexuality (Forster 155) and enters psychiatric treatment that uses hypnosis. The treatment fails to change him, and he finally embraces his sexuality.

The attempt to change via therapy occupies the center of Edmund White's novel *The Beautiful Room Is Empty*, a sequel to his autobiographical novel *A Boy's Own Story*. The earlier novel takes the hero through his childhood and into his adolescence. The sequel opens during the mid-1950s, which have come to symbolize the relative peace and stability following the turbulence of World War II. White also points out that the 1950s were years of discomfort and persecution for minorities and "misfits." Nonconformists' vulnerability was symbolized by the McCarthy "witch hunts" against suspected Communists and homosexuals. The novel ends in 1969, with social pressures to conform being challenged by Hippies, radical student groups, the civil rights/black power movements, and the new women's liberation movement. *The Beautiful Room Is Empty* chronicles the effects of the then-dominant psychological theory of homosexuality as a mental illness upon the unnamed first-person narrator and upon his friends. One friend even resorts to a short-lived marriage in an attempt to change, or at least pass as heterosexual. The groundless belief that marriage or sexual intercourse with women will lead a homosexual man to become heterosexual also is ridiculed in other gay novels, as in the case of the protagonist of *The City and the Pillar*: "Jim believed that should he ever have a woman he would be normal. There was not much to base this hope on but he believed it" (Vidal 195). Such strategies are not uncommon in actual experience: "Masters and Johnson (1979) were surprised to find that twenty-three percent of homosexual females and males had previously been married; . . . some felt that marriage would help them overcome their same-sex feelings" (Coleman, "Marriage" 93, 95). Yet any homosexual who seeks out repeated heterosexual encounters in the mistaken belief that a preference for heterosexual experience inevitably will emerge sooner or later "through sheer force of habit" is bound to be disappointed (Fisher 23). Marriage does not magically banish homosexual desire. In fact, survey results indicate that over half of men who have homosexual encounters in public rest-rooms are married (Brown 109). Perhaps the most common results of such a strategy are not change in sexual orientation but rather hypocrisy and compulsive, self-destructive, impersonal sexual encounters. In a group for gay or bisexual married men, Coleman found that all thirty-one "reported having previously in some way attempted to eliminate their same-sex feelings," often through therapy (Coleman, "Marriage" 95). Our unnamed hero does not marry (or even have sex with women, for which he feels no desire), but he admits that he is tempted to marry Maria and escape from the loneliness and anguish that people around him ascribe to living as a homosexual. He enters therapy to change.

One price White shows that gay people paid for internalizing the diagnosis of being "sick," which was applied to them virtually without question during the 1950s and the 1960s, was disavowal of and distrust of their feelings. The effort to appear to be heterosexual often led to a ceaseless inner vigilantism against betraying any homosexual traces. This leaves the hero of *The Beautiful Room Is Empty* feeling that he must impersonate a male heterosexual adult. This destroyed self-confidence in one's impulses and instincts. It sabotaged the ability to be natural and relaxed. Peter Fisher entered therapy to change his sexual orientation but found that he was so afraid of unintentionally manifesting his homosexuality that he lost the ability to do or say anything spontaneously (Fisher 96).

At that time, almost all the media echoed the psychiatric verdict. Self-loathing among homosexuals was widespread and was reinforced at every turn. The self-righteously homophobic stance of the media is reflected in the editorial run by the magazine for which our hero works, which rails against the fashionable tendency to regard homosexuality as " 'a *different* way rather than a *lesser* way. . . . Homosexuality is not a sophisticated or naughty aberration but a pathetic malady' " (White, *Room* 192; emphasis in original). White's fictional magazine article closely matches the wording of Martin Duberman's review, published in *Partisan Review* in 1968, of Mart Crowley's play *The Boys in the Band*. Duberman's review states that the play,

> despite all its chic analytic references and its set acknowledgments that hysteria, depression and self-hatred are the main components of gay life, nonetheless subtly glorifies that life. . . . [The boys] are, moreover, capable of True Love, . . . which is romantic bullshit, and dangerous to boot—for it will help to confirm homosexuals in the belief that theirs is merely a *different* not a *lesser* way. (Duberman 418; emphasis added)

White's allusion is especially apt in that Duberman could have been the double of the hero of *The Beautiful Room Is Empty*. Despite his vehement homophobia, Duberman was sexually active with men when he wrote the review. Recently he admitted that he became sexually active with men in the mid-1950s (Duberman, *About Time* 187). He was not happy about this, as a 1957 entry from his diary indicates: "I wish to change . . . but parallel with this desire runs the stronger current of neurotic drive and compulsion, thwarting most of my efforts to change. I can neither give up my homosexual activities, nor devote myself guiltlessly to them" (359). Duberman, who has been "an openly gay journalist, playwright and critic" since the early 1970s, now describes himself "as a radical/gay activist" (xiv, xvi).

The homophobic former policies of the *New York Times* documented in Chapter One show that *Partisan Review* was not the only homophobic high-brow publication in New York City at that time. As noted in Chapter Two, the *New York Review of Books* used the terms "queer," "faggot," "Sodom," "pederasty," and referred to homosexuality as being "against the laws of heaven and earth" in its review of *City of Night* (1963; Chester 80, 83).

Homophobic messages have been conveyed not only by the media and institutions, but perhaps most devastatingly of all by gay people's families, particularly their parents. Many gays would no doubt like to turn to their parents for comfort and understanding during their periods of greatest alienation and perplexity. Unfortunately, just when gays and lesbians are most disturbed by their own sexuality, their parents typically are unable to comfort them, because they are faced with a "coming-out" process of their own as the parents of a lesbian or gay child. Parents often react with Denial: "My son [or daughter] could not possibly be homosexual." The road to Acceptance is as long for parents as for their gay children. Parents of lesbians and gays have formed the self-help support group Parents and Friends of Lesbians and Gays (P-FLAG) to come to terms with having homosexual children. Through that support, they can learn to let go of unrealistic expectations for their children and to accept them for who they are.

The protagonist of *The Beautiful Room Is Empty* thus is not alone in finding his self-esteem assaulted by the obvious disapproval of his mother and father just when his need for someone to bolster his shaky self-image is greatest. His parents withhold emotional support and encouragement from him. This humiliates him. Obviously they believe that his homosexuality can be changed, and they spare no efforts to bring this change about, even resorting to giving him grueling physical labors to perform, telling him, as he says, that this might "drive the queerness out of me" (White, *Room* 42). His mother tells him that obviously his therapy is changing nothing for the better. On the contrary, she tells him he is becoming, if anything, " 'more and more effeminate' " (127). She further goes on to reveal the cruelty parents can display in their single-minded determination to eradicate their children's homosexuality at any cost: " 'I've read of some interesting hormone treatments for your problem' " (127). Note that she is too ashamed to specify the "problem." Thus she conveys her revulsion by refusing to name the "love that dare not speak its name." She explains to him that if he has female hormones implanted into his leg, the estrogens would eradicate his sex drive completely. As she puts it, "they neuter you and soon you're free to lead a normal life" (128). Essentially, she would prefer to see her son castrated rather than to have him be gay. Some gays must endure serious pleas from their parents to undergo aversion therapy and similar tortures that simply do not work in the long run. Many of the deepest wounds to gays come from their families, who often unthinkingly uphold the homophobic attitudes with which they themselves were raised. In this, gays and lesbians differ from other minorities, whose families share the same minority status. Most of the closest relatives of homosexuals are heterosexual. Other minorities' families can face bigotry and discrimination together with the understanding and mutual support that develops through shared experience. Even individuals with physical defects usually receive understanding from their families, but "unlike physical defect, there remains always the suspicion that we could rid ourselves of [homosexuality] if we wanted to enough" (Altman, *Oppression* 28).

White portrays internalized homophobia and self-loathing. He shows how these were reinforced by the media and by the families of gays. Nonfictional accounts mirror White's depiction. Howard Brown confesses that during the 1960s he "still accepted many of the psychiatric clichés about homosexuals—that we were emotionally impaired narcissists who could never really love as fully as heterosexuals, that we were innately superficial and irresponsible" (Brown 22). Earlier in his life, Brown had believed psychoanalysis could cure him of his homosexuality (Brown 151). Other gays have also written of psychoanalytic experiences similar to those depicted in *The Beautiful Room Is Empty*. Peter Fisher writes that his analyst told him flatly that he was not homosexual and that if he tried hard enough for long enough, his heterosexuality would emerge because "there were no major obstacles." Fisher went along with this psychiatric advice wholeheartedly and came to date "girls . . . as though my life depended on it. . . . After a year and a half, I left therapy thinking I had been cured" (Fisher 95–96). Fisher dated women without satisfaction for years, but his homosexual thoughts and behavior continually resurfaced, which caused him guilt and anguish. This convinced him that he was "a very sick young man. I was right—it took me years to get over my psychoanalysis" (Fisher 96).

How does such therapy supposedly bring about a change in sexual orientation? Typically, the homosexual patient is instructed "to give up homosexual experiences, to avoid the company of gay people, and to continue therapy, at least until he [feels] ready for a lasting heterosexual relationship" (Brown 112). Patients are instructed to avoid their gay contacts at all costs. Analysts seem to understand that those with a homosexual orientation come to accept that they are gay only after overcoming their negative attitudes about homosexuals and homosexuality. This occurs through contacts with gays with whom they can identify (Weinberg 121), so the first step is to isolate the patient from gays. As was shown here in Chapter Two, Denial often rests on the inability to identify oneself with the negative stereotypes of homosexuals. Those in Denial can engage in homosexual behavior without considering themselves to *be* homosexual. Contact with the gay subculture allows them to recognize that homophobic stereotypes are false. It also allows them to interact with potential gay role models. Analysts require that sexual contacts as well as social contacts with homosexuals be avoided. Fisher was told "to avoid any further homosexual experiences at all cost" (95). Even homosexual fantasies are forbidden, which apparently was the intent behind a prohibition of masturbation. Fisher was told that masturbation "would weaken the strength of my 'heterosexual drive' " (95). The need for a reference group is crucial in forming a stable sense of identity, and thus being able to find a social group with which one is comfortable may be "a pull to the gay world" even stronger than sexual opportunities (Weinberg 160). One study of men who now identify themselves as gay showed that "fifty percent defined themselves as homosexual when they began associating with other homosexuals" (Troiden 369).

The psychiatric profession has acknowledged that homosexuals come to reconcile their homosexuality with their sense of self via gay reference groups, but there is no widely accepted idea of what causes homosexuality. Although many conflicting theories of the origins of homosexuality have been proposed, none of these has been verified empirically. (Careful empirical research that refutes psychoanalytic theory and popular beliefs regarding the causes of homosexuality is documented in *Sexual Preference: Its Development in Men and Women*, by Alan P. Bell, Martin S. Weinberg, and Sue Kiefer Hammersmith.) The cause (or causes) of homosexuality remains mysterious. The profession cannot agree on theoretical issues of the formation of sexual orientation, let alone on specific measures that supposedly would change it.

Even though Freud himself explicitly opposed efforts to change sexual orientation and indeed wrote in a letter in 1935 that "it is nothing to be ashamed of, no vice, no degradation [and that] it cannot be classified as an illness" (Freud 423), he never agreed with the idea of a homosexual orientation as a fixed and unchangeable aspect peculiar to a specific group of people (Altman, *Homosexualization* 40), although this idea had already gained some currency by the late nineteenth century. "The interpretation of homosexuality as a form of innate pathology was at first resisted" (Greenberg 416), but much medical literature advanced this belief around the turn of the century. "Physicians complained that homosexuals used this literature to justify their resistance to change" (Greenberg 417). Freud believed in the "polymorphous perverse" nature of all people's sexuality and felt that universal homosexual impulses are usually repressed as part of the normal maturation process. Failure to do so was a sign of "arrested development," clearly suggesting that it is "better" to repress homosexuality than to give it free rein. But "whatever its origin," Freud maintained (unlike some of his followers) that "homosexuality is not a sickness" (Greenberg 425). Yet those who judge that Freud was correct in his theories of repression and sublimation often place much importance on the repression of homosexuality (Altman, *Homosexualization* x). But repression is one thing; elimination of homosexual tendencies is another. Freud himself "refused to analyze patients [simply] because of their homosexuality unless they were also neurotic" (Greenberg 426). But some psychiatrists still claim that they can change their clients' sexual orientations, though increasing numbers admit this is impossible. Freud would view psychiatric claims to alter sexual orientation more skeptically than do many of his followers.

Ignorance of gay people and vagueness about what exactly a psychiatric "cure" of homosexuality might mean are rife among those psychiatrists quick to label gays as sick and in need of "cure." They are often remarkably ignorant of gays, including those in their own profession. Frequently, lack of insight and of therapeutic effectiveness are hidden behind a smokescreen similar to that surrounding the claims of the "ex-gay" ministries. "Ex-gay" ministries hide their failures. So do psychiatrists, resulting in inflated statistics of supposed "cures." Perhaps even more fundamentally, they never specify exactly what a change in sexual orientation means:

> Does it mean that the formerly exclusively homosexual patient is now having occasional heterosexual experience while continuing to have homosexual urges and fantasies? Does it mean that he is able to marry and have children? Does it mean that he has given up sex altogether? Until a definition is offered and generally accepted, claims of cures are virtually meaningless. (Brown 217)

Those proclaiming psychoanalytic "cures" of homosexuality wildly exaggerate and distort the evidence much as do those who claim spiritual "cures." The typical pattern, when one sifts through the supporting data, according to Fisher, is that the analysts screen hundreds of homosexual applicants who turn to psychiatry for a "cure" for their homosexuality and out of these select "fifty who seem 'highly motivated' to change and whose homosexuality is not too 'severe.'" After years of treatment, perhaps thirty drop out, while of the twenty remaining "eventually thirteen or fourteen decide that they have been 'cured,'" which means such things as the willingness to marry; a few may even report having had sexual experiences with women (Fisher 108). But how deep or satisfying is this supposed "cure" of homosexuality? Typically, no assessment is made to determine if those who have been "cured" are happier for it or even if the "cure" lasts much at all beyond the period of treatment. Despite a "cure" rate even on these terms of no more than seven percent, "prestigious psychiatric journals announc[e] that a new method of treatment can guarantee a sixty-seven percent cure for homosexuals" (Fisher 108). Not even such drastic measures as castration and lobotomies yield a higher rate of "cure" (Fisher 108), although the fact that they have been employed makes one wonder who is really sick, the homosexual or those committed to "curing" him.

Eventually, patients grow weary while waiting for the promised "cure" to materialize. In his own therapy, Brown says he was assured by his therapist "that my heterosexual side was bound to emerge, sooner or later," but despite Brown's earnest desire, this never happened, and his attempts to stimulate his heterosexual desire by trying to sleep with women failed (Brown 213). In *The Beautiful Room Is Empty*, Sean, who had been the protagonist's boyfriend, enters a therapy whose premise is that everything people do is part of playing a game. The degree of Sean's desperation to change and his willingness to deceive himself in the process is revealed by one character's comment about Sean that he feigns sexual excitement over his analyst, Dale, " 'who could be his mother and has ankles thicker than his waist' " (White, *Room* 187). Such desperation in the search for evidence of "cure" breeds self-deception.

The biggest problem with psychiatric and religious attempts to change homosexuals to heterosexuals, aside from their obvious homophobia, is that they do not work. Such efforts are futile. They also are enormously costly emotionally, psychologically, and often financially. They undermine self-esteem, creating a deep distrust of one's most basic emotions and impulses, and often foster acute alienation and elaborate schemes of self-deception. They leave in their wake great frustration and bitterness.

Such lingering feelings of resentment are evident in White's portrayal of the psychiatrist Dr. O'Reilly, who takes large quantities of amphetamines each morning to wake up and drinks bourbon at the day's end to wind down. White draws O'Reilly heavy-handedly, but then the techniques used upon homosexual patients by the O'Reillys of the psychiatric profession *are* heavy-handed. Even if White's depiction of O'Reilly smacks of the "some-day I'll write a novel about this town" syndrome (as vowed by the lesbian protagonist in the movie *Desert Heart*), it does dramatize an important figure in recent gay novels, the "god that failed." White's characterization (or caricature) no doubt epitomizes the contempt many gay people feel in retrospect after lengthy, costly therapy has failed to "cure" them, despite glib assurances to the contrary, such as Dr. O'Reilly's pompous claim, "I'm the only one who can save you, my boy" (White, *Room* 57).

O'Reilly tells the protagonist about the causes of his homosexuality. Many equally speculative theories were—and still are—taken seriously, although they wildly contradict each other and nothing can account for these contradictions. The narrator's subsequent bitterness is hinted at by the gullibility with which he initially accepts O'Reilly's wild speculations that he had had sex with a man named Tex primarily not out of sexual desire but out of a desire to defy his mother, who caused him to act out his "homosexual impulses" (White, *Room* 39). O'Reilly's absurd theorizing is exposed mercilessly, just as he had mercilessly inflicted it upon the narrator: "What I desire most was a man; desiring men was sick; therefore, to become well I must kill desire itself. 'Or kill men!' O'Reilly shouted, triumphant, half rising from his chair behind the analytic couch where he usually dozed . . . [or] fiddled with his drink" (58). It is hard to imagine that anyone with a strong sense of self-confidence would listen to such nonsense and believe it, or would regard such an alcoholic wreck of a man as an authority figure. White's point is that as a result of being told repeatedly that they are sick and sinful and in need of cure or healing, gays suffer from low self-esteem. The financial interests of such psychiatrists as O'Reilly are served by keeping their patients insecure, keeping them divided against themselves, tormented, and dependent, keeping them, in short, as paying customers. O'Reilly continues with his preposterous theory: " 'You want to murder men! You . . . think I'm sleeping, . . . but even when I'm dozing I'm listening, putting the pieces together in the preconscious, creative part of my brain. You want to murder men by sleeping with them. The stiff cock is the torero's sword. There's a lot of bullfighting imagery here' " (58). This sounds more like bullshit than bullfighting, but no doubt this is White's implication.

Under O'Reilly's shadow, the protagonist remains isolated from others, and his therapy certainly does not facilitate his forming close ties with others. He socializes chiefly with others who are on the fringes of society, such as bohemian artists and Chinese exchange students. His interactions with others are superficial and restricted. He is particularly secretive and guilt-ridden about his sexual encounters. He discovers the "tearooms" on his college campus, and loiters there incessantly spending all his free time— hours daily—cruising for fleeting impersonal sex. He admits, "I was obsessed" (48). These encounters only reinforce his sense of shame and self-loathing, which in turn make impersonal sex his only conceivable sexual outlet, apart from a one-time session with his fraternity brother, Mick, which occurs while both are extremely drunk. Throughout his period of obsessive cruising of the campus's men's rooms, the protagonist continues his therapy with O'Reilly. During this time, it seems inconceivable to the protagonist that he might come to accept his homosexuality and integrate it into the rest of his identity and life.

The protagonist of *The Beautiful Room Is Empty* has a few discussions with people who try to get him to accept himself and stop his fruitless attempt to change his sexual orientation. Maria, his long-time friend, tells him that he is destroying himself by his refusal to accept being gay, even though being gay " 'isn't such a big deal' " (White, *Room* 185). The narrator realizes that O'Reilly is becoming unhinged, and in avoiding confronting this, the narrator develops a series of psychosomatic illnesses severe enough to require his hospitalization. While hospitalized, the protagonist talks with a graduate student in psychotherapy, who asks him why he is in therapy. He says he wants to change his "object choice" and notes that the graduate student then "looked me intently in the eye, and now I could see that he, too, must be homosexual. 'But people don't really change,' he said. 'It's useless to try. It's more a question of adjusting. . . .' 'Oh, no,' I said, angry. 'I *am* changing, I *must* change' " (131). Soon after this conversation, the narrator concludes that he will remain in torment unless he confronts O'Reilly. The narrator finally does so, and O'Reilly sheepishly admits that their work together has not been successful and that work with a different therapist might help more. Right after ending his therapy with O'Reilly, our hero has his first personal sexual encounter, with a man whose name is Fred. This experience stands in marked contrast with his many prior sexual experiences with men whose names he never knew and whose faces he often could not see, separated from them as he was by the partitions between toilet stalls. After this more than simply physical encounter, he loses his nerve and so he never calls Fred after they make love. White is too realistic and too skillful an author to show his hero leaping overnight from impersonal sex to a committed relationship. Yet White's juxtaposition of O'Reilly's exit with the hero's first tentative romance surely suggests that his character simply could not form an emotionally satisfying gay relationship while he was in therapy. This had left him with endless anonymous and degrading sexual contacts instead.

A lesser author than White might have been tempted to have his hero recognize the flaws in O'Reilly's reasoning as soon as O'Reilly suffers a nervous breakdown and is hospitalized. That would make for an economy of plot, but it would reduce an inner conflict to an interpersonal melodrama. O'Reilly merely serves to reinforce the internal homophobia his patient held prior to entering therapy; had our hero felt secure in his sexual identity to begin with, he would have rejected O'Reilly's authority and his bogus claims right from the start. Most gay men have difficulty in coming to accept their homosexuality, and vacillate in this protracted process. White is realistic, therefore, in depicting the way his hero's Bargaining strategy persists after O'Reilly's inglorious exit as his analyst.

Some time after moving to New York City in 1962, White's hero meets Sean and has his first gay love affair. But neither he nor his lover Sean has worked through his own homophobia, although our hero starts to become uncertain about why he is supposed to feel ashamed. Yet Sean finds their deepening relationship conflicting with his desire not to be homosexual. The protagonist suggests to Sean that they "start therapy and go straight together—slowly, I hoped" (White, *Room* 183). Both enter group therapy (in separate groups) with a psychotherapist named Dale. During the course of the therapy, Sean ends the relationship. But then an unexpected thing occurs. Instead of placing full credence in Dale's efforts to get him to become heterosexual, the narrator begins in retrospect to view his recently ended relationship with Sean, his first steady boyfriend, differently. His habit of dismissing his own feelings and denying their validity left him unprepared for what he calls "the virulence of my love" (191). In the face of virtually insurmountable obstacles, namely internal and external homophobia, his love for Sean and his abortive attempt to forge a relationship with him begin to seem noble. His long-pent-up Anger surfaces as he begins to question his own homophobia and that of others. This occurs during a group therapy session in which another group member, Simon, a Russian immigrant who believes castration or lobotomy is fit punishment for what he terms "sexual perversion" (184), finally goes too far when the hero cries over Sean and all Simon is interested in is his relationships with women. The narrator becomes so enraged that the other members of the group have to pull him away from Simon. The narrator breaks forth from the life of repression, suppression, guilt, and hypocritical, impersonal sexual encounters in men's rooms. He finally ceases his half-hearted attempts to change into a heterosexual, something that was never in his nature. His personal metamorphosis is followed shortly by a momentous turning point in recent gay history.

White's novel ends with the eruption of the riot at the Stonewall Inn in Greenwich Village on the night of June 27, 1969. The riot was precipitated by what started as a routine police raid upon a gay bar, neither an isolated nor even a new occurrence, as raids in New York City upon what are now called gay bars were conducted at least as early as the nineteenth century. A police captain testified in 1899 that he succeeded in closing an "Artistic club" on West Thirtieth street by raiding it "two or three times," managing as a result to convict "all the Nancys and fairies that were there" (Katz 45). On this night, however, something happened that had never happened before in New York during a police raid on a gay bar: two hundred homosexuals gathered and taunted the police. Then the crowd threw at the police "bricks, bottles, garbage, even a parking meter. . . . It was the first time homosexuals had united to fight back against . . . their oppressors" (Brown 20). This event and the spirited resistance of the gays there have come to symbolize the birth of the contemporary gay rights movement. Since then increasing numbers of gays and lesbians have refused to cower before homophobia, personal and institutional. In a sense, at three in the morning, among a group of two hundred mostly effeminate homosexuals, gay pride was born. The drag queens were among the bravest in battling the police. This event is commemorated each year at the end of June in Gay Pride marches in cities nationwide and abroad. Within weeks of the Stonewall Rebellion, the Gay Liberation Front was formed, and the gay liberation movement swiftly gained momentum. "By 1973, almost eight hundred gay and lesbian organizations had formed" and by the end of the 1970s there were several thousand (D'Emilio and Freedman 319, 323).

Stonewall marked the beginning of the end of the "homosexuality as illness" theory, which until then had dominated psychological theory about homosexuality. That theory had burdened the life of the protagonist of *The Beautiful Room Is Empty* for years. As a result of the greater assertiveness of gay psychologists and psychiatrists since Stonewall, the board of trustees of the American Psychiatric Association voted on December 15, 1973 to remove homosexuality from its official *Diagnostic and Statistical Manual of Mental Disorders*. Brown wryly observes, "Since it is doctors who ultimately determine whether people are mentally ill or well, the board's vote made millions of Americans who had been officially ill that morning officially well that afternoon. Never in history had so many people been cured in so little time" (200–201). Not long thereafter, in 1975, the American Psychological Association officially removed homosexuality from its classification as a mental disorder. Nevertheless, as in the religious sphere, some practitioners remain adamant in upholding "the theory that homosexuality is equivalent to psychopathology" (Alexander 6). Those people are increasingly in the minority, however. Homosexuals are no longer seen as psychologically impaired. Rather, it is those who are prejudiced against gays and lesbians who are seen as impaired (Alexander 6). In other words, homosexuality is now increasingly regarded as a normal part of human sexuality, while homophobia is seen as dysfunctional. The fact that homosexuality is no longer considered to be a mental disorder has led to a shift in the type of research being done on sexual orientation. Less research is now devoted to comparing homosexuals with heterosexuals ("deviants" versus the "normal") and more is devoted to "examining the diversity which exists among homosexuals in attempts to more clearly understand the variability in homosexual adjustment" (Brady 7).

In a one-hundred-eighty-degree turnabout, psychiatrists "retained the category of 'dystonic homosexuality' [solely] for people who are disturbed by or who would like to change their sexual orientation" (Altman, *Homosexualization* 3). In short, the very desire to change from homosexual to heterosexual by using a Bargaining strategy, fostered for years by psychiatric theory and practice, suddenly was categorized as a psychological impairment. With homosexuality as such no longer considered to be a mental disorder, those who have accepted their homosexuality are now regarded as "healthy homosexuals," a term that until recently would have been regarded as an oxymoron. In 1987, even " 'ego-dystonic homosexuality,' that is, homosexuality considered unwanted by and disturbing to an individual, also has been removed as a mental disorder" from the latest edition of the American Psychiatric Association's *Diagnostic and Statistical Manual of Mental Disorders* (Hopcke 5). "The net effect of . . . the APA's removal of any form of homosexuality as a mental disorder is to depathologize homosexuality once and for all" (Hopcke 5). This reversal would have been virtually unimaginable even a few decades ago.

EXERCISE: IDENTIFYING THE GUILT TRIPS UPON WHICH BARGAINING RESTS

Bargaining, the attempt to change one's sexual orientation, stems principally from a religious belief that homosexuality is a sin or the psychological teaching (now generally abandoned by psychiatrists and psychologists) that homosexuality is an illness. A person's desire to change his or her sexual orientation thus rests mostly upon guilt and the fear of ridicule or rejection from others. For us to feel guilt, we must first have witnessed others expressing negative judgments about homosexuals and homosexuality. Although not all gay people attempt Bargaining, many of us have had statements like the following hurled at us by others who have tried to persuade us to change. Which of these sound familiar? Have you encountered other guilt trips that are not listed here?

You should change because . . .

RELIGIOUS GUILT TRIPS

homosexuality is sinful.

the Bible condemns homosexual acts.

any sexual act other than that which can result in procreation is wrong.

fornication is wrong.

any sexual act except that between husband and wife is wrong.

homosexuality is unnatural.

you must learn to control and channel your sexual energies.

the desires of the flesh are evil.

you cannot be both homosexual and spiritual.

PSYCHOLOGICAL GUILT TRIPS

homosexuality is an illness.

homosexuality is just a phase on the road to a mature adult sexual adjustment.

homosexuals are fixated at the anal or oral stage.

homosexuals are immature.

psychological maturity can come only through relationships with members of the opposite sex.

homosexuals are narcissistic.

homosexuals have not resolved their feelings towards their parents.

Religious and psychological authority figures who are pressuring gay people to change typically compound their guilt trips when the hapless individual's attempts to change prove unsuccessful. Additional guilt trips may then be launched:

You can change, so if you are not changing, you are . . .

not really trying hard enough.

resistant.

self-indulgent.

weak; you have no will power.

not really a spiritual person.

in an arrested state of development.

Once we start to question, doubt, and challenge those who are trying to get us to change, their attempts to shame us lose power. Their power over us rests upon their ability to shame us and to destroy or to impair our self-esteem.

EXERCISE: RECOVERING FROM BARGAINING

Those who have suffered at the hands of homophobic religious organizations or individuals may seek support from religious groups that affirm a positive sense of gay identity while allowing the individual to operate within a religious context. Gay synagogues exist in some places, and the Metropolitan Community Church ministers primarily to the gay and lesbian community and friends and families of lesbians and gays. The following support groups for gays and lesbians exist within various Christian denominations: Affirmation (Methodist), Affirmation (Mormon), Dignity (Roman Catholic), Integrity (Episcopal), Kinship (Seventh-Day Adventist), Lutherans Concerned, and Sovereignty (Jehovah's Witnesses). Those who have had negative experiences within Fundamentalist churches may find support in Fundamentalists Anonymous, a nondenominational support group modeled on Alcoholics Anonymous for those (gays and lesbians included) who are recovering from the abuse and shame they received while participating in various Fundamentalist groups. Spiritualities outside the monotheistic tradition sometimes deliberately create a supportive environment for gays and lesbians. Some, like the Lavender Pagan Network, focus upon exploring, reclaiming, and creating specifically gay and lesbian myths and rituals.

Those who have undergone psychotherapy with homophobic therapists may now more readily find therapists who are supportive and nonjudgmental of gays and lesbians. Qualified therapists may help gays and lesbians build a healthy sense of self-esteem.

5

Depression: *Dancer from the Dance*

Are we having fun yet?

Eventually, most men who have denied their homosexuality, become infuriated by the injustices homosexuals face, and even, perhaps, tried to change their sexual orientation lapse into a state of resignation. Reluctantly, they admit to themselves, "I probably am homosexual, and there is nothing I can do to change this." Depression sets in. In the coming-out process, as in the mortality process, the overwhelming feeling in the stage of Depression is one of great loss (Kübler-Ross 75). Such a sense of loss permeates and shapes Andrew Holleran's elegiac romance, *Dancer from the Dance*. The unnamed narrator of this novel reflects upon and reexamines the personal meaning he has attributed to the figure of a glamorous deceased gay man, Malone. The handsome, well-bred, and Ivy League–educated Malone realizes that he is gay in his late twenties and abruptly leaves his law career to immerse himself in the post-Stonewall gay scene in Manhattan in the 1970s. His elusive pursuit of love and sex in Manhattan's gay enclaves becomes his full-time occupation. Sutherland, an older and outrageously effeminate gay man, serves as Malone's "fairy godmother," his guide to the gay world. Malone, who never rids himself of his internalized homophobia, becomes promiscuous and jaded. Sutherland overdoses at an elaborate party he has staged for Malone on Fire Island, and Malone disappears the same night, either drowned in Long Island Sound or burned to death in the fire at the Everard Baths. Malone, a "doomed queen," fascinates the narrator for a time, but ultimately he rejects such a self-destructive figure as a role model. The narration thus reflects the narrator's working through of his own Depression about being gay.

In the mortality process, Depression is both a reaction to what has already been lost (such as job and physical capabilities) and a preparation for the loss of "everything and everybody [the dying person] loves" (Kübler-Ross 76–77). Some persons with AIDS must confront issues from their mortality and their coming out simultaneously. Although most gay people entering the stage of Depression in the coming-out process are not on the verge of death, they, like the dying, must also leave much behind: illusions, others' expectations, hopes of conforming to "normal" sex and gender roles, and aspects of self-image that conflict with a gay identity. Thus they pass through a symbolic death. Gay fiction often portrays a literal death as the only means of escape from such conflicts, reflecting the guilt and self-hatred of the characters (not to mention the authors). Altman rues the large number of corpses in gay literature and the absence of living-happily-ever-after endings, as in the camp comment of Michael in *The Boys in the Band:* " 'You show me a happy homosexual and I'll show you a gay corpse' " (Crowley 128). Some have seen the deaths of Malone and Sutherland in *Dancer from the Dance* as reinforcing the homophobic literary convention that homosexuals in fiction have a terrible reckoning to face. Brief episodes of contentment and pleasure contrast with pointedly unhappy endings. Altman judges the characters in *Dancer from the Dance* to be similar to "the sad, scared, guilt-ridden queens of *Boys in the Band*" (Altman, *Homosexualization* 16). Gay novels that buck this convention, such as E. M. Forster's posthumously published *Maurice* (written in 1913 and 1914, but not published until 1971), have been criticized for their "they lived happily ever after" endings.

Cognitive dissonance and guilt are "the components of depression [that relate] most strongly to internalized homophobia, and in particular to one's feelings about one's own homosexuality" (Alexander 92). One's attitudes about homosexuality influence how much one feels one is losing by embracing a gay identity. The extent of internalized homophobia determines the severity of Depression and impaired self-esteem. "Concerns about disclosure of one's homosexuality [are only] secondarily important in relation to depression" (Alexander 88).

People enter the stage of Depression when they can no longer maintain their Denial, and when they either have bypassed the Bargaining stage or have abandoned it after it has failed to work. Depression and Anger may alternate as negative feelings are directed internally and externally, respectively. Initially in this stage people may only admit reluctantly, "I probably am gay," but then may come to feel, "I am gay. There is nothing I can do about it, though I am not happy about it." Unlike those in previous stages, they no longer fight being gay, but their feelings about being gay nevertheless remain ambivalent. They become resigned, accepting that being gay is something beyond their control.

Depression feeds on internalized homophobia and lingering internal conflicts between self-image and sexual identity. In his study of internalized homophobia among gay men, Ronald Alexander's "hypothesis stated that high levels of internalized homophobia in gay men would be directly proportional to elevated levels of depression. This hypothesis was supported" (Alexander 79). In his study of the coming-out process, Richard R. Troiden found that "perceived levels of happiness increased with the crystallization of a sense of identity" (371), suggesting that those in the stage of Depression have not yet completed the process of what Troiden terms Gay Identity Acquisition. Many gay men find themselves, Thomas Weinberg discovered, perplexed by a dilemma created by American cultural values: "The men in our sample reported their most prevalent conflict to be that between being a man, as our society defines it, and being a homosexual" (295). Proust's Baron de Charlus, in *Remembrance of Things Past*, is one of the most notable of the many fictional characters who embody this conflict and suffer immensely from it. Charlus is drawn to the society of elegant women, appreciates their wit and charm, and poses as a great seducer of women, yet he is sexually drawn to men. As with others carrying on a double life, Charlus has difficulty keeping his sexuality secret. Charlus is discovered while being whipped in a male brothel. Proust apparently believed that male homosexuals are always effeminate. Gay men, in Proust's view, thus necessarily experienced sexual frustration: The masculine men who attracted them were heterosexual, while sexually available homosexual men were effeminate and therefore unappealing. Andrew Holleran, unlike Proust, apparently sees no necessary connection between male homosexuality and effeminacy. Yet Holleran's Sutherland, like Proust, does associated male homosexuality with effeminacy. Sutherland flaunts his rejection of stereotypical masculinity by playing the role of flippant, effeminate queen to the hilt. Yet Sutherland's effeminacy is unusual among the gay male characters in *Dancer from the Dance*.

Cass's model of the coming-out process contains a stage that she terms "Identity Tolerance," which resembles Kübler-Ross's stage of Depression. During Cass's Identity Tolerance stage, a homosexual identity is reluctantly and tentatively embraced or tolerated, rather than being accepted. Weinberg found in his study of the coming-out process among gay men that the realization that one is, "indeed, 'really' homosexual" does not always indicate happiness about this or acceptance that this is permanent and final; some men remain ambivalent (Weinberg 289). The person entering the Identity Tolerance stage "seeks out homosexuals and the homosexual subculture" to overcome isolation and alienation (Cass 229). Others have also recognized the importance to the coming-out process of being exposed to the homosexual subculture. Frederick Suppe, for instance, says this vital step in the coming-out process follows declaring one's homosexuality to significant others and refusing to pretend to be heterosexual around them. Suppe argues that one accepts one's identity as a homosexual only after "becoming acculturated into the gay subculture" (Suppe 84).

Dancer from the Dance depicts how several newcomers become absorbed into the gay milieu. Yet the very name of Malone, the main character, may suggest that his attempts to overcome his feeling of isolation through participating in the gay subculture prove unsuccessful. If the M in Malone is read as "am," then Malone's name signifies "[I] am alone." Malone's very name represents one of the most enduring homophobic myths: that homosexuals are condemned to loneliness, particularly once youth fades. (Malone is thirty-eight years old at the time of his disappearance.) Much pulp gay fiction reinforces such stereotypes, indicating that many in the gay community still believe, or at least tolerate, such characterizations of being gay. In his discussion of *Vermilion*, a paperback novel written by Nathan Aldyne and published in 1980 by Avon Books and marketed to the urban gay male reader, Adam Mars-Jones notes, "The most obvious characteristic of the community which produced and consumes *Vermilion* is fear . . . fear of isolation and fear of dependence" (40). Such fears are understandable, Mars-Jones reasons, in a community that is constantly marginalized by society.

Upon first entering the gay subculture, the quality of newcomers' contacts with other gays is crucial: negative experiences may lead to the feeling " 'If this is what being a homosexual is all about, then I do not like being a homosexual' " (Cass 230–31), a sentiment Malone never entirely shakes, as is amply evident in *Dancer from the Dance*. Malone asks Sutherland, his slightly older friend and guide to the gay milieu, whether he loathes being gay. Clearly, promiscuity, impersonal sex, and other aspects of life that are frequently more visible in the gay subculture conflict with moral attitudes gay men have before coming out "that they have previously learned and had never seriously questioned" (Weinberg 289). Conversely, positive experiences may lead the person to go from thinking "I probably am homosexual [though I am unhappy about it]" to thinking "I am a homosexual," and integrating this into a positive self-identity, thus entering the stage of Acceptance (Cass 229–31). Although Malone never completes this transition, the unnamed narrator does so in the process of telling Malone's story. The narrator idolizes but then finally rejects Malone as a gay role model, at first identifying with Malone's self-loathing and internalized homophobia, yet eventually repudiating them in a necessary part of his rite of passage to Acceptance of being gay.

Depression occurs in the coming-out process when, as a result of internalized homophobia, being gay is viewed as a sentence of exile from an idealized, or at least respectable, heterosexual world. The central proposition of E. M. Forster's posthumously published novel *Maurice* "that ho-mosexual fulfillment is incompatible with conventional involvement with society is borne out by most contemporary treatments of the theme" (Adams 109). Such a sense of being cast out, of not being able to fit into the het-erosexual world, plagues Malone. This perception can be magnified by the isolation from the straight world possible in the "gay ghettos" that grew phenomenally in the decade after Stonewall. Gay men in America can now "live entirely in a subculture of bars, baths and gay-owned businesses" (Mars-Jones 14). Gay ghettos have existed quietly in large American cities for many decades. As Havelock Ellis noted in 1915, "The world of sexual inverts is, indeed, a large one in any American city, and it is a community distinctly organized" (quoted in Katz 52). Thus the emergence of a gay male urban subculture is not merely a post-Stonewall nor even a twentieth-century phenomenon. The urban gay male subculture was well established, though discreet, in London by the early eighteenth century. In a curious anticipation of the Stonewall riots, "In 1725, the patrons of one London molly-house fought back when the house was raided" (Greenberg 349). (Molly-houses were roughly equivalent to today's gay bars. Open to the public, they were all-male taverns in which clients could drink, and, in some, dance together and even have sexual encounters in private rooms). By the 1830s, there were "all-male social clubs" in New York City, but "the London molly subculture could not spread to the United States until cities were large enough. This point was reached only after the Civil War" (Greenberg 355, 383).

The characters in *Dancer from the Dance*, attempting to overcome their loneliness and alienation from society at large, move through Manhattan's gay society of the 1970s and deliberately avoid straight society. They have distanced themselves from their families and places of origin and built up support networks with other gay people. David Bergman has seen Holleran as extreme in his view of the need of separating gay and straight worlds: Holleran "is alone in throwing up his hands in desperation of even bridging the gap between family life and gay life (Bergman 192). Bergman insists that Holleran's characters have not separated psychologically from their families at all, despite the ostensible distance. Bergman labels "all of Hol-leran's denizens of the gay underworld . . . [as] mama's boys in disguise" (191). The characters in *Dancer from the Dance* avoid heterosexist milieus, the centers that generate the homophobia that oppresses the narrator of *The Beautiful Room Is Empty.* But in rejecting their families and the dom-inant heterosexist culture, they can't escape from the homophobia they carry within themselves; they merely ghettoize it. Such internalized ho-mophobia surfaces during Malone's trips from gay circles in Manhattan to those on Fire Island. Malone idealizes the large white houses and their inviting front yards as he is driven through Sayville and his romanticized images of such places and all they represent of family, security, and respectability haunt him. To him the taxis driving through Sayville en route to summer retreats from Manhattan on Fire Island seem "like vans bearing prisoners" (Holleran, *Dancer* 24). They feel like people banished from Sayville and tantalized by their fleeting glimpses of such an idyllic-seeming town with its big houses, lawns, and gardens. Holleran, in writing of these trips from New York City through Long Island, ironically reverses the trips made to New York City through Long Island by the characters in *The Great Gatsby*, another novel of elegiac romance. The social acceptance Malone seeks eludes him, just as it eludes Gatsby. Other similarities between these two novels are discussed below.

Malone and Sutherland, in leaving their cramped quarters in Manhattan, find themselves on Fire Island in equally cramped surroundings. Holleran's metaphor of prison suggests that the sexual license that flourishes in the hothouse environments of the discotheques of Manhattan and Fire Island does not lead Malone to true freedom, to a sense of the soul set free, but to its opposite. Such sexual license merely provides a temporary escape from Depression. At the outset of the novel, as in this passage, the narrator identifies with Malone's wistful yearning for the happiness he associates with the straight world, a happiness from which he feels excluded due to his sexual orientation. Malone has left the straight world and knows he can never reenter it on its own terms. This depresses him. All of Malone's partying, flaunting of social and sexual conventions, and sexual promiscuity are merely elaborate attempts to mask his sense of loss. Malone, like those around him, is free to indulge his wildest sexual fantasies virtually without restraint, and he does so. Yet this fails to satisfy him. Malone, depicted as a romantic at heart, searches for love and turns a cold shoulder to all that does not promise to lead to love. The pursuit of love becomes his full-time occupation and his overriding obsession. The elusiveness of his quest demoralizes and disillusions him. Given such things as, in most cases, the absence of children to hold gay couples together, as well as the unavailability of legal marriage as an option between same-sex partners in the United States (despite legal challenges from the American Civil Liberties Union and the legality of same-sex marriages in the Netherlands and Denmark), there is less to hold same-sex couples together than there is for straight couples. For this reason, "the illusion of love is more important for homosexual couples than for heterosexual ones" (Altman, *Homosexualization* 189). But Malone sabotages his stable relationship with Frank by seducing other men, and he fails to reestablish another ongoing romantic relationship. Malone's initial delight in transitory sexual encounters, which leads him to be unfaithful to Frank, wanes. As Holleran notes in *Ground Zero*, "The thousandth trick is not what the first one was" (117). Malone grows tired of endless numbers of sexual encounters that leave him feeling exactly the same afterwards as he had felt before. He wonders how so many men cope with such " 'perfectly meaningless sex' " (Holleran, *Dancer* 141). Malone embodies a larger dilemma facing modern gay fiction, namely the conflict between conventional notions of romantic (and often monogamous) love and contemporary sexuality, with its endless series of sexual partners, each of whom must compete with those who have gone before or may come after.

Sexual promiscuity may serve as a coping strategy for Depression. "Promiscuity seems to me often a matter of habit as much as anything else; many homosexuals, like some heterosexuals, learn early that sex is an easily available palliative for boredom or self-doubt" (Altman, *Oppression* 16). "Sexual activity can . . . be a 'fix,' a way to bolster a damaged self-concept and temporarily feel good about oneself" (Coleman, "Stages" 38). The obsessive pursuit of sex may function as a drug-like escape from introspection, particularly if the sexual encounters are fleeting and impersonal, thereby requiring no soul-searching or emotional commitment. For Malone, sex becomes addictive. The more sex he has, the more he wants. This leads him from bed to bed, and from beds to the bathhouses. He dispenses with the requirement that his sexual partners be handsome or even ordinary looking, and finds himself having sex even with ugly men. "He made a vow to sleep with everyone just once. . . . He was a prisoner of love" (Holleran, *Dancer* 128). In *Ground Zero*, Holleran proposes that "*Once more* (or *Once Is Not Enough*) is the *mantra* of promiscuity" (116). This can result in obsessive compulsiveness about attracting the next trick by becoming or remaining a physically or sexually desirable commodity on the "meat market." Malone works out religiously in a gym.

Promiscuous sex can easily lead to an avoidance of emotional intimacy, to the treatment of people as disposable sexual commodities to be "consumed" and then discarded. In gay male fiction, this is reflected in the "presentation of sex as performance, sex as marketing, sex as status, sex as anything but need" (Mars-Jones 37). As one model in *Dancer from the Dance* says, if growing a beard doesn't attract the boy he's fallen in love with, maybe a moustache will: " 'It's all just a matter of packaging' " (Holleran, *Dancer* 164). But a "sexually attractive person isn't a person without needs, simply a person whose needs are appetizing to others. At best, and with a lot of help, a sexually attractive person can dodge the unrewarding task of examining those needs" (Mars-Jones 34). For Malone, the need to be desired virtually consumes him. Much in the gay subculture has fostered the commodification of gay male sexuality. "A gay bar may be a subcultural meeting-place, but it is first and foremost a commercial establishment, and the sexual possibilities, like the bowls of peanuts so freely offered, are there only to make you drink more" (Mars-Jones 28).

Consumerism, the accumulation and consumption of material commodities, like promiscuity, can serve as a coping mechanism for Depression. Consumerism and promiscuity stem from similar conditions and values. It even has been argued that "the new homosexual could only emerge in the conditions created by modern capitalism" (Altman, *Homosexualization* 93). The gay community epitomizes the shift of the overall economy from one of self-denial, frugality, and capital accumulation to hedonism, planned obsolescence, and frenzied consumption. In the last few decades, "rather than requiring self-restraint to permit capital accumulation, the economy now required high levels of consumer spending to forestall recessions" (Greenberg 460). Greenberg links the emergence of modern gay culture with this material abundance and with a rise in hedonism, "the recreational use of drugs and alcohol, the blurring of traditional gender roles . . . , and the abandonment of traditional restrictions against sexual expression" (460). More relaxed attitudes towards homosexuality have accompanied the shift to a belief in sexual pleasure as a legitimate end in and of itself, along with greater tolerance for premarital sex, divorce, birth control, abortion, and pornography (462). In this environment, a shopping spree, like a fleeting impersonal sexual encounter, can provide the illusion of escape from self. Malone assembles an enormous wardrobe to dress for "the handsome stranger" he may meet (Holleran, *Dancer* 124–25). The fantasy of finding a perfect man resembles the fantasy of wearing the perfect outfit. The "handsome stranger" is no less a commodity, something to be consumed, than is an article of clothing.

Holleran does not skirt the issue of the commodification of sex in gay male culture. He takes it to its most extreme manifestation. Prostitution is the ultimate commodification of sex. Sutherland pimps for Malone, who works as a call boy, apparently willing to satisfy any of his clients' requests, no matter how bizarre, even those that entail enemas or fist fucking. Although gay men are not the only people who bring heightened expectations to sex, gay male culture epitomizes and intensifies the trend towards the commodification of sex prevalent in consumer-oriented societies. In such societies, people view sex "as a solvent of all problems," with the resultant "stress on sexual fulfillment" undermining marriage and committed relationships of all kinds (Altman, *Homosexualization* 83). As Adam Mars-Jones asks in mock horror, "What would happen if gay men formed relationships? They might stop frequenting [gay bars], for one thing, and they might stop renting [apartments from gay slumlords]. They might move out of the subculture, to the suburbs even. They must be saved from themselves" (28).

The narrator's correspondent in *Dancer from the Dance* makes precisely such a move out of the urban gay male subculture. He thereby rejects the values of the urban gay enclaves of the 1970s. Yet much of gay male fiction glamorizes such commodification of sexuality. Adam Mars-Jones, for instance, says of the novel *Vermilion*, in what could apply equally well to Malone's view of gay life in *Dancer from the Dance*, that the constant pursuit of casual sex is portrayed as an inevitable part of urban gay male life (31). The difference is that *Dancer from the Dance* implicitly critiques that value system, via the rejection of Malone as a role model by the narrator and his correspondent, whereas *Vermilion* advocates and celebrates it. In *Vermilion*, the character Mark becomes an embarrassment because he does not slip into sexual relativism; he actually believes "that it is possible to prefer one person to another, even in bed" (Mars-Jones 28).

Promiscuity as an escape from Depression offers only a temporary relief: the promise, through being found sexually desirable, of a fleeting distraction from low self-esteem and guilt. Significantly, such impersonal sex does nothing to combat internalized homophobia. On the contrary, it reinforces it, as is reflected even in the settings in which it takes place in *Dancer from the Dance*. This is nowhere more evident than in the scenes set in the Everard Baths. Such bathhouses "were usually dirty and tawdry—appropriately, given the sense of guilt and furtiveness associated with homosexuality" (Altman, *Homosexualization* 80).

Substance abuse is another coping strategy for the Depression faced by gay people who, like Malone, have not yet come to Acceptance of being gay. Promiscuity and consumerism promise escape or distraction from nagging inner problems. So does substance abuse. Drugs and alcohol facilitate the entrance into the realm of fantasy. Exposure to the gay subculture appears necessary to forming a positive gay self-image, but this acculturation process contains hazards. Drug and alcohol abuse are common in the gay world and serve as props to bolster the shaky sense of self common among those new to the gay world. Alcoholism and drug abuse are more common among homosexuals than among heterosexuals: "According to statistics published by the Pride Institute in Eden Prairie, Minnesota, thirty-three percent of the gay and lesbian community is chemically dependent, as compared to about twelve percent of the general population" (Griffin 2). Substance abuse arrests the process of personal growth and maturity. "One stumbling block to completing the tasks of the exploration stage successfully is the use of intoxicating agents to anesthetize pain or to shore up a weak self-concept" (Coleman, "Stages" 37). Alcohol and drug abuse flourish along with other difficulties that result from internalized homophobia: "Lesbians and gay men . . . generally internalize [homophobic] attitudes long before they become aware of their own homosexual orientation. . . . [C]onjectural detrimental effects of this 'internalized homophobia' include depression, low self-esteem, substance abuse and suicide, guilt, difficulties with relationships, and various impairments in identity development" (Alexander 85). Many gays have commented upon the link between chemical dependency and the stigma of being gay and a corresponding lack of self-acceptance. A Pride Institute counselor, Michael Witt, says, "the need for escape is . . . [intensified] by being gay, because of our inability to accept ourselves" (Griffin 2). References to substance abuse crop up more and more frequently in *Dancer from the Dance* as the narrator gradually ceases idealizing Malone and Sutherland. The narrator begins noting that everyone familiar with Sutherland knows he is destroying himself through his constant shooting up. At his final party, Sutherland, in his typical campy manner, asks the discaire what drugs he is taking, adding, " 'the hostess and the discaire [should] be on the same drug' " and wondering if the drug of the evening should have been on the invitations (Holleran, *Dancer* 223). Despite this flippant attitude, drugs prove fatal to Sutherland the very next morning, as, oblivious to the dangers of mixing drugs at random, "half-asleep, he reached reflexively for another pill" causing his heart to stop beating a few moments later (Holleran, *Dancer* 233).

At first it might seem counterintuitive if not reactionary to equate with Depression the heady decade after Stonewall. The new gay liberation movement was flourishing. In increasing numbers, gay people were rejecting the closeted nature of gay life prior to the Stonewall riots. Annual gay pride celebrations commemorating Stonewall sprang up in several cities. The AIDS crisis had not yet devastated and decimated those living the gay life in the fast lane. Yet a sense of doom hangs over Holleran's depiction of gay life in the 1970s. Politicized gay circles disapproved of the novel. The Gay Activists Alliance staged protests upon the publication of *Dancer from the Dance* for not being "sufficiently correct ideologically" (Altman, *Homosexualization* 159). Nevertheless, Altman maintains that the protests and criticisms by gay activists on gay businesses and on "novels such as *Dancer from the Dance* in which the commercial scene of discos and baths is such an important element, miss the point," given the need to have stable institutions in which to make first contacts and the need to come out in an environment sheltered from the larger society (Altman, *Homosexualization* 21).

Perhaps the members of the Gay Activists Alliance might have reacted with less hostility had they viewed the novel from within its literary context, that of the elegiac romance. This form shapes *Dancer from the Dance,* as do the framing elements of the epistolary prologue and epilogue. Both suggest that the narrator comes to abandon his identification with Malone without rejecting a gay identity or condemning gays in general. The epistolary prologue and epilogue establish, via the correspondent who now resides in the deep south, that not all gay men live in urban gay meccas such as New York and San Francisco, nor do all who do so behave as Malone does. The narrative is in no sense intended to represent "typical" gay men.

Many outstanding twentieth-century novels are elegiac romances, in which the first-person narrator reflects upon the life of a deceased hero, as the narrator of *Dancer from the Dance* reflects upon Malone, initially idealizing him but ultimately rejecting him as a role model. Typically, glimpsed from afar, at first the hero appears in many ways to be larger than life and, to the narrator, seems to embody great glamor and romance. Nevertheless, the tale is finally one of the hero's failure and loss, and the rejection of him as a hero or role model. Malone's life, like Sutherland's, ends in failure; both men destroy themselves. If this were all that the novel is about, it would indeed reinforce the myths of gays as perhaps superficially clever and amusing, but deeply disturbed people who kill themselves in the end. Holleran's novel does no such thing. Holleran never equates Malone with all gays nor does he condemn gays or portray gay life as inherently self-destructive. Via the narrator's changing perspective of Malone, he shows how gays can reject self-destructive gays as role models and work through the phase of Depression. Malone epitomizes the Depression that results when a person carrying the baggage of internalized homophobia comes to realize that he, unequivocally and irrevocably, is gay. This leads to feeling resigned about being gay or as if "doomed" to be gay. The narrator and the reader are meant to realize that such attitudes are indeed self-destructive. But this does not mean that Holleran's novel is intrinsically homophobic. On the contrary, the narrator rejects the internalized homophobia that Malone represents. Examining the twentieth-century literary form that shapes *Dancer from the Dance*, namely the elegiac romance, helps to clarify this.

Focusing upon the increased understanding the narrator gains, the elegiac romance unites elegy and quest romance. The heroic quest becomes internal and psychological, a matter more of personal growth than of external conquest. In this tradition, both the narrator's quest and that of the narrator's hero are "generated by a sense of loss" (Bruffee 48). The tale, while seemingly an exercise in hero worship for both narrator and reader, leads both to reject such uncritical adulation. As Lawrence Buell notes about this type of narrative:

> the hero is characterized in such a way as to renew the observer's (and the reader's) faith in the possibility of a degree of grandeur we had more or less assumed to have faded from the contemporary world; to indulge that dream for awhile; and yet finally to keep from full identification with it by viewing it as illusory and/or destructive. Thus the encounter with the hero is finally turned into a learning experience for the observer. (101)

Holleran's decision to write within the tradition of the elegiac romance could be served only by examining a deceased gay "hero" whose quest for true love had ended in Depression and failure. While it might be argued that there is something homophobic about choosing to write about such "doomed queens," this is to ignore the broader issue inherent in all elegiac fiction of overcoming hero worship (the tendency to project one's fantasies upon others) and achieving a more personal individuation (to use the Jungian term). Is Holleran upholding venerable anti-gay stereotypes in this novel? Is he implying that embracing homosexuality leads to sexual license, unhappiness, loneliness, and self-destruction? Certainly many have read this novel as a general attack on gay life and its supposed superficiality and self-destructiveness. Yet Holleran's novel indicts only one style of gay life, one whose wild surface abandon barely masks deep-seated Depression about being gay stemming from lingering internalized homophobia. Although this lifestyle proves self-destructive, gay life need not be. In fact, Holleran is engaged, through his narrator, in showing that self-destructive patterns of behavior, such as drug abuse and impersonal sex, may be rejected as part of one's life without rejecting a gay identity as such.

The fictive narrator's correspondent, whose letters appear in the prologue and epilogue to the novel, functions as a mentor or older brother/ guide to the narrator, as Sutherland does to Malone. In no sense does this correspondent deny his homosexuality nor try to change his sexual orientation. But he has rejected the type of gay life he formerly led in New York, in which he had encountered Malone and Sutherland. He thus has rejected the attitudes and lifestyle symbolized by them. He writes that he wants to distance himself completely from his former life, to which he cannot return. (The protagonist of Holleran's subsequent novel *Nights in Aruba*, published in 1983, has made the break and has withdrawn increasingly from his former life in New York City.) But in announcing his intention to make this break, he is not trying to change his sexual orientation. Unlike the narrator of *The Beautiful Room Is Empty*, he is not in a Bargaining phase. He is merely trying, as a gay man, to live in another place, and in another way. He thus indicates his rejection not of being gay, but of the pressure to conform to a particular gay stereotype represented by the life he had lived in New York City. The narrator's correspondent says, "we are not doomed because we are homosexual[;] we are doomed only if we live in despair because of it," as they did on Fire Island and in Manhattan (Holleran, *Dancer* 249). This correspondent suggests that he has transcended the Depression afflicting Malone, the Depression that the narrator of the novel is trying to work through in the process of narrating Malone's story.

Holleran makes explicit, both in the epistolary prologue and the epistolary epilogue to his novel, that he did not intend his novel to be representative of ordinary, more or less successful gays, but about what he terms "doomed queens." "Most fags are as boring as straight people. . . . But the failures—that tiny subspecies of homosexual, the doomed queen . . . fascinates me" (Holleran, *Dancer* 18). Those are the people the novel is about.

Yet the fictional narrator's curiosity is not merely literary or academic: At the outset, personally he identifies strongly with Malone. The narrator seeks to make sense of his own life and experience through discussing Malone, and in doing so, he frees himself from his obsession with Malone and transcends this identification with him. The narrator writes to his correspondent in the prologue: "I am a doomed queen" (Holleran, *Dancer* 17), indicating his (possibly unconscious) identification with Malone and underscoring that the novel is at least as much about his own journey as it is about Malone. He goes on to say, "I would LIKE to be . . . happily married . . . but I'm not! I am completely, hopelessly gay!" (Holleran, *Dancer* 17). This sounds remarkably similar to the attitudes he attributes to Malone in Malone's taxi ride through Sayville. We cannot regard the identical attitudes ascribed to Malone simply as Malone's. Clearly, at the outset, such homophobic attitudes are projected onto Malone, with whom the narrator indirectly identifies. By the end of the novel, however, he has rejected Malone as a role model and, presumably, has rejected the homophobic, self-destructive element of his own nature that he had projected onto Malone. Symbolically, the self-destructive aspect of his personality dies once he finishes writing the novel, his elegy for Malone. The hold Malone had over his psyche is released.

Malone, ostensibly the novel's central figure, at first is depicted, as are most heroes, as charismatic. Like a tragic hero, he falls from a great height. Like most charismatic figures, he seems larger than life, extraordinary. He comes from a privileged background. He shows an unusually deep faith in childhood. He attends exclusive schools. After completing his education at Choate and Yale, he pursues the law career that is expected of him, but finally leaves it all to devote himself to one of the most elusive of human endeavors: the pursuit of love. He is thus seen as a romantic hero on a quest. In his journey, as is true of most figures who embark upon odysseys in quest romances, Malone finds an older man who helps and advises him, namely Sutherland, a WASP from an upper-middle-class background who lives the bohemian life in Manhattan's gay community. The two travel through the demimonde, the world of super-trendy discos, summers on Fire Island, ultrafashionable parties, the baths, and other cruising grounds, with their promise of endless, impersonal promiscuous sex. Sutherland even pimps for Malone, which certainly, at least in conventional fiction, would symbolize Malone's utter degradation, his final fall from grace and privilege. Surely this shows Malone's final rejection of the values upon which he was raised and the privileged station reserved for him so long as he follows the rules he scorns by working as a call boy. All that he has rejected floods his memory when on a call Malone encounters a former Choate schoolmate. Instead of having sex, they look at an old Choate yearbook. Malone comes back and reflects on his memory of his former way of life, captured by the photograph. He realizes that he had "erased that photograph, bit by bit, until that person had vanished utterly" (Holleran, *Dancer* 199). Holleran goes on to suggest that most homosexuals tend to make such a break with their former world. Malone's inability to bridge his former life and his present one, as well as his all or nothing separation of gay and straight worlds, reflects his internalized homophobia. A more self-accepting gay person would not need to maintain such a complete division between gay and straight. To Malone, though, the alienation from his former life and former self is absolute. Like a tragic hero, he has lost virtually everything, having fallen from an extraordinarily privileged position. Despite the

unnamed narrator's knowledge of Malone's fall from the world of respectability, Malone is portrayed, especially at first, as if seen through rose-col-
ored glasses, as the last of the true romantics.

We learn near the end of the novel that Malone has grown weary of the
superficial charms of the gay party and disco scene, which reflects the narrator's own disillusionment with Malone as a role model. After Malone has
lived several years of this particular gay life, Sutherland throws a huge
party in a palatial home on Fire Island. Malone reveals there how very
jaded he has become. John Schaeffer, who has a crush on Malone and is
seventeen years his junior, serves as a foil to Malone. John, smitten with
infatuation and showing signs of falling in love, dances with Malone. Rather
than prompting in Malone feelings of elation, this leads Malone to mock
and belittle John's love, as Malone no longer believes in love in the way
John does. "They faced each other at opposite ends of an illusion" (Holleran, *Dancer* 229). Malone deliberately tries to shatter what he takes to
be John's illusions about love, partly by talking in a campy manner. Ad-
miring the party, John says he is glad Malone likes the party, but Malone
tells him he loathes the party. John asks why and Malone explains, " 'Because . . . I'm thirty-eight. . . . I'm in mid-passage, darling. . . . I'm
menopausal. . . . I'm a *jaded queen*' " (Holleran, *Dancer* 227; emphasis in
original). The narrator says this speech is delivered to demystify Malone to
John, but actually it serves to demystify Malone to the narrator and to the
reader. Malone uses camp to destroy his masculine allure and sabotage his
image of desirability. Camp developed out of the need many gay people—
and gay writers—felt to deliver coded messages that would be interpreted
differently by gays and straights. "Camp pits both nature and society against
art" (Bergman 112); it is highly artificial and self-conscious. "Camp, with
its brittleness and insistent triviality, is a conversational style that is perceived as compromising, however enjoyable, by contemporary gays; over-
indulgence in camp is felt somehow to be letting the side down" (Mars-
Jones 24). Later that night, Malone, feeling his youth fading, disappears
from the party, never to be seen or heard from again. (Presumably, he has
drowned in the Atlantic or been burned to death in the fire at the Everard
Baths later that night.) Sutherland dies of a drug overdose. Both self-destructive lives end in premature death. All these events have transpired
before the novel opens, so the order and manner in which they are narrated reflect the unfolding of the narrator's reassessment of Malone and the
life he symbolizes.

Even from the novel's outset, the fictional narrator repeatedly alerts the
reader that we learn of Malone and Sutherland only through the narrator's
retrospective account, which must be largely conjectural or fanciful. As the
fictional narrator says of Malone, with perhaps unconscious insight, "He
lived perhaps in my memory" (Holleran, *Dancer* 33). How does the narrator know of Malone's conversation with John, for instance? As the narra-

tor admits, Malone "was just a face I saw in a discotheque one winter" (Holleran, *Dancer* 23). Like a hero in a fairy tale, he is more the embodiment of an archetype than a specific individual. This distance is necessary for the psychic role that Malone plays in the narrator's imagination. "For a gay reader, the hero of a novel can just as easily be a role-model or a pin-up, a subject of identification or an object of desire. But he can be both these things only if his behaviour remains studiedly vague" (Mars-Jones 37). In this sense, such a hero must be like the protagonist of a folk tale or fairy tale, who may be described, for instance, as the handsomest youth in the kingdom, but whose features must not be described in detail, lest the description not match the individual reader's image of what an exceptionally good-looking person looks like. Although the narrator says he thinks "Malone was the handsomest man I'd ever seen," the narrator goes on to admit or to claim, "But then I was in love with half those people" and states that he never even exchanged two words with any of them (Holleran, *Dancer* 36). The narrator's recreation of Malone's life and Sutherland's life is suspect if read as biography, for it is framed (in the prologue) as what it is: a novel, a narrative fiction. We must not view the portrayal of Malone and Sutherland as objective or fully informed, but as essentially the fictional narrator's projection of his own complex personality, mixed with fantasy created out of fragments of knowledge gained largely through hearsay. So too, as with most elegies, this novel is less a meditation on the dead hero than it is a charting of the narrator's learning experience, the process by which the narrator reexamines his fantasy of his hero, which has grown to mythic proportions. The narrator's obsession requires self-analysis, and this self-analysis is the true subject of the novel.

Malone is, like a figure in a dream, a self, possible self, or aspect of the narrator's self from which the narrator distances himself by telling his tale. The narrator must reclaim his own power by withdrawing his projection from his hero and facing the dilemma that has preoccupied him, which his hero had come to represent. Telling the tale allows the narrator to gain the critical distance and self-knowledge that he needs.

Why does Malone, someone our narrator knew but slightly, have so enduring a hold on the narrator's imagination? This question is one that pertains to all elegiac romances, in which not even death can free the narrator's mind from its inexplicable fascination with the deceased hero. In the process of narrating the story, the fictional narrator works through his process of grieving so that he may resume his own life without being haunted by the ghost of the vanished hero. The elegiac romance finally, then, is told for the sake of the narrator. Thus the shadowy nature of the nameless narrator (aside from the prologue and epilogue) should not trick us into ignoring that this novel is, after all, his tale, not Malone's.

As do other narrators of elegiac romances, our narrator gradually rejects his hero, Malone, the glamorous gay man he had seen from a distance and regarded as a role model. Transcending hero worship is necessary for the narrator's own mature sense of self to unfold. This process of withdrawing his projections involves casting off cherished beliefs and forging a new sense of identity. "Elegiac romance may sometimes, therefore, be painful to read. The action of the narrator's tale involves loss, grief, disappointment, disillusionment, and guilt. Telling the tale involves the anguish of coming to terms, literally and figuratively, with these feelings" (Bruffee 57). It is always painful to dispense with heroes, for then we must look within for strength and guidance. Elegiac romance follows this shift away from hero worship:

> The *necessary conditions* for elegiac romance fiction are the narrator's protracted hero worship of his friend, and his friend's death before the narrator begins to tell the tale. The *occasion* of the narrator's tale is his irretrievable loss of his hero. The *ostensible purpose* of his tale is to memorialize his lost hero. The *real purpose* of his tale is to recover the coherence of his own interior world, lost when he lost the screen, so to speak, upon which he had projected his fantasies. (Bruffee 51).

Although this form is traceable to Joseph Conrad's *Lord Jim,* the most immediate prototype for *Dancer from the Dance* may be *The Great Gatsby,* a novel by F. Scott Fitzgerald. *Dancer from the Dance* holds a particular similarity with certain earlier elegiac romances, including *Gatsby,* Conrad's *Heart of Darkness,* and Robert Penn Warren's *All the King's Men,* all of which show how an entire society or civilization has gone wrong or become hollow at the core. But the parallels with *The Great Gatsby* are especially striking. Malone, like Gatsby and all other heroes of elegiac romances, has died before the narrative begins. Initially, Malone, like Gatsby, is built up as a mysterious, highly romantic man seen from afar.

Although both Malone and Gatsby are characterized as exceptionally good-looking, neither's appearance is described photographically. One character says of Malone, "Malone is all of them, all of those boys, those summers" (Holleran, *Dancer* 194). As the narrator confesses, he never describes Malone's appearance "in a story that is really about physical beauty more than anything else" (Holleran, *Dancer* 133). Holleran suggests in *Ground Zero,* "The thrill of homosexuality is finally an aesthetic thrill" (35). Gatsby's appearance is similarly vague. When Nick Carraway first sees Gatsby, all he notes is that Gatsby has his hands in his pockets and that "something in his leisurely movements and the secure position of his feet upon the lawn suggested it was Mr. Gatsby himself" (Fitzgerald 21). Gatsby's appearance is nowhere described at all specifically. F. Scott Fitzgerald wrote to Max Perkins, "I myself didn't know what Gatsby looked like" (quoted in Sarotte 221).

Another similarity between *Dancer from the Dance* and *The Great Gatsby* is that the opening paragraph of the narrative portion (after the epistolary prologue) of *Dancer from the Dance* contains the narrator's reflection upon an observation his father once made. In the opening paragraph of *The Great Gatsby*, Nick Carraway, the narrator, quotes his father. Neither father is mentioned again in the novel. Surely such a similarity could not be merely coincidental; Holleran's allusion to Fitzgerald's work seems intentional.

Clothes also function similarly in both novels. The narrative of *Dancer from the Dance* begins with the narrator's trip to Fire Island to sort through Malone's clothes. Malone's wardrobe is catalogued down to his forty-four pairs of shoe trees, his twenty-eight bathing suits, and his thirty-two plaid shirts, all of these (and other clothes) being merely those he had chanced to take with him to his temporary summer weekend getaway. This description of Malone's clothes probably alludes to the scene in *The Great Gatsby* in which Gatsby "took out a pile of shirts and began throwing them, one by one, before" Nick Carraway and Daisy Buchanan (Fitzgerald 93). The clothes are used both by Malone and by Gatsby as props in what to each becomes an ultimately unsuccessful pursuit of love. The outer, material abundance (numerous shirts) stands in contrast with these characters' inner emptiness and frustrations.

The narrator's quest for information about Malone is matched by Nick Carraway's series of revelations about Gatsby. Characters ask other characters what they know of Malone, where they first met, and so on. "At first we thought he was a medical student; then we heard he worked on Seventh Avenue. . . . Then someone said he . . . was being kept by an Episcopalian bishop; . . . Malone went through as many guises as the discotheques we danced at" (Holleran, *Dancer* 117–18). Similarly, rumors multiply about Gatsby: that "he's a nephew or cousin of Kaiser Wilhelm's" (Fitzgerald 33), that he was a German spy in World War I (44), and so on. Gatsby, Nick tells us, inspired "romantic speculation" (44).

Even Malone's talent for making people feel special is like Gatsby's. Malone "made you feel you were being . . . selected, for some confidential revelation" (Holleran, *Dancer* 56). Gatsby, Nick tells us, had "one of those rare smiles . . . [that] concentrated on *you* with an irresistible prejudice in your favor" (Fitzgerald 48).

Yet as the story unfolds, for all Malone's charms, the narrator gradually shifts from adoring Malone to belittling him and rejecting him as a role model, just as Nick Carraway exposes, little by little, the flimsiness of Gatsby's pretenses, such as his claim of being an "Oxford man," reflected in his preposterous affectation of referring to Nick as "old sport." Nick learns of Gatsby's true, humble origins. The narrator's correspondent writes in the epilogue to *Dancer from the Dance*, "Let us not . . . dignify Malone too much: He was in the end a circuit queen" (Holleran, *Dancer* 249). By now the narrator has made a one-hundred-eighty-degree turnaround in his stance regarding Malone, from hero worshiper to iconoclast. This narrative thus re-creates this shift, first attributing to the hero great glamour and then piece by piece showing why that glamour was misplaced, so that the reader can relive the narrator's self-discovery and disillusionment by experiencing it as he does. We too, like the narrator, embark upon an odyssey of self-discovery, casting off false idols along the way.

Dancer from the Dance turns out to be more about the personal journey of self-understanding of the unnamed narrator than it is about Malone, even as *The Great Gatsby* can be seen to be more about Nick Carraway than about Jay Gatsby. The narrator moves closer to accepting a gay identity without being depressed by this through the very recounting of the story of Malone's descent to his doom. As the narrator distances himself from his hero, he gains greater self-confidence. He withdraws his projection of an idealized sense of self from Malone and modifies it and claims it as his own, with his ex-New York correspondent going before him and articulating the reasons for his own move away from the lifestyle symbolized by Malone. Malone comes to be viewed as a god who failed, whose outlook and vision cease to inspire. Yet to the end he is portrayed as essentially the romantic hero on a quest for the ineffable, whether this is his childhood search for a life consecrated to Christ or his adult search for an ideal male-male love. The quests prove elusive; Malone finds himself disappointed by both ideals (Holleran, *Dancer* 221). That the two ideals could successively dwell in the same breast does not strike Holleran as paradoxical, as is clear from a statement that he places in the mouth of a fictional character in *Ground Zero*, which apparently we are meant to take essentially at face value:

> What many do not realize is that the age of promiscuous, anonymous sex was also a *sentimental, romantic* age! [To] the real romantics . . . sex that is rational, circumscribed, premeditated is not *sincere*. Sex to them must be a surrender, a loss of self. . . . They are searching, through physical love, for what Saint Theresa experienced through mystical trances. (Holleran, *Ground Zero* 157–58; emphasis in original)

Malone's very romanticism and his idealism, perhaps his chief charms (apart from his looks), are finally seen as impractical. Malone's ideal of love—and that of many other gay men with similarly extravagant expectations—is out of reach of any lover other than the perfect love who dwells in his romantic imagination. "Did we all suspect that half the beauty and shimmer of that life was in our own hypnotic hearts and not out there?" (Holleran, *Dancer* 245).

Malone is gone. He is either dead or elsewhere. His disappearance proves as mysterious as his very presence had been. This is fitting for someone seen from a distance who serves in the narrative as the screen for others' projections, especially once the sense of self he represents has been outgrown. At last the narrator can let go of his memories and fantasies about Malone. The elusive quest that Malone represents, for romance and glamour, for excitement and escape, for the thrills of sexual pursuit and the brief euphoria of drugs, ceases to fascinate and attract the narrator. Such strategies for coping with an underlying sense of Depression about being gay generally lose their allure among those who come to accept being gay and to integrate this self-identity into their day-to-day lives. So too, in forming and stabilizing a mature sense of adult identity, including a secure sense of sexual identity, the need for hero worship diminishes. Such an inner shift to a stable sense of sexual identity as a gay man has already occurred in the protagonist of Paul Monette's novel *Taking Care of Mrs. Carroll,* which exemplifies the final stage of the coming-out process, Acceptance.

EXERCISE: EXAMINING ONE'S ATTITUDES ABOUT THE GAY COMMUNITY

In coming out, Depression involves ambivalence, internalized homophobia, impaired self-esteem, and a sense of resignation about being gay. Usually discovering "I am homosexual and there is nothing I can do to change that" is greeted with reluctance or, at best, resignation. Self-image as a homosexual is often projected upon the gay subculture. Those who have the most trouble accepting their homosexuality tend to view the gay community the most negatively (as is the case with Jody and Farragut in *Falconer*). One's experiences in and attitudes about the gay subculture also affect self-image. Positive experiences in the gay world can lead to Acceptance, while negative experiences can reinforce Depression and produce a sense of being a "doomed queen." *Dancer from the Dance* focuses upon the self-destructive aspects of the gay subculture of the 1970s, as represented by the figures of Malone and Sutherland.

To what extent do you agree with the following attitudes of Malone about the gay subculture, as presented by the narrator of *Dancer from the Dance?*

Joining the gay community means. . .

being in exile from the straight community.

that one is an outcast from society.

that society at large despises you.

cutting oneself off from family and former friends and associates.

becoming economically marginal and living by one's wits.

living in a world of bars and bathhouses.

that one must acquire an enormous wardrobe.

that one must do all one can to be sexually attractive.

that one is on the cutting edge of fashions and trends.

drinking alcohol and taking other drugs.

that one goes from one transitory sexual encounter to another.

that one never will be able to maintain a long-term sexual relationship.

that one is bohemian.

that one must live in an urban gay ghetto.

that one will become jaded, bored, and disillusioned.

that one will secretly loathe being gay and wish one could be respectable.

that one will destroy oneself one way or another.

6

Acceptance:
Taking Care of Mrs. Carroll

"I'm not into closets."

—Paul Monette,
Taking Care of Mrs. Carroll 107

Paul Monette uses a unique and offbeat plot in *Taking Care of Mrs. Carroll* to establish several points about Acceptance of being gay and about establishing and maintaining successful long-term gay relationships. Rick, the narrator, is called early in the summer of 1975 by his ex-lover, David. Rick, who is forty-five years old, has not seen David, now thirty, since their relationship of three and a half years ended five years previously. David, on the rebound from his breakup with Neil Macdonald, his relationship subsequent to the one he had had with Rick, has taken the position of houseboy for Mrs. Carroll, an eighty-two-year-old eccentric widow. Mrs. Carroll has written her children out of her new will to preserve her extensive oceanside acreage (of beach, woods, marsh, and a dairy farm) from the development that inevitably would result should her children inherit the land. But she dies before signing her will. The novel's characters assemble on the Carroll estate and cagily plot to see that Mrs. Carroll's last wishes concerning her property are carried out, thus "taking care of Mrs. Carroll," as the novel's title expresses it. To keep their illegal scheme from being discovered, they avoid contact with the outside world for the whole summer. As Labor Day approaches, they succeed, and so prepare to disperse. The novel ends. The entire action of the novel takes place during the summer of 1975, apart from flashbacks and other methods of exposition of prior events, such as Rick telling David how he had met Madeleine when he was twenty-eight, in 1958.

Of course, this plot structure and setting help Monette to limit his cast of characters and to eliminate all that are inessential. Within *Taking Care of Mrs. Carroll,* a tightly written novel with this relatively small cast, Monette makes skillful use of foils and parallels to define his characters and to establish his points about successful gay male individuation and long-term gay relationships. Aside from Mrs. Carroll, whose death is established within the first four words of the novel's opening sentence ("When Mrs. Carroll died" [Monette 3]), only eight characters appear "on stage" at the Carrolls' summer house: five gay men, two straight men (Phidias, the estate's caretaker, with whom Beth Carroll had carried on an extramarital affair for forty years; and Donald Farley, Mrs. Carroll's straight-laced lawyer), and one extraordinary woman, Madeleine Cosquer. Now in her seventy-fourth year, as far as Rick can tell, Madeleine is a legendary French movie star and chanteuse of the stature of Garbo, Piaf, and Marlene Dietrich. Madeleine symbolizes the archetypal feminine, with which Rick has developed a mature relationship. Rick's self-acceptance makes this close friendship with Madeleine possible. (It is also highlighted in other novels by Paul Monette, such as *The Gold Diggers* and *Afterlife.*) "This acceptance of oneself as a gay man enables the kind of closeness and intimacy between women and gay men that many heterosexual men notice (and perhaps envy) and that many women find enormously enjoyable and freeing" (Hopcke 153–54). Such rapport between women and gay men has long been recognized, as is evident, for example, in the writings of Edward Carpenter (1844–1929), who refuted the notion that male homosexuals hate or fear women. On the contrary, he argued in *The Intermediate Sex,* Uranians (gays) "are by their very nature drawn rather near to women, and . . . often feel a singular appreciation and understanding of the . . . other sex" (198).

Rick, the fictional narrator and main character, delights in the company of his friend of many years, Madeleine Cosquer. Rick has long since integrated being gay into his sense of adult identity. He epitomizes the final stage of the coming-out process, Acceptance. His long-term relationship with David rests on a firm foundation of Acceptance. "The taking of a lover *confirms* gay identity" (Troiden 369), just as it does in Peter and Nick's relationship in Monette's novel *The Gold Diggers.* Like those in the Acceptance stage of the mortality process, Rick "is neither depressed nor angry about his 'fate' " (Kübler-Ross 99). Monette has this forty-five-year-old character contemplate his past, his entrance into middle age, and the prospect of old age without any of the maudlin fears of aging often attributed to gay men. Rick differs in this regard from the hustlers depicted in John Rechy's novels, to whom being noticeably over twenty or so is a disaster to be postponed for as long as possible. Monette manages that rarity in serious gay fiction: a happy ending in which gay male ex-lovers reunite as a couple, with the promise that this time they will actually get it right. Perhaps even more remarkably, Monette does so without sentimentalizing the relationship or making it seem implausible. Monette said in a recent interview, "I am fundamentally a writer of love stories" (Fenwick 59). In short, Monette tackles head-on the major homophobic clichés that have plagued most gay fiction.

Taking Care of Mrs. Carroll thus refutes the claim made by Georges-Michel Sarotte in *Comme un Frère, Comme un Amant* (1976), which first appeared in its English translation as *Like a Brother, Like a Lover* in 1978, the year of publication of *Taking Care of Mrs. Carroll*. Sarotte claims that despite the gay liberation movement, America is so riddled with taboos against homosexuality that "no harmony can exist between the homosexual dream . . . and American reality. . . . The inability to create viable couple archetypes is the most tangible proof of this failure" (303). Despite Sarotte's contention that the American "dream" of homosexual love has not been realized successfully in American literature, such is certainly no longer the case. Moreover, it was not the case even at the time at which Sarotte wrote (1976). Sarotte mentions the followers of Buechner and Isherwood as failing to embody this dream, but despite this assertion, it did become reality for several in Buechner's circle, notably the poet James Merrill. Sarotte conveniently ignores the politics and economics of publishing. It may be true that traditionally "the homosexual in literature has generally been a tragic figure, doomed to a bitter, unhappy and lonely life" (Altman, *Oppression* xi), but this simply cannot be blamed on any supposed inadequacy of homosexual writers' imaginations or literary abilities. Until recently, most publishers resisted or refused to publish any positive portrayal of gays. Authors had to pander to public preconceptions, misconceptions, and prejudices about homosexuality in order to see their works published. No wonder homophobic stereotypes were upheld. The financial and social pressures upon the publishing business produced predictable results. Even those who oppose homophobia looked at gay literature in the mid-1970s and found it wanting. Roger Austen, a committed foe of homophobia, laments "the decline and perhaps even the 'death' of traditional gay fiction over the past fifteen years [1962–77]" (199). Austen, writing in 1977, failed to predict that gay fiction would flourish in the following decade. This boom in gay fiction was heralded by the publication the very next year (1978) of, among other novels, *Dancer from the Dance* and *Taking Care of Mrs. Carroll*.

Sarotte betrays his homophobia not only in his critique of gay literature but also in his views on the causes of homosexuality. He dredges up the hackneyed cliché of an enduring "mother fixation," as well as the equally unilluminating notion that "the failure of introjection" of an adult male role model "is the basic cause of . . . homosexuality" (Sarotte 169, 213). Such notions have been disproved by empirical research; Bell, for instance, concludes that a boy's relationship with his mother has "only a limited influence on his sexual orientation in adulthood" (5) and that "the quality of the father-son relationship (like that with the mother) is not a very good predictor of a boy's eventual sexual preference" (56). With stunning vagueness, Sarotte traces what he terms the "homosexual instinct" to "childhood emotional insecurity" (Sarotte 260). As Stephen Adams notes, even though Sarotte ostensibly avoids judging homosexuality as a moral depravity, he insists that the works of homosexual writers fall victim to "their own neuroses and self-hatreds, thereby confirming the view of homosexuality as a pathological failure to achieve maturity, as an impaired form of masculinity" (Adams 12). Such homophobia as Sarotte's has become increasingly conspicuous and offensive to gays as self-acceptance has grown stronger in recent years. Rick, like real-life gays in Acceptance, does not fit Sarotte's psychological portrait of the homosexual. Rick integrates the masculine and feminine elements in himself. He develops a mature understanding of the nuances of human interactions, both in his friendships with men and women and in his love for David. Monette's success in depicting Rick and his relationships in a plausible way calls into question Sarotte's sweeping generalizations.

Rick gets on well with his coconspirators on the Carroll estate, but they are cut off from outsiders. This geographical isolation symbolizes the social isolation from mainstream society that many gay people face. Dennis Altman soberly observes that the type of pluralism that society recognizes does not extend to "acceptance of real diversity in sexuality, in gender roles, and in family structures" and thus complete acceptance of homosexuality eludes those who demand it (Altman, *Homosexualization* 210). Certainly acceptance from straight people helps facilitate coming out, but "change in self-feeling and self-acceptance . . . tend to be the results of acceptance by and support from gay people rather than 'straights' " (Weinberg 303). The geographic isolation of the characters on the Carroll estate has many literary precedents. Adams maintains that as full integration into society is frequently denied to homosexuals, "the homosexual novel is typically a description of a journey away from the everyday world" (109). The use of pastoral or exotic settings can be seen in gay fiction written by E. M. Forster, Gore Vidal, James Baldwin, Christopher Isherwood, William Burroughs, Andrew Holleran, Edmund White, and C. F. Borgman, among others. It applies to lesbian fiction, such as novels by Rita Mae Brown and Alice Walker, as well as to gay fiction. Both Djuna Barnes' *Nightwood* and Thomas Mann's "Death in Venice," for instance, use Roman Catholicism in Europe to suggest decadence or freedom from a Protestant ethic that makes heterosexual marriage a badge of honor. Altman maintains that in the American gay novel, homosexual themes typically are treated in settings of wilderness or retreat from society, whereas in British novels, homosexuality characteristically is depicted within society. The American gay hero remains a loner even when placed in the urban landscape, as is evident in the novels of John Rechy (Altman, *Oppression* xiii–xiv). There are exceptions to Altman's generalization: in *Maurice,* for instance, the gay lovers have no chance of being received into English society. (Altman probably had no opportunity to consider this exception, as *Maurice* was not published until 1971, the year when Altman's book was published.)

On the Carroll estate, the characters in *Taking Care of Mrs. Carroll* build a surrogate family, a step necessary for the many gay people whose parents, at least initially, are anything but supportive and understanding upon finding out they have a gay child. Monette's fiction mirrors his own experiences in this regard. Monette calls his fifteen closest friends—"half men, half women, half straight, half gay"—his "family" (Monette, *Borrowed Time* 25); his biological family's reaction to seeing the galley proofs of *Taking Care of Mrs. Carroll* was to say "they would have to sell their house and leave town" (Monette, *Borrowed Time* 54). The cohesive alternate society built by the characters in *Taking Care of Mrs. Carroll* resembles the new social networks many gay people built in coming out. While Malone, according to the narrator of *Dancer from the Dance,* mourns being cast out of the straight world, in *Taking Care of Mrs. Carroll* Rick scarcely thinks about his parents and the other presumably nonsupportive straight people whose company he has left behind. (Parents of gay characters are also absent in Monette's novel *The Gold Diggers.*) Rick has built up an effective support network among gay and non-gay men and women. Rick has left behind the "gay ghetto" mentality that besets Malone in *Dancer from the Dance,* one sign of his completion of the coming-out process. Cass calls the final stage of her Homosexual Identity Formation model the Identity Synthesis stage. When a gay person reaches this stage, there is typically a breakdown of "them and us," straight versus gay feelings (Cass 234). The individual who has publicly and privately come out comes to see his homosexuality as only one part of a larger self. In this process, he realizes that "some heterosexuals can actually accept homosexuality more fully than some homosexuals" (Brady 28; Brown 242). Phidias is more comfortable around Rick, Aldo, and David than is Tony.

Rick has created a surrogate family and effectively has left his biological parents out of his present life. This parallels the experience of many gay people, who often use the word "family" to indicate not their biological relatives but the gay and non-gay people who provide them with emotional support on a day-to-day basis. "Indeed, finding a family of sorts has become the chief interest of characters in much gay fiction" (Hall 26). If such surrogate families seem to be artificial constructs, some recent television melodramas with gay characters have shown that the same is true of biological families. "One of the unintended effects of *An Early Frost* [a 1985 television movie about AIDS] is to narrate how the family is itself an ideological construct[,] which in turn reproduces discursive conflicts to the point of agonized contradiction" (Leo 46). This process of forming surrogate families, which is less common among straight people, is often misunderstood by them. When President and Mrs. Bush met six men with AIDS in 1989, for instance, "Mrs. Bush asked [one of them] whether his family was being supportive. He answered . . . 'My real family here is Joseph, my lover.' . . . Mrs. Bush seemed confused" (Wylen 42). Rick notes cynically that we can do without our families of origin, in which we allow our fears of loneliness to imprison us. He admits he has not seen his North Shore father in years. Rick reflects that the parents of gay men are either absent or as shadowy as the children they do not have. Indeed, in many gay novels, gay men's families of origin play little or no role.

Gay novels often omit or minimize mention of gay characters' interactions with their families. Many gay novels, however, adhere to the standard Bildungsroman form, tracing the hero's development from his childhood through his separation from his family and his formation of an adult identity. This necessarily involves exploring family influences upon the hero's subsequent development. Gay novels of other types sometimes pursue the importance of the ongoing connection between adult gays and their families of origin.

A Boy's Own Story is a Bildungsroman, as is *Totempole*. In *A Boy's Own Story,* by Edmund White, the protagonist ages from his childhood only through his mid-adolescence, and therefore, throughout the novel, his family is central. Sanford Friedman's *Totempole* traces the life of Stephen Wolfe, its gay hero, from age two to age twenty-four. The first half of the novel pivots around his relationship with his father, mother, brother, and his family's domestic servants. Even in *A Boy's Own Story* and *Totempole,* however, the prominence of family does not lead to glamorization of it. Marital tensions and arguments loom large, resulting in the former novel in divorce, and in the latter in the threat of divorce. But depicting family prominently, however negatively, is hardly typical, and in many gay novels the gay characters' families are almost entirely absent.

In some recent gay fiction, though, authors have challenged the convention of ignoring gay men's families. Gay male characters' relationships with their families of origin are at the heart of the novels by the late Robert Ferro, as is evident even in their titles: *The Family of Max Desir* (1983), which traces several generations of a gay man's family, and *Second Son* (1988), which devotes far more space to the gay character's family than to his lover. A young gay man's relationship with his parents is also the major theme of David Leavitt's *The Lost Language of Cranes* (1986). Christopher Isherwood's novel *A Meeting by the River* (1967) hinges upon the relationship between two brothers, one of whom is a closeted homosexual. However, such novels as Ferro's, Leavitt's, and Isherwood's are atypical. This is unfortunate, for two reasons. First, for many gay men, one of the hardest parts of coming out is telling their parents and siblings. Fictional treatment could help gay men and their families resolve difficult issues. Second, gays do have families, contrary to the rhetoric of the political Right, which suggests that families are always entirely heterosexual. To the extent that the families of gays are ignored, the political Right can use its rhetoric of "family values" to deny gay people their rights. The AIDS crisis, for instance, affects not only gays (and others) but also their families.

In the conspicuous absence of his biological parents, however, Rick finds in Madeleine Cosquer a surrogate-mother of sorts, or, to be more precise, a female friend old enough to be his mother. Not only is Madeleine twenty-eight years Rick's senior, but also, near the end of the summer, Rick learns that in 1930, when she was twenty-eight, Madeleine had a baby boy that she put up for adoption. This son would now be forty-five, Rick's age. Rick wonders if he could be that child. At least briefly, Rick entertains the idea that Madeleine might be his biological mother. In a Dickensian plot twist, Rick belatedly learns that Madeleine and Phidias had been married in 1930 and that Madeleine's child was Phidias's as well. This causes Rick to imagine Phidias being his father. Perhaps conceding that such Victorian plot twists are overly sentimental for modern readers, Monette establishes that there is no factual basis for believing that Madeleine is Rick's biological mother. Madeleine belittles Rick for entertaining such notions.

Nevertheless, for the duration of the summer, Madeleine plays the role, if not exactly of mother, then that of the lady of the house, particularly in her impersonation of Beth Carroll. This is the pivotal element in the plan to get Beth Carroll's will signed. Afterward a plausible "disappearance" of Mrs. Carroll can be arranged, whose body has already been buried in secret in a remote spot on the estate. Phidias is doubly linked to Madeleine-as-Beth, both as the actual former husband of Madeleine, and as the former lover of Beth. With his former conjugal or quasi-conjugal connections with the two matriarchs, Phidias, the only straight man to be part of the inner circle, becomes its ersatz patriarch. He becomes a father figure for Rick and the other men for the summer. In any case, Madeleine has occupied a very important role in Rick's life, not only during this summer, but also throughout the seventeen years of their friendship, especially for the thirteen years in which she has been staying at his place each year during her annual concert series in Boston. One might say that Madeleine serves for Rick as an anima figure, the embodiment of the ideal feminine.

One of the psychological tasks all men face in their individuation is the integration of the anima into consciousness. For gay men, this necessity may become especially urgent. As Hopcke argues, "For gay men, . . . a connection with the positive side of masculinity may be achieved only once some resolution of the issues of femininity can be found" (Hopcke 143). A straight man may find this facilitated through his projection of his anima upon the woman (or women) he marries and/or loves. For a gay man, the projection of the anima often occurs through the idealization of a famous, larger-than-life woman. Ken Bartmess, through extensive analysis of the dreams of gay men, has identified archetypal figures distinctive to gay male psyches, including what he has termed the diva archetype. As he notes, "[One] gay archetype that has emerged for me is the diva, a strong dramatic woman. She might take the form of movie or opera star and has dual aspects—a powerful guide or the Queen of the Night, a bitch. She is an interesting figure to look for in both of her manifestations" (Bartmess, quoted in Thompson, "Soul Making" 245). This accords with one widespread stereotype that "gay men are supposed to be enthralled with older movies, elevating such stars of the past as Judy Garland, Bette Davis, Joan Crawford, Gloria Swanson, and others to the cult status of goddess" (Hopcke 38). This stereotype underlies such gay novels as Manuel Puig's *Kiss of the Spider Woman*, in which the gay character Molina is obsessed with the glamorous heroines of movies he has seen, as well as Gore Vidal's *Myra Breckinridge* and *Myron*, particularly the latter, which offers an extensive commentary upon old movies.

Hopcke uses religious language to describe this phenomenon, which dovetails not only with the religious aura surrounding the diva archetype but also with Jung's feeling that the gay man is often "endowed with a wealth of religious feeling" (Jung, quoted in Hopcke 38). This only seems paradoxical to those steeped in centuries of Western homophobia and sex-negative conditioning traceable to Greek dualism. James Nelson asserts, "We can be both fully spiritual and fully sexual" (171). To a Christian, the doctrine of the Incarnation confounds any absolute dichotomy between spirit world and material world, or the divine realm and the human realm. In practice, the union of opposites represented by the Incarnation remains to many a radical concept.

Monette portrays Madeleine Cosquer, the seventy-three-year-old movie star and chanteuse, as an embodiment of the diva archetype in its aspect of guide, whereas Beth Carroll (at least according to her son Tony) seems to have personified the malevolent aspect of the diva. She was a cold woman who used her wealth to withdraw into her own estate, which she ran as an autocrat would without interference. Beth Carroll isolated herself from the world, whereas Madeleine delights in her travels and her public appearances. Even at her age, Madeleine still has a devoted group of loyal followers, and still attracts an audience, smaller perhaps, "mostly gay, faithful as postulants" (Monette, *Taking Care* 27). Monette's religious language in the simile "faithful as postulants" suggests the sacred task of the anima: to serve as a man's soul guide, as Beatrice does for Dante in *The Divine Comedy*. Many (though by no means all) female movie and television stars as well as singers have gathered a devoted gay male following similar to Madeleine Cosquer's, showing the pervasiveness and power of the diva archetype among gay men. The gay following of such stars often is drawn to both the positive and the negative aspects of the diva archetype. This is evident, for instance, in the camp humor of female impersonators, such as Charles Pierce, who in his routine as Joan Collins says, "All I know how to do is wear clothes and be a bitch." That both aspects of the diva are opposite sides of the same coin is hinted at in *Taking Care of Mrs. Carroll* by the former sexual affair between the two women. Madeleine Cosquer, it turns out, had had a lesbian affair with Beth Carroll several decades previously. Although this and Madeleine's other affairs with women are not well known, this is not due to concealment on Madeleine's part, but because the public "has chosen not to notice" (Monette, *Taking Care* 39).

Madeleine plays her part as star to the hilt, but she does not lose her detachment while doing so. She is not one to confuse the distinction between her private life and the legend her fans cherish. Her sense of irony allows her to continue to play the role of the beautiful woman in love. Madeleine astutely assesses, cultivates, and capitalizes upon her own continued popularity. Rick watches her annual Boston concert year after year and concludes that though some signs of aging are impossible to hide, Madeleine, through her careful art, projects the illusion of being "a woman arrested in full flower," as if she were the embodiment of the myth she has created (Monette, *Taking Care* 71).

The late Mrs. Carroll, as the only female character other than Madeleine, serves as foil to her. Mrs. Carroll's life is reflected upon by many of the characters, for various reasons. Phidias quietly mourns his illicit beloved of forty years while ensuring that her wishes regarding her property are honored. Madeleine relives her affair with Beth through reading Beth's diaries. Beth Carroll, though the wife of a New England starched-collar type, posthumously and ironically, through her bisexual past, links the various sexualities, past and present, of the assembled cast. In her person, she establishes, via her former sexual affairs with both Madeleine and Phidias, another connection between them apart from their youthful marriage to each other, long kept secret. Beth Carroll also serves as a reminder to the reader that gays have no monopoly on sexual relations that flourish without benefit of the clergy's blessing or legal recognition. A further irony is that the various legal marriages of Madeleine, Beth, and Phidias all prove unhappy and/or short-lived, whereas the adulterous affair of Beth and Phidias lasts happily for many decades, until their union is split asunder by death. Monette here subtly undermines the unthinking equation of licit relationships (legally sanctioned marriages) with longevity and happiness and the corresponding assumption that illicit relationships (including all gay relationships and extramarital affairs) are unstable and short-lived. This obliquely sets the stage for favorable prospects for Rick and David's staying together in the long term.

How can we come to know Mrs. Carroll, this absence at the center of the Carroll estate and indeed of the novel itself? It is her death that precipitates the gathering that the novel recounts and thus the reunion of Rick and David. This question plagues Madeleine, who must impersonate her old friend in order to pull off the crucial meeting with Donald Farley, the lawyer, to sign Beth Carroll's will. The aging movie star must summon her consummate skills for yet another performance. Madeleine rifles Beth's diaries in quest of background information and clues as to how to play this most demanding of roles convincingly. What she finds infuriates her: endless guest lists, menus, and details about place-settings. In short, the diaries contain a meticulous chronicling of events in which personal feelings have been left out. A rare exception is Beth's entries during her trip to Paris, in which she and Madeleine were together. Madeleine is infuriated when she finds the gushings of a star-struck schoolgirl. Rick wonders how much of the past can be recaptured and ponders the elusiveness of the truth. Beth Carroll proves surprisingly inscrutable. Her past cannot be reconstructed from the impenetrable reserve of her diaries and from her taciturn former lover, Phidias. Mrs. Carroll, in yet another way unifying the novel, represents the difficulty of recovering the past experienced by all the novel's characters. Representing the past becomes no less a matter of interpretation and artifice—if not downright fraud—than Madeleine's impersonation of Beth Carroll.

Perhaps the perception of life as a complex set of choices and unrecoverable former circumstances becomes acute at the initial onset of middle age, at approximately the age of forty, at which time it may become imperative to reassess the choices one has made during one's youth. Three of the gay male characters in *Taking Care of Mrs. Carroll* are forty-five years old: Aldo, Tony, and Rick. Daniel J. Levinson and his colleagues conclude, "At around forty-five (plus or minus two years) . . . [a man] can no longer give so much energy to reappraising the past and reintegrating the polarities. . . . The main tasks now are to make crucial choices, give these choices meaning and commitment, and build a life structure around them" (Levinson et al. 278). Aldo seems already to have built such a structure. Rick does so in the course of the summer, recounting the process in his narrative. Tony fails to do so.

Aldo is Madeleine's manager and perhaps her most ardent fan. Tony Carroll, the youngest of Mrs. Carroll's three children, whom Rick describes as a "washed-out closet case," shows up unexpectedly at an inopportune moment and almost destroys the conspirators' scheme. Of course, there is also Madeleine's friend Rick, the narrator. That all three share the same age naturally invites comparisons between them and allows (the author and) the narrator to reflect on how very different gay men of forty-five can be, at the age at which, as Gail Sheehy notes, "a man will generally stabilize" (293). The three certainly wear the mantle of gay identity differently as each settles into middle age after the mid-life transition. By this time of life, most men have long since made their peace with their sexual orientation, to the extent that they are ever likely to do so. Surprising numbers overcome the obstacles and embrace a gay sexual identity. The move towards self-acceptance seems to be an intrinsic part of maturing, when the peer pressures that seem crushing during adolescence diminish; "many people naturally grow more comfortable with themselves as they grow older" (Fisher 238).

Aldo, Madeleine's manager, is flamboyantly and unapologetically effeminate. Madeleine has described him to Rick as "an old queen who's been looking all his life for a pet movie star" (Monette, *Taking Care* 79), leading Rick to think of Aldo as "an elderly queen" (26). Rick is thus surprised to realize, upon meeting Aldo, that they are the same age, forty-five, though Aldo looks older. Aldo's first line upon bursting into the Carroll house is "Mary, there isn't a soul at the front desk" (103). Aldo's dialogue runs to camp, unlike that of the other gay men in the novel. He is in his element handling Madeleine's wardrobe and whipping up gourmet meals that are presented on the plate like artistic compositions awaiting the photographer from a culinary magazine. In short, Aldo is prissy and effeminate. He epitomizes one negative stereotype of gay men as soft, rounded, and "nellie." He is what many homosexuals fear they might be or become: the exact opposite of the ideal of masculinity in a culture that commodifies sexuality and ascribes virtually magical powers to sexual attractiveness and virility. Men like Aldo are not desired by the (usually closeted) men who place personal ads in search of "straight-acting" and "straight-appearing" men. Such closeted men dread being judged effeminate by others and so avoid the company of nellie queens, fearing "guilt by association" should they socialize with men like Aldo. The drag queen's style of high camp, which mortifies closeted homosexuals, insecure in their own sense of their masculinity, may permeate the insistent sexual bravado of effeminate queens. Ultimately, such men are seen finally as unmanly and therefore sexless. Rick accordingly dismisses the sexual innuendos of this type of gay men as hollow, seeing camp and its shock value as substitutes for sex used by those who cannot attract sexual partners. At first Rick places Aldo in the same category with "the dizziest gay men, the reckless, boy-hungry types" (Monette, *Taking Care* 107). But Rick is secure enough in his own sexual identity not to be threatened or embarrassed by Aldo. Rick is not like the closeted homosexuals who secretly suspect that the existence of queens demonstrates what they are loathe to contemplate: that their own homosexuality is somehow unmanly. Such closeted men would cut Aldo and those like him because they (probably unknowingly) project their internalized homophobia upon effeminate gay men. Rick, on the other hand, develops a rapport with Aldo, and acknowledges his individuality, refusing to dismiss him offhandedly as just an effeminate queen, admitting there is much more to Aldo than that. Contrary to the literary clichés of the nellie queen, Aldo is not depicted as secretly unhappy or self-destructive beneath his seamless and amusing banter. Aldo is quite content with who and what he is.

Tony Carroll, another forty-five-year-old gay man, serves as a foil both to Rick and to Aldo. Although Rick is as masculine as Aldo is feminine, both fundamentally accept being gay. Tony, however, loathes being homosexual. But the others do not ridicule Tony even though Rick and Aldo are utterly absorbed by the many ways in which he reveals his internalized homophobia and self-hatred. Rick says that he, Aldo, and Madeleine are "appalled by the way in which Tony was gay. *His was the fate the rest of us had escaped*" (Monette, *Taking Care* 204; emphasis added). Clearly, Tony represents a figure of "what might have been" for Rick and Aldo, hence their almost morbid fascination with him. As gay men of the same generation, they realize how unchecked self-loathing might have wreaked havoc upon their lives had they not come out and come to accept being gay. Tony serves as a foil, showing how far the other gay characters have come out. Although all three are gay and forty-five, both Rick and Aldo have used their early adulthood to find ways of expressing their sexuality that feel comfortable to them. Yet Tony Carroll, though his youth is gone, continues to lead the tortured and closeted life that many gay men cast off in adolescence or early adulthood. Tony Carroll brings back to mind for Rick his own former adolescent self-loathing. Tony is stuck in his psychosexual development, whereas Rick and Aldo have reached a mature sexual adjustment. Tony, however, is unable either to come out fully or to return to more complete Denial. He seems to vacillate endlessly between Anger and Depression. He cannot forgive his mother, nor let go of the lingering resentments that gnaw at him. He feebly tries to drown his guilt and rage in Dewar's Scotch, which he carries with him in half-gallon bottles.

Tony also demonstrates how difficult, if not impossible, it is to help others take the next step in their coming-out process if they are unable or unwilling to do so. If coming out may be likened to what Joseph Campbell refers to as the hero's journey, that is, as a process of initiation into a new adult identity, then one could note that though the hero has helpers on his journey, he is not compelled to venture forth. The hero may ignore his call (as Campbell indicates in *The Hero with a Thousand Faces*). Tony has received his "call," the insistent internal message letting him know he is homosexual, but he spurns the help that is offered to him in this painful process of initiation and transformation of identity. David offers himself sexually to Tony, in an effort to help him come out. Although Tony accepts the offer, he pays David back for his concern afterwards by hurling a lamp at his face in a fit of self-revulsion. Rick tells David that "he couldn't take care of people who made a career of hurting themselves" (Monette, *Taking Care* 230). Madeleine and the others see Tony as gay at once, in one of the greatest ironies of the gay world: It is often those who try the hardest

to conceal their homosexuality from others who are the most instantly identifiable as homosexual. Although his sexual orientation is no secret to per-
ceptive observers, Tony stays in the closet. Rick muses that he cannot bring
himself to tell Tony, "Just open the door and walk out[;] it isn't locked"
(Monette, *Taking Care* 233). Were he to take this step, he might find that
his loneliness, like the loneliness of the hustler/protagonist in John Rechy's
City of Night, is self-imposed and thus reversible. Peter Fisher said in
retrospect, after a long and painful coming-out process, that he finally realized he had always been a homosexual and that this was inextricably and
undeniably what he was: "It was not a grudging or reluctant acceptance.
For the first time in years I really liked myself. I found it hard to believe
that I had spent so many years struggling and growing steadily unhappier
when the solution was so simple: all I had to do was be myself." (244)

Unlike Tony, Rick has long accepted being gay. Rick is settled in for the
summer in the remote summer house upon the sprawling seaside Carroll
estate, which even lacks that modern staple for "killing time," a television
set. Thus Rick is at leisure to reflect upon his past, as are the other characters. Madeleine, spurred on by her perusal of Beth Carroll's diaries, seizes
the summer as an opportunity to begin writing her memoirs, though, like
Beth's diaries, these carefully edit out certain facets of her personal life,
such as her friendship with Rick. Surrounded by people reappraising their
personal pasts, Rick is entering middle age, the onset of which is a time
proverbial for introspection and soul-searching. Having spent his entire adult
life in Boston, Rick now is far from the madding crowd and his familiar
haunts. He briefly thinks about his years of sexual promiscuity prior to his
meeting David and what John Clum terms "the peculiar alienation of the
brief sexual encounter" (163), (which, as Clum notes, was a particular focus
of the poetry of Tennessee Williams). The intimacy and depth of commu-
nication Rick established with David made his impersonal sexual encounters, in retrospect, seem unfulfilling. For Rick, David is without peer. Rick's
elusive pursuit of love, which he never describes in detail, perhaps because
it leaves him little or nothing of enduring value, sounds like Malone's career of love in *Dancer from the Dance.* Using some inherited money, he
leaves his home on the North Shore and devotes fifteen years to the elusive
pursuit of love. He finds that fifteen years of going from one fling to another slip past quickly until David's arrival, after which, "for a few years,
love won" (Monette, *Taking Care* 30). The part of Rick's past most press-
ingly confronting him is his relationship with David. They had been lovers
for three and a half years when David left. The five years they have spent
apart have not dampened Rick's ardor. Slowly, Rick admits to himself what
is obvious to everyone else: He still loves David.

At first Rick thinks his desire for David stems simply from a wish to
recapture his lost youth. David, at thirty, seems unimaginably young. But
Rick's attitudes about aging, a stereotypical gay fear, mellow in the course

of the summer. He realizes he has avoided the company of old people, other than Madeleine, who "took good care and stayed young. Of course it was self-defeating of me. I had ended up being the oldest person I knew" (Monette, *Taking Care* 253). For Rick, the gay male's intensification of the society-wide cult of youth is embodied in his recollection of a body-builder—that stock figure of narcissism—with whom he had a fleeting sexual encounter on a train. Rick says the bodybuilder has a plan to commit suicide upon turning sixty, the age after which he figured he could no longer maintain his body satisfactorily. But Rick doubts the bodybuilder would ever commit suicide, dismissing his plan as a youth's empty boast. In the course of the summer, Rick apparently makes his peace with leaving his youth behind. This shift in perspective is symbolized, perhaps, by Rick's decision not to return to Boston, in which he spent his youth cruising the bars for fifteen years. He comes to let go of the past's hold upon him. Although Monette's novel is set in 1975, just as *Dancer from the Dance* is set in the mid-1970s, and although both novels were published in 1978, *Taking Care of Mrs. Carroll* is not an elegiac romance. Mrs. Carroll is not even the ostensible heroine, and, although it opens with her death, the book is not an elegy at all.

At first, Rick's narrative reads as if it might become a lament for his lost love, his singular and passionate attachment to David. David admits to having many abortive love affairs after leaving Rick, but David says he found himself running away from anyone who wanted a commitment. David asks Rick, " 'Is that what you do?' " Rick responds, " 'No. I fall in love every couple of decades. And I don't run away' " (Monette, *Taking Care* 59). Of course, Rick here is really reminding David, "I didn't run away from you. You left me." Monette also subtly indicates that vestiges of internalized homophobia may be found even in the language used between two male lovers who accept their homosexuality by David's avoidance of the masculine pronoun in referring to a typical man he had picked up. (David uses "they" instead.) This habit of exercising caution in revealing the gender of same-sex sexual partners stems from fear of reprisals, a subtle form of oppression facing gays, even in sheltered moments. The summer retreat on the Carroll estate never quite becomes an escape to a never-never land.

Monette further avoids sentimentality in his depiction of Rick and David's relationship by establishing Rick's initial reluctance to resume sexual relationships with his former lover. Rick and David refrain for several weeks from having sex. They prepare themselves emotionally first. The change is gradual and plausibly motivated. This is no pornographic, hop-in-the-sack-at-the-drop-of-a-dime fiction, despite the frankness with which the sex scenes are described. "The characteristic that defines sexual scenes as pornographic is their relative unbelievability" (Austen 179). Rick's holding back from his own sexual desires surfaces linguistically in his use of several negatives when he describes seeing David in the nude: "I'm *not* pretending that I *didn't* remember David had *no* clothes on, but *until then* it *didn't* mean anything to *me*. . . . I *don't* mean to say that I *wasn't* turned on at the sight of him" (Monette, *Taking Care* 116–17; emphasis added). But here Rick, via the litotes, is not distancing himself from facing being gay as is the Cuckold in John Cheever's novel *Falconer*. Rick accepts being gay. He is no prude.

What Rick does fear is the reemergence of his deep and long-term love for David and the loss of emotional control this would create. He is trying in advance to reduce the pain of parting from David at summer's end. Rick struggles to keep from expressing his past feelings, paradoxically, precisely because he refuses to let go of the past. By keeping his love for David in the past, he can narrate his love story in the way he wishes, forgetting what he chooses to forget, embellishing and reshaping it to his heart's content, just as Beth Carroll told what she wanted to tell in her diaries, and just as Madeleine Cosquer artfully cultivates her image in her memoirs. Thus Rick can tell himself over and over about his great romance and its sad ending. So long as the story remains private, inside his own head, Rick can exercise word-for-word control over its beginning, middle, and end. The outcome is already set: David left him. Apart from that tragic denouement, he can edit and reorder the script of his memories to his heart's content. As Rick says, early on in his narrative, "To think your life is a story may be just the right illusion" (Monette, *Taking Care* 12). But he must choose between maintaining such control and living in the moment. The serendipity of a close emotional rapport comes from letting go of the desire for control. So does the frenzy of sexual abandon, which can sometimes reach its wildest point within the context of a deep emotional bond. Rick must choose which is more important to him: romance or love. He can control the story of his romance, but he cannot control David, nor can he compel him to return. Rick realizes after the summer is more than half over and after he and David have resumed being lovers that if he prefers to have an "inner movie," a story, romance, or memory of what his love for David was like, rather than the feelings of being in the moment, then he is unable to love. Rick realizes that it would be a mistake to settle for the sad but predictable story of the ill-fated romance rather than the exciting, frustrating, unpredictable, and open-ended reality of an ongoing relationship. Settling for the story of a dead past would be worse, Rick realizes, than embracing, as he had done for fifteen years, "the fiction of freedom" that gay bars offer. By the end of the summer, Rick has rejected romance and chosen love. David tells Rick that romantics cling to the past and that as Rick is no longer doing this, he is " 'not a romantic anymore' " (Monette, *Taking Care* 272).

The abandonment of the desire to control in favor of trust in the other and trust in the moment develops slowly in Rick. It is as if he reorients his attitudes towards love and romance as part of a vow to himself: I won't make the mistakes with David I made years ago. For one thing, he steers clear, insofar as he is able, of the demon of possessiveness. Aldo asks Rick, " 'Is that boy out in the yard yours?' 'No,' [Rick says], bristling. 'I don't own anyone.' " Aldo glibly replies, " 'So he *is* yours' " (Monette, *Taking Care* 105). Rick does not display possessiveness in response to David's sexual gesture toward Tony. Rick also abandons his insistence on being "top man," which has been associated at least since the time of ancient Greece with dominance and the masculine role (as Foucault, Boswell, and others have shown). In their love-making Rick and David now begin reversing and alternating sexual positions, making themselves into "the equal lovers we wanted to be" (Monette, *Taking Care* 138).

Perhaps the single most important element in Rick's reorientation regarding romantic love surrounds the issue of taking care of others. Monette hints at this in his choice of title for the novel, *Taking Care of Mrs. Carroll*. Monette contrasts "taking care of" others with loving them. Although Rick does not say so explicitly, he is apparently the adult child of an alcoholic. He refers to the "drunken" home he left. Evidently he is a codependent, as is often the case among adult children of alcoholics, who typically suffer from low self-esteem as a result of neglect and abuse. A codependent tackles his feeling of low self-esteem by gravitating toward neediness in others, so he can ignore his own needs, his own pain, and his own low self-image by focusing on others and taking care of them. Feelings of self-worth become measured by what is done for others, by deeds and accomplishments, by what one does rather than who one is. In the past, Rick has waited for crises to "be given to me to take care of people" (Monette, *Taking Care* 267), being willing to smooth things over with outsiders and authority figures when troubles arose. Rick is a caretaker. The past attempt at relationship between Rick and David failed because each was trying too hard to take care of the other. David ran away a dozen times with other men, and Rick was only too eager to welcome him back each time and to take care of him, until David ran away for good. Thus Rick thinks he was taking care of David. Evidently, others see things differently. Phidias says to Rick that David is " 'good at taking care of people. . . . [M]ake sure he doesn't make do with taking care of you' " (Monette, *Taking Care* 141). This prompts Rick to wonder, "Had David thought I needed taking care of . . . ? I thought I took care of *him*" (142). By the end of the summer, Rick realizes that he is loved for who he is, not for what he does. He doesn't need to take care of anyone any more. Mrs. Carroll is dead and buried and her will is signed. The group has finished taking care of Mrs. Carroll. The living can take care of themselves. Having let go of the need to take care of David, Rick can now love David, and their love promises to last for a long time. Paul Monette said in an interview in the *Advocate*, "I don't want to put out the message that the *only* way to live happily is to live in love, but that's how it's been for me, and it all starts with coming out" (Lassell 35).

EXERCISE: MEASURING ACCEPTANCE

Rick's Acceptance rests on having built effective support networks with other people to whom he has disclosed his homosexuality and who accept him as he is. It also stems from his having come to terms with the masculine and feminine sides of himself and others. To what extent do you share the following attitudes held by Rick?

STATEMENTS OF ACCEPTANCE

I am glad that I have been honest with myself and others about my sexuality.

I have built effective support networks of people who accept me as I am.

"Family" to me means those who love and accept me.

Most (or all) of the people who are important to me know that I am gay.

I don't really care who knows that I am gay.

I can enjoy friendships with both men and women.

There is something special about female stars or "divas" that gay men appreciate.

Effeminate gay men do not threaten me. Different people have different ways of expressing the masculine and feminine sides of themselves.

I realize that, ultimately, each of us is the author of his own life story, just as Madeleine is the author of her memoirs.

Youth isn't everything. Growing older is a part of life that I accept.

The homophobic stereotype that homosexuals are lonely is simply not true.

I don't need to be in a relationship to feel good about myself.

I don't need to control other people's actions or attitudes to feel good about myself and my life.

I can handle the emotions of being in love and being in a loving sexual relationship with another man.

7

Implications:
Gay Novels and Gay Identity

> Coming out is a long and complex process, one that involves not merely the assertion of a gay identity, but the creation of new standards of behavior that will allow us to live in ways we are only beginning to imagine.
>
> —Dennis Altman, *The Homosexualization of America, The Americanization of the Homosexual* 273

Gay novels of the past few decades chart the emergence of a self-affirming gay identity in the midst of a generally homophobic society. The ways in which realistic gay novels create a meaningful sense of gay identity pertain to issues being debated among theorists of narrative generally. Leo Bersani sees a connection between the concept of a unified self and the realistic narratives that help shape such a sense of self. Jay Clayton notes that in narrative, as in all realistic art, what is represented is sifted through a filter of importance in which some characters and events are given leading roles, while others play supporting roles. "According to Bersani, narrative is 'intimately linked' to the mimetic impulse . . . because of the way it organizes the people and events it depicts. . . . Thus narrative has something to do with our very sense of perspective" (Clayton 42–43).

Gay men are depicted in gay fiction differently now than was the case even a few decades ago. Although the "coming-out novel" is not an obsolete genre, in contemporary gay fiction it is often taken for granted that gay characters have completed the coming-out process. Some recent gay novels chronicle coming out, as this remains for many gay men a long process filled with difficulties. But once the struggle is over, what does it mean to be a man who has come to Acceptance of being gay? Gay theory approaches the question from "essentialist" and "constructionist" positions. Although these terms may be new, David Bergman notes that "constructionist and essential arguments have competed for the support of gay people" since the eighteenth century (18).

Homosexual behavior appears to have existed in all cultures. Many have been tempted to speak of a distinct gay identity that has existed throughout history. Such people are known as "essentialists." Among gay men, this attitude generally prevails today. Prominent essentialist writers and theorists include John Boswell and Arthur Evans. Yet the concepts of homosexuality and of gay identity are relatively recent ones. The "constructionists," who currently dominate gay academic discourse, have argued that gay identity is a social construction, and a recent one, and that it therefore does not make sense to refer to "gay people" apart from particular social, economic, political, and historical conditions. There is much evidence for that view. Nevertheless, even though the term "homosexual" did not exist until the late 1800s, "[a] few Renaissance authors wrote of sexual orientation as a relatively stable trait and discussed it within a framework of causal determinism" (Greenberg 407). The emergence of a distinct gay male urban subculture can be traced back in America to the existence of "all male social clubs" from the 1830s on. In England, the emergence of molly-houses (the forerunners of today's gay bars) in the late seventeenth century marked the emergence of a distinct male homosexual culture (Greenberg 348–55).

Essentialists sometimes gloss over historical and cultural differences. Applying the concept of gay identity, at least as this has been shaped and defined by a distinct urban subculture within English and American societies of the past few centuries, to other cultures and other historical periods is somewhat problematic. In non-Western societies, and in the West in ancient times, "the only societies in which homosexuality may have been encouraged as a matter of civic virtue were warrior societies, not the pacifying ones we are remembering or imagining" (Blau 116). Altman argues that without a gay subculture there can be no such thing as gay people as we now understand the term. Such subcultures emerged in the eighteenth and nineteenth centuries in Western Europe, according to Foucault (Altman, *Homosexualization* 49). For most of Western history the notion of a separate homosexual identity simply did not exist. The Bible, for instance, discusses homosexual acts, but in no place mentions the idea of a homosexual sexual orientation.

Even cultures that recognized a distinct social role for men we would now call gay, as, for instance, the berdache role in many traditional Native American tribes, did not classify people as either heterosexual or homosexual (or, in some cases, as bisexual), as routinely occurs in contemporary America. In Native American culture, the berdache role was never simply a matter of sexual behavior. It was a well-defined androgynous social role involving "reversal of the customary sex roles—cross-dressing, cross-working, cross-speaking—as well as homosexual activity" (Katz 282). The men who had sex with the berdache were regarded as "normal," fully masculine men. Some of the chiefs had male berdache "wives." Homosexual relations also existed between "apparently 'normal' males," although Western observers were less likely to notice these (Katz 282). Some have seized upon the berdache as an embodiment of a gay male archetype. Therefore "the recovery of the history of Native American homosexuality is a task in which both Gay and Native peoples have a common interest" (Katz 284).

Great caution should be used in "exporting" modern notions of gay identity to cultures that never recognized such a concept. The essentialist notion of gay identity imposes modern sexual ideology upon periods and cultures that lacked exact equivalents of such notions.

Constructionists, on the other hand, tend to downplay the fixed elements of homosexual attraction, focusing instead on the ways in which different societies' values affect the way people conceive of their sexuality. Some constructionists may even gloss over the "perceived non-voluntary component of identity" (Epstein 24). The unfolding of gay identity at times seems to happen despite, not because of, free individual choice. Most men react very negatively upon discovering homosexuality within themselves and they often resist acknowledging it for years.

Coming to accept a gay identity as a positive aspect of self requires embracing an ideology of sexual identity that runs counter to that of the heterosexist society. In contemporary gay culture, Epstein argues, this has come to resemble the formation of a mythology akin to that shared by various national or ethnic groups in America. Of course, there is one major difference: as Herbert Blau argues in *The Eye of Prey*, "no homosexual is raised *as* a homosexual" (119; emphasis in original). For this reason, Blau finds it inappropriate to compare gays with, say, blacks or Hispanics. Yet every people needs a mythology of its origins, its identity, its purpose, and its destiny. The gay male community has been systematically deprived of a positive shared mythology, yet ancient and pre-Christian mythologies do provide a rich variety of gay archetypes. Perhaps it is natural that attempts to forge such a gay mythology, drawing in part on those frequently neglected sources, would emerge at this historical moment, in gay fiction as well as in some gay theory. Some "essentialists" have been explicit about doing so, as is evident even in the titles of several recent books, such as *Visionary Love: A Spirit Book of Gay Mythology,* by Mitch Walker; *Gay Spirit: Myth and Meaning,* edited by Mark Thompson; and *Myths and Mysteries of Same-Sex Love,* by Christine Downing.

The trickster archetype and its raw sexual energy have been tapped by Joe Orton and other gay authors. "Orton's favourite literature was trickster tales" (Lahr 134). Orton and Arthur Evans are among those gay authors who have explicitly drawn upon Dionysus, a trickster figure from Greek mythology, to challenge patriarchal notions of masculinity and sexual identity. Both have worked with Euripides' play *The Bakkhai*, in which Dionysus ridicules the one-sidedness of the patriarchal ideal, represented by the doomed Pentheus, upon whom Dionysus exacts a bloody revenge. Evans provides his own translation of the play in *The God of Ecstasy: Sex-Roles and the Madness of Dionysos*. Orton's play *What the Butler Saw* is a reworking of *The Bakkhai* (Lahr 15).

Rictor Norton also draws from Greek mythology to understand gay identity. He sees in the love of Hercules for Hylas a model for the literary depiction of homosexual male love. In *The Homosexual Literary Tradition: An Interpretation*, Rictor Norton examines literature dating from 3300 B.C.E. to 1700 C.E., proposing what he terms a "Hylas Ritual," consisting of five stages:

1. The Challenge (ritual contest);
2. The Sacred Precinct (such as a sacred grove in which a ritual initiation occurs);
3. The Lament of the king for the absent boy-surrogate (as reflected in David's love for Jonathan and the love of Achilles for Patroclus);
4. The Sacrifice (combat and dismemberment);
5. The Feast (eating "the flesh and blood of the slain boy-surrogate) (Norton 94).

Norton also examines the figures of Ganymede, Cupid, Adonis, and Narcissus and their abiding influence upon homoerotic literature, but does not trace the literary influence of these archetypes in the literature of the eighteenth, nineteenth, or twentieth centuries.

Attempts to trace and lay claim to a gay mythology have not been limited to literary and mythological sources. Research has been conducted into anthropology and comparative religion as well. Anthropologists and comparative religionists have long noted a widely held belief, present among peoples throughout the world, "that unusual powers of divination and prophecy were to be found in homosexual folk" (Carpenter 260). This is evident in the works of George Catlin and Sir James Frazer, among others. Catlin, "who spent eight years traveling among Western Indians during the 1830s" (Williams 107), was one of the first Westerners to report in detail about the sexuality and religious roles of the Native American berdache. Frazer, in *Adonis, Attis, and Osiris*, traces the homosexuality of prophets attached to religious sanctuaries in the ancient Middle East (Carpenter 257–58) and in *The Golden Bough* traces many homoerotic religious practices and beliefs. Even the enemies of homosexuals (such as members of the Inquisition) have long linked homosexuality with a distinct spirituality. "Many societies have linked homosexuality with magic. The witches of the Middle Ages as much as the shamans of some Indian tribes, and the court jesters who gave their name to the Mattachine Society are all examples" (Altman, *Oppression* 56).

Contemporary gay writers are continuing the task, started by pioneering gay writers such as Edward Carpenter, of reexamining and reviving the traditional attribution of a unique spirituality to the people now called gay. Carpenter notes

> the constant connection between the *choupan* and the *angakok*, the *ke'yev* and the *shamon*, the *berdache* and the witch-doctor, the ganymede and the temple-priest, and the correspondences all over the world, the *basir* among the Dyaks, the boy-priest in the temples of Peru, the same in the Buddhist temples of Ceylon, Burma and China (272)

and concludes that "all these cases seem to point to some underlying fact, of the fitness or adaptation of the invert for priestly or divinatory functions" (272). Carpenter ventures that "there *is* an organic connection between the homosexual temperament and unusual psychic or divinatory powers" (268). "Many societies have linked homosexuality with magic. The witches of the Middle Ages, as much as the shamans of some Indian tribes and the court jesters who gave their name to the Mattachine Society are all examples" (Altman, *Oppression* 56). Harry Hay named the homophile group he founded in 1950 Mattachine to suggest gays' spiritual past. The Faery Circle, founded in San Francisco in 1975, and the later Radical Faerie movement also assert gays' spiritual gifts.

The essentialist versus constructionist controversy has preoccupied many gay scholars and thinkers for some time. Steven Epstein has argued that this debate "may well have outlived its usefulness" (Epstein 11) and many express both constructionist and essentialist views without conscious awareness of the contradictions between them. Despite scholars' opposing positions on this issue, "both essentialist and constructionist views are ingrained in the folk understandings of homosexuality in our society—often in a highly contradictory fashion," that is, people often leap from essentialist to constructionist positions inconsistently (Epstein 11). Epstein cites the example of a woman who wrote to Ann Landers the she was worried

> that her fourteen-year-old son may be "seduced" into homosexuality (folk constructionism) by the boy's friend, who she has "no question" is gay, because of his "feminine mannerisms" (folk essentialism). Ann reassures the mother that the only way her son would turn out to be gay is if "the seeds of homosexuality were already present" (folk essentialism). At the same time, she questions the mother's certainty about the sexual orientation of the friend, claiming that it is "presumptuous" to label a fourteen-year-old as "gay" (folk constructionism). (Epstein 11–12)

The coming-out process depicted in the gay novels of the last several decades in America should be seen as the product of a particular historical and cultural moment, defined by distinct views of romantic love and sexuality, and homosexuality in particular. Homosexuals bear the brunt of Western societies' suspicion of extramarital sexual love. Negative attitudes towards sexuality can be traced at least as far back as St. Augustine. Foucault has shown that sexual excess was viewed negatively even during the classical age of Greece (Foucault, II 44, 48, 64). Such distrust of sexual passion is still part of the Western cultural heritage. For instance, Dennis de Rougemont, in exploring the courtly love tradition and its influence on subsequent notions of romantic love, asserts that "passion means suffering" and that "passionate love is a misfortune" (2). Given a more sex-positive society, and a society more accepting of homosexuality and homosexuals, the process of coming to accept a gay identity would no doubt be less emotionally and psychically taxing for gay men. In any case, Altman, a constructionist who, like Freud, denies that homosexuals are a distinct class of people, insists that "the development of a sense of gay identity is a phenomenon peculiar to America," where political and social self-identification with racial, religious, and ethnic groups outweighs class consciousness (Altman, *Homosexualization* ix).

Jay Clayton, in a discussion of desire and narrative, tosses up an essentialist viewpoint as a clay pigeon, calling into question the supposedly fixed nature people attribute to sexual desire even by those who regard such desires as the desire for material possessions as a social construction (36). Some may straddle the fence by concluding

> that desire is constant but that manifestations of desire in social forms change over time [but] the analyst cannot separate desire from its manifestations. . . . Desire . . . is what happens to need when it enters history, language, culture, and society. Desire names the way in which individuals transform their needs under the pressure of the particular social conditions. (Clayton 50)

Clayton therefore insists that desire is a social construction. "To view desire as historical requires that one not merely say that the way desire is invested in narrative changes but that the economy of desire changes too" (52).

Within the gay community, current conceptions and behaviors surrounding sexual identity are radically different from those prevalent prior to the riots following the police raid at the Stonewall Inn in June of 1969, with the terms currently and formerly applied to gay men leaving a linguistic trail of these changes. The emergence of gay liberation was made possible, in part, by several decades of attempts to challenge homophobic laws and attitudes. Organized attempts in America to lobby for homosexual rights can be traced back forty-five years before Stonewall. "The first well-documented emancipation organization of American homosexuals is the Chicago Society for Human Rights, founded by Henry Gerber and chartered by the state of Illinois in 1924" (Katz 336). Attempting to minimize the perceived differences between homosexuals and heterosexuals was one way in which the homophile movement of the 1950s and the 1960s responded to a society that regarded homosexuals as "deviants" and "perverts." The epithets applied to gay men at that time reflect that attitude, such as those that appear in William Burroughs' novel *Naked Lunch* (1959): buggers (143), catamites (79), cocksuckers (82), deviants (35), faggots (82), fags (2), fairies (50), fence straddlers (88), fruits (4), homosexuals (49), male hustlers (115), pansies (135), perverts (211), queens (28), queers (27), sexual deviants (188), swishes (62), Transitionals (85), transvestites (85), and undesirables (164). The terminology used to designate homosexual men reflects perceptions of gay men by themselves and others. Mark Thompson describes "the natural progression in the long derivation of words used to describe us: *Uranian, invert, homosexual, homophile, queer, faggot* and, now, *faerie*" ("Tribe" 275). Although the latter terms are a proud claim of the distinctive aspects of a gay identity, the "accommodationist" homophile position was that the only difference between homosexuals and heterosexuals is in the gender of their sexual partners. "We're just like everyone else, except . . ." was the plea for tolerance, if not respect. Harry Hay states that the "position [that] 'we're exactly the same' characterized the whole Mattachine Society from 1953 to 1969" (Katz 417). Yet such accommodationists were anything but cowardly; the heroism of those willing to come forward during the time of Senator Joseph McCarthy and the purge of homosexuals from the State Department should not be overlooked. Furthermore, some gay activists still sincerely believe the accommodationists' claim that homosexuals are not inherently and invariably different from heterosexuals apart from sexual orientation itself. Dennis Altman and the social constructionists maintain to this day that other differences people ascribe to homosexuals are not intrinsic to their sexual orientation. Constructionists point out that sexual orientation is itself a modern concept scarcely more than a century old and that secondary traits of homosexuals are social constructions, ways of conceiving of sexuality peculiar to a social structure defined by historical and sociological forces.

Since the birth of the gay liberation movement and the mushrooming of Gay Pride festivals and marches, efforts have been made to forge a distinct gay identity. In the 1970s this sometimes entailed a rejection of the accommodationist rhetoric and beliefs of the earlier homophile movement in favor of gay separatism. "Gay ghettos" grew around Christopher Street in New York and Castro Street in San Francisco. "Gays only" signs were painted on the boardwalks leading to a wooded area on Fire Island that was dubbed "The Meat Rack" in recognition of its notoriety as a gay cruising area. But some felt unsatisfied by forming a sense of gay identity merely in opposition to heterosexist institutions and values, such as marriage and (supposed) monogamy. Many asked, What is distinctive about being gay? In the absence of readily available gay role models, many have turned to gay novels for clues. Some have found that narratives set in present society are insufficient to answer questions about gay identity and have advanced the notion of a timeless essence to gay identity. In doing so, they admit that much gay history has been repressed, making it difficult to document and reconstruct.

Nevertheless, John Boswell has traced gay history back two thousand years, and Arthur Évans has traced it back over three thousand years, with surprising (and, to be sure, controversial) results. In *Christianity, Social Tolerance, and Homosexuality: Gay People in Western Europe from the Beginning of the Christian Era to the Fourteenth Century,* Boswell charts the gradual rise of homophobia within the Church, but maintains that there was widespread tolerance of gays within and by the church during its early centuries. Evans, in *The God of Ecstasy: Sex-Roles and the Madness of Dionysos,* traces the almost universal worship of the goddess and the horned god that flourished c. 4500–1200 B.C.E. and the suppression of this worship by Indo-European invaders after 1200 B.C.E. Evans argues that the status of women and gay men steadily eroded as the worship of the Indo-European warlike sky gods displaced worship of the goddess and the horned one. Evans argues that Euripides' *Bakkhai* was a warning against the imbalances inherent in patriarchal belittlement of women and of the feminine aspect of men.

The essentialist versus social constructionist theories of gay identity continue to be debated, but this debate recedes in importance if both viewpoints are seen as attempts to understand what it means *at present* to be gay. Both essentialists and constructionists seek self-understanding. How gay men think about their sexual identities clearly has changed enormously during the last quarter century, and these changes have been accompanied by a transformation and a blossoming of gay literature. Gay fiction, composed largely of realistic narratives set in contemporary society, both reflects and produces changes in gay self-conceptions. Gay genre writing also is flourishing. Gay science fiction and gay detective fiction, for example, now boast many titles. Gay men are telling different stories about themselves as the gay community comes of age. Classic coming-out novels and the anguished ruminations of guilt-ridden closeted homosexuals, for the most part, became dated period pieces as the secretive, self-loathing homosexual underground of the 1950s and 1960s gave way to gay liberation in the 1970s. Militant gay rights activism and manifestations of gay pride and solidarity intensified with the outbreak of the AIDS epidemic and in reaction against governmental foot-dragging in response to it under the Reagan administration in the 1980s.

Gay novels that attempt the self-creation of gay identity have had to reject many traditional forms of narrative. Porter Abbott notes that "the oldest narrative of identity, older than the quest, . . . is the narrative of parents begetting children" (40). Narratives of procreation, such as those that figure prominently in the Old and New Testaments, imply that social stability and individual and collective identity are formed by generation following generation in traceable genealogical lineage. Not surprisingly, procreation and narratives of procreation are conspicuously absent from gay fiction. Gay fiction erases not only the act of procreation but also the origins of self in that act. The parents of most gays and lesbians are not gay or lesbian, and thus cannot function as gay or lesbian role models, and often are unable to offer support to their children as they struggle with their homosexuality. For this and other reasons, many gay novels omit mention of the parents of their gay characters. Whether mentioned or not, parents and families of gays often pose problems and difficulties to those who are struggling to come to respect themselves as gay people. David Bergman notes that gay novels currently lack "integrating myths that will help bring together the sexual world and the familial world" (196). Several recent gay novels do address this problem directly by highlighting the relationships gay men have with their families of origin. Robert Ferro's novels *The Family of Max Desir* and *Second Son*, and *The Lost Language of Cranes* by David Leavitt, are a few notable examples of novels that explore gays' relationships with their families. In any gay Bildungsroman, such as Edmund White's *A Boy's Own Story* or Sanford Friedman's *Totempole*, as in non-gay novels of that form, the family of origin and its influence upon the subsequent adult identity of the hero are also crucial. In many gay novels, however, a surrogate family based on friendship is introduced and figures more prominently than the biological relatives of the protagonist. Figures from older and younger generations may be absent, or, if present, may be represented by intergenerational friendships (such as that between Rick and Madeleine Cosquer in *Taking Care of Mrs. Carroll*) rather than by parents, children, or other relatives. Although gay heroes are often cut off from their families, they are also often carrying old wounds from their families that cry out for resolution. "Family problems can be a major block to self-acceptance" (Fisher 238) even to those many gay men who are to some extent estranged from their families. David's struggle with his father looms large in the background of *Giovanni's Room*, for instance, even though David's father is, as it were, "off-stage" in America, while David lives in France.

As gay sex is nonprocreative, assuming a gay identity usually implies a break in the procreative chain, and thus the claims to create, to endure, and to leave a mark must rest on other acts. Thus the links with preceding and future generations that are taken for granted in many traditional narratives are severed in gay fiction. Gay fiction is engaged in self-creation in the moment. Gay fiction, like existential fiction, often seeks the "erasure both of [the] procreative father and the linear procreation of narrative [in an] attempt, in effect, to pull time up into oneself" to understand self, being in the moment (Abbott 41). Such narratives draw away from the external world to create Wordsworthian "spots of time," moments of heightened awareness of oneself in conjunction with the cosmos that impart a sense of transcending chronological time and temporally based narrative structures. In *Naked Lunch*, William Burroughs subverts not only romance, marriage, and procreation but also the linear plot structure of a typical narrative. Sexual acts between man and woman lead not to family ties and reproduction (the extension of self in time through subsequent generations) but to death. Burroughs repeatedly juxtaposes images of orgasm with death by hanging. The progressive unfolding of events through plot (time) is replaced by a unified, unchanging, pervasive nightmarish vision. Burroughs' novel, like the experience of drug abuse it chronicles, is an attempt to opt out of ordinary narrative structure. The act of writing itself becomes a buffer against life experienced as narrative. As Burroughs says in the introduction to *Queer*, "I achieved some immunity from further perilous adventures . . . by writing my experience down" (xiv). But if self is divorced from the world, the creation of self becomes even more imperative in fiction. Burroughs says of Lee, the main character of *Queer*:

> What Lee is looking for is contact or recognition, like a photon emerging from the haze of insubstantiality to leave an indelible recording in Allerton's consciousness. Failing to find an adequate observer, he is threatened by painful dispersal, like an unobserved photon. Lee does not know that he is already committed to writing, since this is the only way he has of making an indelible record, whether Allerton is inclined to observe or not. Lee is being inexorably pressed into the world of fiction. He has already made the choice between his life and his work. (Burroughs, *Queer* xvi)

Most gay writing entails the erasure of narratives of procreation and the Oedipal struggle, but without effacing conventional narrative structure entirely. Rather, it rejects patriarchal forms of narrative in favor of alternate narrative strategies. Realistic gay fiction must create not only a self but an environment in which gay identity can unfold. Being must unfold in time and place. It is not enough for it to be glimpsed in peak moments or "spots of time." "Both narrative and mimesis are strategies for placing us within a historically constructed world. . . . Narrative locates us in a network of connections that makes our world intelligible and gives our actions a context" (Clayton 45). Narratives attempting to create or instill a positive sense of gay identity rest on perceived connectedness, a characteristic that distinguishes novels of acceptance from those filled with alienation and isolation, that is, novels of Denial, Anger, Bargaining, and Depression. As the social constructionists have argued, being gay as we now think of it is dependent upon the existence of a social milieu in which it is possible to be gay. Our very self-definition depends upon our social relationships. "The identifications involved in reading also have a social dimension. . . . [N]arratives must appeal to us not only as individuals but also as members of social groups" (Clayton 48). Gay fiction about gay identity serves to create a communal, and not just an individual, sense of self.

The gay community has gone through a coming-out process, just as have gay individuals. Although homophobia has not disappeared, increasingly it is being challenged. Partly as a result of the AIDS crisis, and partly as a result of gay activism, gays are more visible in the media than ever before. Most people are much more aware of the existence of gay people than was the case a generation ago. Such slogans as "Silence = Death" proclaim the refusal, in the face of the decimation of gay men due to AIDS, to be silent, invisible, and ignored. In short, more and more gay men are refusing to stay in or to return to the closet. "The essence of gay liberation is that it enables us to come out" (Altman, *Oppression* 217). The protests of Queer Nation and especially of ACT UP (The AIDS Coalition To Unleash Power) have sparked controversy within and outside the gay community due to their confrontational tactics of civil disobedience and disruption, such as the silent protest held within St. Patrick's Cathedral in New York City a few years ago during a sermon by Cardinal O'Connor. Despite the controversy, the history of women fighting for suffrage and blacks fighting for civil rights shows that "unpopular minorities take their rights by making a nuisance of themselves, not by politely asking for them" (Altman, *Homosexualization* 139). This is as true for gay writers and artists as it is for others. Support from publishers and recognition from critics have only recently been forthcoming. With the easing of taboos against homosexuality since World War II, explicitly gay novels have emerged. These are a far cry from the veiled homoerotic subtexts of classic American quest fiction. Despite greater critical recognition and acclaim, gay fiction remains distinctly a minority tradition, and some literary critics still adhere to the homosexuality-as-deviation position, although typically expressing their homophobic biases less baldly than they dared a few decades ago.

There are powerful forces that would like to turn back the clock and strip the gay community of its few hard-won rights. Although several states now have gay rights laws, most do not. Statutes prohibiting consensual sexual acts between adults of the same gender remain on the books in almost half of the states in America. The government's lackluster response to the AIDS crisis, the homophobia that erupted in response to the exhibition of the photographs of the late Robert Mapplethorpe, and the Supreme Court's 1986 ruling in the *Hardwick* case are all causes for concern among those trying to secure and maintain gay rights.

Persons with AIDS are literally fighting for their lives. The sluggish pace

of the government's response has made many realize how deeply entrenched is society's homophobia and how much more remains to be done
to secure gay rights. As Paul Monette notes in *Borrowed Time: An AIDS
Memoir,*

> The course of our lives had paralleled the course of the movement itself since
> Stonewall, and now our bitterness about the indifference of the system made
> us feel keenly how tenuous our history was. Everything we had been to-
> gether—brothers and friends beyond anything the suffocating years in the
> closet could dream of—might yet be wiped away. If we all died and all our
> books were burned, then a hundred years from now no one would ever know.
> So we figured out we had to know and name it ourselves, tell each other
> what we had become in coming out. (227–28)

In the controversy that erupted in 1989 over the public exhibition of the
photographs of the late Robert Mapplethorpe, Senator Jesse Helms tried
to deny future public funding for any and all homoerotic art, regardless of
artistic merit or critical acclaim. Helms argued that homoeroticism necessarily constitutes obscenity. Many in America now appear willing to permit
unprecedented forms of censorship.

The Supreme Court's 1986 ruling in *Hardwick* also gives cause for alarm
to those who would like to establish a more secure legal foundation for gay
rights. Justice White's majority opinion in *Hardwick* states that "family,
marriage, and procreation" are forms of sexuality protected from state interference, but "sodomy" between consenting adults in the privacy of their
own homes is not. Blackmun's dissenting minority opinion upheld the "lib-
erty interests of privacy and the individual" (Caserio 273). Caserio deftly
observes that neither side can "permit to homosexuals a space of appearance in the public realm. While the court majority justifies supervising—
and even eliminating—homosexual privacy, and while the court minority
defends homosexual privacy, both sides agree that homosexuality is only a
private matter" (Caserio 273–74). Effectively, then, "both sides of the court
maintain a long ideological tradition that homosexual life . . . is and should
be a closeted life" (Caserio 274).

Powerful forces would like to shove gay men, gay life, gay art, and gay
literature back into the closet. What effect would this have on gay identity?
If successful, this attempt would cause the complex issues surrounding gay
identity to be ignored. The discourse on homosexuality would return to the
focus upon isolated and illicit sexual acts. This would reverse "the greatest
single victory of the gay movement" in the 1970s, namely the success in
shifting "the debate from behavior to identity," which had the effect of
"forcing opponents into a position where they can be seen as attacking the
civil rights of homosexual citizens rather than attacking specific and (as they
see it) antisocial acts" (Altman, *Homosexualization* 9). Being gay is not simply a matter of sexual acts. Indeed,

the question of sexuality does not stand by itself, but is at all points interactive with other politics or economics which are for the most part not specifically or obviously erotic ones, such as the network of class and gender positions enforced in the culture, of people's various ways of inhabiting these positions, especially in their respective relations to their own and other people's bodies and bodily lives, to their work, and to language and writing. (Moon 251)

Gay writers and gay theorists have just begun the tasks of formulating what gay identity means, an undertaking with implications for the well-being (or lack of it) in the lives of gay men. Promising pioneering efforts are being made. For example, Robert Hopcke, in *Jung, Jungians, and Homosexuality,* provides the first full-length, systematic treatment of Jungian attitudes towards homosexuality. His discussion of the archetypes of the masculine, the feminine, and the androgyne in gay male culture offers leads for further research into the analysis of gay male fiction and gay culture. Such explorations of gay identity are not merely academic. The notion of gay identity, though new, is important for gays. "Identity plays a central part in organizing one's life. To have a clear, firm, secure identity free of guilt and ambivalence is not just a matter of how one conceives of oneself and feels about oneself. It simplifies one's life" (Weinberg 302). Gay men who have come to Acceptance do not want to return to the tortured existence of the closet and the numerous complications of "passing" as heterosexual.

Yet many homosexuals fall prey to the pressures to remain in the closet, at great cost to their emotional and psychological well-being. By no means do all homosexuals take an assertive attitude. Many have internalized society's homophobia and shame and thus remained paralyzed when it comes to fulfilling their desires. Others, for one reason or another, decide not to come out (Altman, *Homosexualization* 17). The progress that has been made in gay rights has often come despite outspoken opposition from such closeted gays, who sometimes express homophobia as a smokescreen to distract attention from their own sexuality. The late Roy Cohn, former assistant to Senator McCarthy, and the late right-wing fundraiser, Terry Dolan, are two prominent examples. Roy Cohn did not challenge McCarthy's public denunciations of alleged homosexuals in high office. Such accusations ruined careers and lives. Letters sent to those on conservative mailing lists warning of the supposedly powerful "homosexual lobby" went out under Terry Dolan's signature. Eyewitnesses report that Dolan was booed upon entering gay bars (to cruise) at the time he was fighting against gay rights. Dolan's hypocrisy "led Larry Kramer to approach Dolan at a gay party, throw a drink in his face, and shout: 'You fuck us by night and fuck with us by day' " (Goldstein 35). Both Cohn and Dolan died from complications resulting from AIDS, which is ironic, given their political opposition to supporters of gay rights, the very people pushing for greater governmental funding for AIDS research and treatment. Many if not most of the men who engage in homosexual acts never come out and embrace a public gay identity (Troiden 371). The homosexuality of many famous men, for instance, has come to light only after they died from complications resulting from AIDS. (Liberace and Rock Hudson are examples of men whose sexual orientation was not known until it was revealed that they were dying or had died.)

Apart from AIDS news stories, gays and gay concerns generally receive only spotty media coverage, although they are no longer consigned to oblivion by the media. In television melodramas, gays are still usually excluded. In televised narratives, "Gay representation perforce must take the form of a disruption of the norm . . . , its presence being a 'dilemma,' a disruption of normal interiority, by definition the home, the stable world of middle-class manners and heterosexual expectations" (Leo 39).

Precisely this notion of homosexuality as a deviation from a (heterosexual) "norm" has been called into question in gay fiction and by gay activists. The challenge from gay militants has been successful, at least officially, in the fields of psychology and psychiatry, which no longer categorize homosexuality as a mental illness. This has reduced, although not entirely eliminated, the need for the defensiveness and special pleading that mark such early gay novels as *City of Night* and *The Sexual Outlaw*. Much gay literature now takes gay identity for granted and focuses on other issues.

Gay literature and the gay community, which until recently were underground phenomena, are suddenly involved in a highly visible process of self-creation. This involves development of gay myths. "A myth arises whenever it becomes dangerous or impossible to speak plainly about certain social or religious matters" (de Rougemont 8). Unfortunately, for many men it is still "dangerous or impossible to speak plainly" about their homosexuality. Myths are powerful. Myths reveal rules of conduct. Formulating gay mythologies of personal and group meaning consists in part of the search for past models. This ranges from research into the existence of gay men in former times and distant cultures, such as the berdaches in Native American cultures, to the elusive quest for a gay stylistic and for homoerotic subtexts in a reappraisal of canonical writers, such as Walt Whitman, Herman Melville, and Henry James, whose homosexuality (expressed or inferred) can at last be discussed openly. Herman Melville is now being claimed as a father of gay fiction, and it is now claimed that Melville loved Nathaniel Hawthorne, though his love was unrequited (Austen 17). Leon Edel has presented convincing evidence for the homosexuality of Henry James in his biography *Henry James: A Life*.

The search for gay mythologies has consisted not only of reappraising past literature and former social arrangements, but also of experimenting with new literary and social forms. Such experimentation is evident in the

Radical Faerie movement as well as in the formal and stylistic innovations of certain avant-garde gay novels. Gay fiction offers possible directions for the evolution of gay identity. This is manifest, for instance, in C. F. Borgman's first novel, *River Road* (1988), the chronology of which roves freely back and forth between 1953 and 2013 and the years in between, optimistically anticipating the time when a cure for AIDS will have been found and boundaries between sexual orientations will have become more relaxed. Other gay novels are grappling with the AIDS crisis and the changes in sexual attitudes and behavior brought in its wake. Although such novels as *Faggots*, by Larry Kramer (1978), and *As If After Sex*, by Joseph Torchia (1984), lament narcissism and promiscuity within the gay male community, more recent novels warn more forcefully about the dangers of "casual" sex. *Horse Crazy* by Gary Indiana (1989) and *Shy* by Kevin Killian (1989) depict how terrifying it can be to become sexually involved with the wrong man.

Given the lack of secure and widespread gay rights in this country, and the strident and entrenched homophobia of many conservative politicians and religious leaders, the emergence of explicitly gay novels of literary merit and distinction in the past few decades is remarkable. It would be unfortunate if gay literature were forced back underground. It is to be hoped that gay literature will continue to flourish in the more forthright climate that allows for the current exploration and unfolding of gay identity. The novels already published point toward Acceptance, charting as they do the often tortuous process of coming out for gay men.

As Rick remarks in Paul Monette's novel *Taking Care of Mrs. Carroll*, " 'Once you've come out of the closet, you know, it's bad form to go back in' " (240).

Glossary

ACAs. See *Adult Children of Alcoholics.*

Acceptance, a term derived from Dr. Elisabeth Kübler-Ross, marks the completion of coming out, in which a gay identity is embraced as an intrinsic and permanent part of self. It usually develops only after contact with positive gay role models and the building of effective social support networks.

Accommodationism and *Assimilationism* are terms applied (mostly by their gay detractors) to those who tend to insist that gay people differ from non-gay people only in the gender of those they sleep with and that gay people should be integrated into mainstream society. These people are called Accommodationists and Assimilationists. Such people often wish to diminish the amount of attention given to minorities within the gay community whose differences from the mainstream of society are most pronounced, such as drag queens or highly effeminate gay men.

ACT UP (AIDS Coalition to Unleash Power) is a direct-action AIDS advocacy group dedicated to increased funding for AIDS research and treatment. It is noted for its controversial protests and confrontational tactics, which have generated much media attention.

Adult Children of Alcoholics (or *ACAs*) are people who, it is believed, share common emotional and psychological traits as a result of growing up with an alcoholic parent or with alcoholic parents, such as low self-esteem and a compulsive need or desire to help others, which is referred to as codependence.

AIDS stands for *Acquired Immunity Deficiency Syndrome,* a disease spread through contact with the body fluids or blood of an infected person, as through intimate sexual contact or sharing a contaminated intravenous needle. After exposure, the incubation period before the onset of symptoms may last for ten years or more. There is no known cure for AIDS. It was first discovered in

1981 and is now believed to have been introduced into the United States in 1978. In the United States, the majority of AIDS cases thus far have occurred among homosexual men. The rate of increase has stabilized among the gay male population, however, and currently the rate of increase of new AIDS cases is rising faster among intravenous drug abusers and heterosexuals than among gay men.

AIDS Coalition to Unleash Power. See *ACT UP.*

Ambisexual (or *ambisexuality*) indicates someone who is neither strictly heterosexual nor strictly homosexual but who is equally attracted to men and women. The word is related to the word "ambidextrous" (indicating someone who is neither left-handed nor right-handed, but equally able to use either hand). An ambisexual person differs from a bisexual person, who is also sexually attracted to both men and women, but who at any given time is likely to be more attracted to one gender than the other, although this may alternate between men and women over the course of the bisexual's life.

Ambisexuality. See *Ambisexual.*

The *androgyne* is an archetype that embodies characteristics of both genders. It is related to the term androgynous.

Androgynous means combining feminine and masculine traits, sometimes suggesting a blurring of biological sex.

Anger is used here to indicate the second of five stages of the coming-out process, as derived from Dr. Elisabeth Kübler-Ross's five-stage model. Anger emerges when attempts at Denial prove ineffective and the prospect of being homosexual is faced head-on for the first time. Rage erupts over the perceived unfairness of being homosexual, given society's attitudes towards homosexuals and homosexuality. Anger involves unhappiness over what is lost in giving up a heterosexual identity, such as approval from society and family, and the clarity provided by heterosexual role models.

Anima is Jung's term for the largely unconscious feminine side of men, which typically is projected onto women, sometimes with a magical or larger-than-life dimension. It has both positive and negative manifestations, for example, Glinda the Good Witch of the North and the Wicked Witch of the West in *The Wizard of Oz.* See also *Archetype* and *Diva archetype.*

Animus is Jung's term for the largely unconscious masculine side of women, which typically is projected onto men.

Archetype is a term Jung invented for important and universal patterns that transcend cultural boundaries and that are embodied in every culture's myths and images, though taking on slightly different forms and nuances in each. For instance, the archetype of feminine love and beauty was formerly represented by a statue of Aphrodite, while in more recent times a poster of Marilyn Monroe might embody the same archetype. (The late Marilyn Monroe is, perhaps revealingly, still often referred to as a "love goddess.") Archetypes have dual manifestations, positive and negative. For example, the Loving Mother, representing unconditional love, is a manifestation of the Mother archetype in her positive aspect. The negative form of the Mother archetype appears, for example, as the wicked stepmother in "Cinderella." See also *Diva archetype.*

Assimilationism. See *Accommodationism.*

Aversion therapy is a form of behavior modification that attempts to break a pattern of behavior by exposing the patient simultaneously both to something that evokes the unwanted response and to some unpleasant stimulus. Aversion therapy has been used in misguided attempts to change homosexuals' sexual orientation, for instance, by showing a homosexual man gay pornography while delivering electric shocks to his genitals or while he is under the influence of a drug that makes him feel nauseated.

Bargaining, a term derived from Dr. Elisabeth Kübler-Ross's research on death and dying, is used here to indicate the third of five stages of the coming-out process. Not all gay men undergo this stage, but those who do agree to do something specific (such as entering psychotherapy or a program run by a so-called "ex-gay" ministry) in the hope that doing so will help change their sexual orientation to a heterosexual one. Empirical evidence indicates that such strategies fail to produce any permanent change in sexual orientation.

Bathhouses that serve a gay clientele are places that typically offer recreational facilities, steamrooms, lounges, and other rooms for cruising and for quick and often multiple sexual encounters. Since the outbreak of the AIDS epidemic, bathhouses in some places have been closed, while in others policies forbidding unsafe sex have been imposed.

Baths. See *Bathhouses.*

Berdache is a term applied by Europeans to the medicine men, shamans, teachers, and healers they encountered in most Native American tribes who crossed traditional gender boundaries by wearing a mixture of men's and women's clothing and by engaging in both women's and men's occupations. Most berdaches would now be termed "gay" and assumed the "feminine" role in their sexual relationships with their male sexual partners. The male sexual partners of the berdaches were regarded as normal men; the berdaches, though viewed as different, were accepted in their tribes and often fulfilled honored ceremonial and spiritual roles.

Bildungsroman is a German literary term designating a coming-of-age story, typically involving a male hero who gains knowledge of the world in a bittersweet manner involving the loss of innocence.

Bisexuality. See *Sexual orientation.*

Bottom is the term applied to the man or woman who is generally passive in homosexual intercourse, especially the partner who is penetrated by the other. (In male couples, the bottom typically assumes the passive position in anal intercourse.) The more active partner is referred to as the top. The term *top* or *bottom* pertains to the sexual position or role of the sexual partner rather than to the dominance or passivity of the individual's personality.

Brainwashing is the systematic, relentless assault upon a person's psyche designed to destroy his or her belief system and sense of self so that in their place a new set of beliefs can be instilled. This form of forced conversion has been used on prisoners of war and members of so-called cults who have been kidnapped by their families for "deprogramming," as well as upon homosexuals.

Bread is a slang term for money.

Butch is a slang term for an exaggeratedly masculine appearance, behavior, or person (whether male or female). Its opposite is *femme*.

A *call boy* is a male prostitute who is "on call," that is, available by appointment (as opposed to walking the streets and being picked up there).

Camp (also *campy, camping*) is a gay slang term that gained wide currency when appropriated in the 1960s by Susan Sontag and others at the height of the Pop Art movement to refer to art and humor that ironically mimic popular culture through self-conscious and often wildly exaggerated self-parody. It has been linked to the elusive notion of a supposed gay sensibility and applied to such things as *Batman* (the television series of the mid-1960s) and female impersonators of Bette Davis and other film stars.

Closet (or *closeted*, and especially *in the closet*) is a term to indicate someone who, although homosexual, has not come out to others, or who may still be in Denial.

Codependent (or *codependence*) indicates a person whose self-worth and self-importance hinge upon helping a dependent person, that is, one who is perceived to need the codependent in order to cope. The codependent person needs to be needed by a needy person. Both persons in such a relationship are dysfunctional, and neither partner has a monopoly on manipulation, guilt trips, or shaming of the other partner.

Cognitive dissonance is an individual's state of psychological conflict resulting from holding irreconcilable yet crucial beliefs (such as "homosexuality is bad" and "I think I may be a homosexual"). It cannot be maintained indefinitely. Some action must be taken to alleviate the distress that stems from the conflict.

Coming out is the process by which one comes to acknowledge that one is homosexual and to accept oneself as a gay person. It is also often used to indicate acknowledging one's homosexual orientation to others.

Coming out is Eli Coleman's name for the second of five stages in the coming-out process. Coming out entails acknowledgment and disclosure of same-sex feelings.

Coming out is also Richard Troiden's name for the third of four stages in his model of Gay Identity Acquisition. In this stage, one labels one's sexual feelings as definitely homosexual.

Commitment is the fourth and final stage in Richard Troiden's model of Gay Identity Acquisition. This involves either the taking of a gay lover or the emotional readiness to do so.

Constructionism (or *constructivism*) is the theory that sexual orientation is created by the social and historical forces present in a particular place at a particular time. Those who hold this position are known as constructionists or constructivists. They are opposed to essentialism and the efforts of essentialists to create or reclaim a (lost) gay history, believing that any such attempt lacks historical rigor.

Cruising (or *to cruise*) is the act of searching for a sexual partner, often for a quick, impersonal sexual encounter.

The *Daughters of Bilitis (DOB)*, the first public organization in the United States devoted to lesbian rights, was founded by Del Martin and Phyllis Lyon in 1955. The first New York chapter of DOB was founded in 1958 by Barbara Gittings.

Denial is the state in which a person has homosexual desires or activity but refuses to admit being a homosexual. Such a discrepancy between feelings, actions, and self-image leads to stress, insecurity, rationalizations, and frequently to self-deception. Some people overcompensate. For instance, a man may cultivate exaggeratedly masculine traits to prove to himself and others that he is not homosexual.

Depression often results when one first realizes that being homosexual is a part of oneself that cannot be changed. This occurs after any attempts to change one's sexual orientation prove fruitless. Low self-esteem and alienation characterize this phase, in which one still feels that being gay is unfortunate or undesirable. Some individuals attempt to mask their Depression through excessive consumption of alcohol, drugs, or other self-destructive behaviors that offer escape.

A *discaire* is a disc jockey in a discotheque.

Dissociation and Signification involve separating a growing awareness of one's own homosexual urges and/or behavior from the rest of one's sense of self to postpone any sense that these might be a permanent part of who one is.

Diva archetype is a term coined by Ken Bartmess. The diva is a powerful, regal, or dramatic woman who might be represented by a film or opera star. As with other archetypes, she has positive and negative manifestations or aspects. The diva archetype holds particular glamour and power among gay men.

A *double life* is a life of duplicity and pretense, such as when one poses as a heterosexual in public, while engaging in homosexual affairs in secret.

Drag queens are males dressed to impersonate females, often in a deliberate attempt to exaggerate female roles to the point of parody. Drag queens were largely responsible for the spirited resistance to the police when the Stonewall Inn was raided on the night of June 27, 1969, which has come to mark the birth of the gay liberation movement.

A *dyke* is a lesbian.

Dysfunctional indicates impaired functioning or unhealthy behavior patterns.

Dystonic homosexuality (also known as *ego-dystonic homosexuality*), or unhealthy homosexuality, is now a term applied only to those so dissatisfied with their own homosexuality that they wish to become heterosexual.

Effeminacy (or *effeminate*) is the state of possessing or exhibiting traits misogynists stereotypically associate with women, such as passivity and weakness, often in an exaggerated fashion. Formerly, in conformity with the patriarchal belief that homosexual men were not "real men," many homosexuals often deliberately or unconsciously imitated the supposed mannerisms of women. Opinion has generally shifted to viewing any alleged effeminacy of gay men as a social construction rather than an inherent attribute of homosexuality itself.

Ego-dystonic homosexuality. See *Dystonic homosexuality.*

An *elegiac romance* is a narrative in which the narrator reflects upon the life of a person who has died and laments his death. Although ostensibly celebrating the deceased hero, who at first is overglamorized, the elegiac romance focuses upon the narrator, who gradually recognizes his initially unconscious identification with this hero. In this process the narrator learns something about himself and ultimately outgrows his need to view his late hero as a role model.

Epistolary means consisting of or pertaining to letters. Thus an epistolary prologue is a prologue composed of letters.

An *epistolary novel* consists entirely of letters written by the characters in the novel.

An *eponymous novel* is one whose title is taken from the name of its protagonist. An example is *The Great Gatsby* by F. Scott Fitzgerald.

Essentialism is the belief that there is an essence to being gay that transcends cultural, religious, or historical boundaries. Those who uphold this position are known as essentialists. Some notable Essentialists are John Boswell, Arthur Evans, and Harry Hay. They are opposed by the constructionists.

"Ex-Gay" movements or *"ministries"* claim that homosexuality is a "sin" that can be "healed" through participation in their programs, that is, that homosexuals can become heterosexuals, or at least learn to refrain from participation in same-sex sexual activities even if homosexual desires linger. Scrutiny of their claims reveals that they have no empirical evidence for any long-term change in sexual orientation.

Exploration is Eli Coleman's name for the third of five stages in the coming-out process. It consists of experimentation.

Faerie (also *faery* or *fairie*) is a term that has been used (usually spelled *fairy*) to ridicule homosexual men for their supposed effeminacy. It also has been reclaimed by some gay men in a self-conscious attempt to link contemporary gay male identity with the spiritual and magical roles held in the distant past by men who would now be called gay. This usage emerged with the founding in San Francisco in October 1975 of the Faery Circle and, later, in 1979, the Spiritual Conference of Radical Faeries.

Faery. See *Faerie.*

Faggot, a derogatory term for a gay man, is derived from the Latin for beech tree, *fagus,* which was a favorite wood used by medieval Christians to burn gay men to death as heretics. The twigs of the beech tree used to ignite the fires were called faggots.

Fairy. See *Faerie.*

Femme is a slang term for an exaggeratedly effeminate appearance, behavior, or person (whether male or female). Its opposite is *butch.*

The *First Relationships* phase is the fourth of five stages in Eli Coleman's model of the coming-out process. As a solid gay identity is not yet in place, such relationships often prove short-lived.

Fist fucking is the insertion of the hand (and sometimes part of the arm) into a partner's rectum for sexual pleasure, caused in part by the stimulation of the prostate gland. Also known as *fisting.*

Fisting. See *Fist fucking.*

A *flashback* is a sudden shift in the chronology of a narrative to an earlier time. It is often introduced by an experience that triggers a character's memory of a former time and place.

Foils are characters introduced or established as opposites in a literary work. The juxtaposition of their differences helps the traits, appearance, speech, values, and/or behavior of each to stand out more sharply.

Gay is a term that indicates more than the presence of sexual attraction towards and/or sexual activity with members of one's own sex. It also indicates the conscious and willing self-identification of oneself as someone whose sexual orientation involves exclusive or primary attraction towards members of one's own sex.

Gay Identity Acquisition is the term Richard Troiden uses for coming out. It comprises four stages: Sensitization, Dissociation and Signification, Coming Out, and Commitment.

Gay liberation is the term embraced by the movement that rapidly emerged and grew, both nationally and internationally, in the wake of the riot at the Stonewall Inn in Greenwich Village, New York City on the night of June 27, 1969. It proposed that sex roles be defined in a radically new way and was marked by a militancy that some felt was lacking in much of the homophile movement it superseded. The gay liberation movement itself has given way to the gay rights movement.

The *gay rights movement,* which superseded the gay liberation movement, has concentrated on legal and political changes, such as electing openly gay and lesbian officials, passing anti-discrimination laws and ordinances, creating penalties for "hate crimes" directed at gays and lesbians, and passing domestic-partner legislation.

A *ghetto* is a place where there can be found a concentration of a minority group that is not easily assimilated into or accepted by the dominant society. Gay ghettos, such as those centered around Christopher Street in New York and Castro Street in San Francisco, grew markedly and gained increased visibility in the decade after the Stonewall rebellion in 1969.

H.A. See *Homosexuals Anonymous.*

The *hero's journey* is a concept popularized by the late Joseph Campbell, the comparative mythologist, who found in the mythologies and folk tales of many peoples the same pattern of Departure, Initiation, and Return. Typically, the hero is a youth on the verge of manhood who must leave his tribe or village and undergo an ordeal that tests his courage and wisdom. This test results in an initiation into the truths of this world (and often into the realm of spirit as well), after which he returns to his place of origin a changed person whose stature has been enhanced.

Heterosexuality. See *Sexual orientation.*

HIV or the *Human Immunodeficiency Virus* is generally suspected as the agent of transmission of AIDS, although this has not been proven. Exposure to HIV occurs through the transmission of bodily fluids (such as blood and semen) through such activities as unsafe sex or sharing of intravenous needles by drug users or abusers. HIV, it is believed, generally leads to the development of AIDS, though this may take ten years or more.

Holy union is the name certain churches are using for gay unions blessed by a religious ceremony of the same name. Most churches shy away from calling such ceremonies "weddings" or such unions "marriages" in the face of the state's unwillingness to grant marriage licenses to same-sex couples. Most churches prohibit the celebration of such ceremonies; others vary from diocese to diocese and from parish to parish on this issue.

Homoerotic (or *homoeroticism*) is a term that suggests subliminal or unconscious homosexual potential (in a person or situation) that may never lead to self-conscious homosexual desire or overt homosexual behavior. It exists consciously only in the eye of the beholder, rather than in the person or character being scrutinized.

Homophile (noun or adjective), meaning one who loves other members of his or her own sex, is a term chosen by those who pioneered the movement for recognition of the existence of and the rights of the homosexual minority in this country. The earliest homophile groups in the United States were the Mattachine Society, founded by Harry Hay in 1950, and the Daughters of Bilitis, founded by Del Martin and Phyllis Lyon in 1955. The homophile movement of the 1950s and 1960s was superseded by the gay liberation movement.

Homophobia (or *homophobic*) is the irrational fear of or hatred of homosexuals and homosexuality.

Homosexual (noun or adjective) indicates sexual attraction to and/or sexual activity with members of one's own sex that is not necessarily accompanied by self-identification as a person whose sexual orientation is that of being attracted exclusively or predominantly towards members of one's own sex. It is thus not exactly the same as being gay.

Homosexual Identity Formation is Vivienne Cass's term for coming out. It involves six stages: Identity Confusion, Identity Comparison, Identity Tolerance, Identity Acceptance, Identity Pride, and Identity Synthesis.

Homosexuality. See *Sexual orientation*.

Homosexuals Anonymous (*H.A.*) is one of many so-called "ex-gay" groups that claims to help homosexuals "recover" from their homosexuality. It models itself very loosely upon Alcoholics Anonymous.

Human Immunodeficiency Virus. See *HIV*.

Hustler. A male prostitute whose clients are men.

Identity Acceptance is the fourth stage in Vivienne Cass's six-stage model of Homosexual Identity Formation. In this stage, homosexual identity is accepted and contacts with other gays are strengthened.

Identity Comparison is the second stage in Vivienne Cass's six-stage model of Homosexual Identity Formation. In this stage, the person thinks "I may be a homosexual" and becomes alienated.

Identity Confusion is the first stage in Vivienne Cass's six-stage model of Homosexual Identity Formation. In this stage, one becomes aware that one's behavior may be homosexual and wonders "Am I homosexual?" This leads either to Denial or to the search for more information.

Identity Pride is the fifth stage in Vivienne Cass's six-stage model of Homosexual Identity Formation. In this stage, greater public disclosure of—and activism tied to—one's homosexuality results from feelings of legitimacy in one's identity as a gay person.

Identity Synthesis is the sixth and final stage in Vivienne Cass's six-stage model of Homosexual Identity Formation. In this stage, the "us versus them" (homosexuals versus heterosexuals) mentality recedes as sexual orientation becomes well-integrated into the sense of self as merely one of many aspects of one's being.

Identity Tolerance is the third stage in Vivienne Cass's six-stage model of Homosexual Identity Formation. In this stage, one reluctantly admits, "I probably am a homosexual" and explores the gay subculture.

Individuation is the term of Carl G. Jung and of analytical psychology for the individual's process of becoming whole by embracing and unifying both the personal and collective unconscious.

Integration is Eli Coleman's term for the fifth and final stage in the coming-out process.

Internalized homophobia is the homophobia (the irrational fear of or hatred of homosexuals and homosexuality) that homosexuals have absorbed from their surroundings and carry within themselves, where it may be magnified greatly by self-doubt and insecurity. Internalized homophobia is a form of self-hatred.

Invert is a derogatory slang term applied to homosexuals, suggesting something twisted in the process of sexual development. Hence the term *sexual inversion*.

Jam is a slang term formerly used to indicate a hustler whose Denial of homosexuality was based on the excuse that he only had sex with other men for the money, not out of desire.

John (or *mark*) is a slang term for the male customer of a hustler or prostitute.

Joint is a slang term for penis. It is also a slang term for prison.

The *Kinsey Report* is the name by which the book *Sexual Behavior in the Human Male* (1948), coauthored by Alfred C. Kinsey, Wardell B. Pomeroy, and Clyde E. Martin, has come to be known. It attempted the first systematic surveying of the actual sexual behavior of adult men in the United States and shocked many people with its indication that homosexual behavior among American men was far more widespread than most people had been led to believe.

Latency is the state of not yet being fully manifest. A latent homosexual is one who has not yet come out, and who may not even be aware of his or her homosexuality.

Liminal means threshold, margin, or borderline, a place gays often occupy.

A *litotes* is an affirmation made obliquely by denying the opposite, as by saying "I wouldn't mind——" to mean "I would like to——." The litotes is usually understood to suggest understatement, sometimes obviously or ironically so. Thus "I wouldn't mind" might better be understood to mean "I would really love to——."

A *mark* (or *John*) is the man who hires a hustler.

The *Mattachine Society*, founded by Harry Hay in Los Angeles in 1950, was a pioneering homophile organization in the United States. It took its name from a group of male musicians who crossdressed and wore masks in public in twelfth- and thirteenth-century France who were called "Les sociétés mattachines." The affiliation of these men with troubadours and others in contact with so-called heretical sects of their day is no coincidence. Harry Hay has long sought a spiritual explanation for gay identity, one that would help answer the questions, "Who are we?" "Where have we come from?" and "What are we here for?"

Mimesis means imitation. It is a key term in Aristotle's theory of literature as set forth in his *Poetics*, the earliest known work of literary criticism. It means that literature should imitate life so as to produce in the reader, listener, or viewer certain emotions, such as pity, empathy, and understanding.

Misogyny (or, in adjectival form, *misogynistic*) is the irrational hatred of or fear of women, which entails devaluation of women and traits and activities supposedly associated with them.

Molly was a slang term for a gay man, connoting the supposed effeminacy of gay men through the use of the female nickname.

Molly-houses were all-male taverns in which gay men could gather, cruise, and sometimes even dance and have sexual encounters in special rooms. Molly-houses began appearing in London after the Restoration in the late 1600s.

Monogamy is the state of restricting oneself sexually exclusively to one sexual partner.

Mother archetype. See *Archetype.*

Nellie is used as an adjective (especially in the expression *nellie queen*) for homosexuals who are perceived as particularly effeminate (as the female name suggests).

Nymphomania is an unusually high sex drive present in a woman or girl.

Orientation. See *Sexual orientation.*

Pansy is a slang term of contempt for a gay man, suggesting effeminacy, that is, that he lacks the strength and toughness of a "real man."

Passing is a form of concealment. It means to succeed in convincing people of being one thing while actually being another. For example, a gay man might pass as heterosexual, or a black person as white.

Patriarchy (or *patriarchal*) is the feminist term for the entrenched male power structure that has overvalued certain supposedly masculine traits (such as aggression, competitiveness, control, dominance, and heterosexuality) to the great detriment of women and gay men.

Pedophile. See *Pedophilia.*

Pedophilia is the sexual love of adults for children. One common homophobic stereotype holds that pedophilia is especially common among gay men, but statistics on reported sexual contact with children do not support this stereotype. Ninety-seven percent of the adults involved are heterosexual men. Someone who practices pedophilia (or who desires to do so) is known as a pedophile.

Person(s) With AIDS. See *PWA(s).*

Persona is a term used by Freud and others to indicate the individual's "mask" or way of presenting the self to the public.

A *pimp* is a prostitute's manager and often serves as liaison or procurer.

Polymorphous perversity is Freud's notion that in infancy, sexual desire is diffuse and unrestrained until, in the course of childhood, societal taboos are internalized and imposed on the self by the superego.

Pre-Coming Out is the first stage in Eli Coleman's five-stage model of coming out. It is marked by Denial and anxiety.

Promiscuity is a lack of selectivity regarding sexual partners. Usually it indicates a large number of sexual contacts.

The *protagonist* is the principal character and hero of the story. The reader is meant to sympathize with his or her trials and triumphs.

PWA(s) stands for *Person(s) With AIDS.* It has replaced other terms felt to be negative in tone, such as "AIDS patients" or "AIDS victims." (Similarly, the expression "persons living with AIDS" generally has replaced the expression "persons dying of AIDS.")

Queen is a slang term for a homosexual man no longer in his first youth whose dramatic style (often a burlesque of a diva's or film star's) commands attention. It is often used to ridicule someone whose sense of self-importance is overinflated, as in the expression, "What a queen!"

Queer is a slang term of contempt for gays that in recent years (like the term *faerie*) has been reclaimed by gays and lesbians by the direct-action group Queer Nation and others. The implicit basis of the insult—that of not fitting in, of being a distinct oddity—has been undercut by the growing awareness since the publication of the Kinsey Report of the prevalence of homosexuality.

A *quest romance* is a tale based on wish fulfillment. Its characters, challenges, dangers, and events have larger-than-life symbolic meanings, often representing either clearly good or clearly evil forces. Its hero or heroine is what we dream of being at our very best (or most attractive, brave, intelligent, or whatever) in our wildest fantasies. The successful quest romance is both "escapist" and psychologically meaningful.

Radical Faerie (or *Fairie*, or *Fairy*). See *Faerie.*

Repression occurs when shame or guilt leads people to push or keep "unacceptable" thoughts, feelings, or desires out of their minds. These submerged energies often reappear unexpectedly, in what Jung termed the "return of the repressed." *Repression* is often used interchangeably with *suppression*, although the terms differ slightly. See also *Suppression.*

Safe sex. See *Unsafe sex.*

Score is slang for someone picked up for sex. If money is exchanged, the score is the paying customer. To score means to pick someone up.

The *secret bargain* is part of the Bargaining stage. It is the unstated assumption that the desired result will be obtained in return for performing a certain action, for instance, that one can become heterosexual by undergoing psychotherapy.

Self-identity is a term for one's own view of who one is, which may or may not match one's public persona.

Sensitization is a term Richard Troiden uses for the first stage of Gay Identity Acquisition. In this stage, a sense of being different, which is not at first interpreted as having a sexual cause, leads to alienation.

Service (verb). To service someone means to gratify him or her sexually.

Sexual orientation is the term now generally used to designate a person's inherent tendency to be attracted to other persons of the same sex (homosexuality), members of the opposite sex (heterosexuality), or persons of both sexes (bisexuality or ambisexuality). The term homosexuality was coined in 1869 and first translated into English in 1881, which indicates that the concept of sexual orientation is relatively recent.

Sexual preference is a term that generally has been abandoned in favor of sexual orientation, as the former term implies that the sex to which one is attracted is a matter of conscious or deliberate choice.

Shadow is Jung's term for the part of the self that could not be consciously acknowledged because of its indifference to or violation of the person's conscious
moral values.

Situational homosexuality refers to homosexual encounters that take place between
heterosexual men when women are not available sexually, as in prisons,
barracks, boarding schools, and other all-male environments. Of course this
may serve as a rationalization or Denial of homosexuality.

Sodomy is a legal term for proscribed sexual acts. Its meaning varies widely by
jurisdiction. In some places, it refers only to homosexual acts, yet in others
it indicates any sexual acts incapable of leading to procreation, for instance,
oral sex between husband and wife.

Stonewall. The Stonewall Inn was a small gay bar in Greenwich Village. On the
night of June 27, 1969, in the course of an otherwise routine police raid,
drag queens and other clients resisted the police and caused a riot. This soon
came to be regarded as the beginning of the gay liberation movement.

Straight means heterosexual, and may suggest restriction. Its antonym is *gay*.

Sublimation is the expression or channeling of ideas, impulses, or attitudes with
which one feels uncomfortable (such as sexual feelings) in disguised form or
through a different outlet. The person sublimating feelings may or may not
be conscious of doing so. Sublimation differs from repression or suppression
in that the energy is released rather than being bottled up in the unconscious.

Substance abuse is the consumption of alcohol and/or other drugs to excess, often
in an increasingly self-destructive manner. Although substance abuse may
be voluntary at first, addiction or compulsion often develops.

Suppression indicates the repression of ideas, thoughts, or feelings from consciousness into the unconscious or the concealment of certain attitudes and behaviors that remain in conscious awareness.

Tearooms are men's rooms used for quick, impersonal sexual encounters.

Top (or *top man*, or *top woman*) is the man or woman who assumes the dominant
position in sex, often the one who is the active partner in anal intercourse
or intercourse involving penetration. "Top" often, but not always, suggests
being butch. The man or woman in the passive position is the bottom. See
also *Bottom*.

Trade was a slang term for the ostensibly macho young men who allowed themselves to be picked up by gay men, usually for money, but who would not
take on any "feminine" role in any sexual encounter. Such "trade" denied
being gay, as in the male hustler's insisting, "I don't really enjoy it myself;
I just do it for the money." Such Denial was ridiculed in the gay saying
"This year's trade is next year's competition," which was widely repeated
from the late 1940s through the 1960s, and which is quoted (in slightly different forms) in *The City and the Pillar, City of Night,* and *The Beautiful
Room Is Empty.* The clear implication of the saying is that the pose of lack
of interest in homosexual sex could not be maintained for long.

Trick (noun) is slang for a sexual partner (usually a stranger) picked up for a casual
sexual encounter. *To trick* (v.) or *to trick with* is to have a casual sexual
encounter with someone one has picked up.

Trickster is an archetype that can be found in many lands, legends, and literatures.

Trickster is a figure of mischief and fun, a deflator of the balloons of the pompous and self-important, the inhabitant on the fringe of society, and often a figure of unbridled (and unconventional) sexuality. The practical joke is the manifestation of trickster par excellence. Trickster tales abound in classical mythology. (Dionysus is a trickster figure.) Children often delight in trickster figures, who challenge or mock the authority of adults. American trickster figures (largely drawn from earlier Native American sources) include Briar Rabbit, Bugs Bunny, and Wily Coyote.

Unsafe sex is any sexual practice that could lead to the exchange of bodily fluids and hence to the transmission of HIV, the suspected cause of AIDS. While there is dispute about the degree of risk involved in certain activities, such as oral sex without a condom, there is a consensus that anal sex without a condom is highly unsafe for both partners, and, due to the possibility of a condom breaking or tearing, even anal sex with a condom has some risk.

Uranians is Edward Carpenter's term for gay men. Carpenter (1844–1929) was a pioneer in advocating understanding and appreciation of gay people and the particular gifts gay people have to offer. This term has fallen out of use.

Works Cited

Abbott, H. Porter. "Narratricide: Samuel Beckett as Autographer." *Romance Studies* 11 (1987): 35–46.

Adams, Stephen. *The Homosexual as Hero in Contemporary Fiction*. London: Vision Press, 1980.

Aldyne, Nathan. *Vermilion*. New York: Avon Books, 1980.

Alexander, Ronald Aden. *The Relationship Between Internalized Homophobia and Depression and Low Self-Esteem in Gay Men*. Unpublished doctoral dissertation, University of California, Santa Barbara, July 1986.

Altman, Dennis. *Homosexual Oppression and Liberation*. New York: Outerbridge and Dienstfrey, 1971.

———. *The Homosexualization of America, The Americanization of the Homosexual*. New York: St. Martin's Press, 1982.

American Psychological Association. *Removing the Stigma: Final Report of the Board of Social and Ethical Responsibility for Psychologists' Task Force on the Status of Lesbian and Gay Male Psychologists*. Washington, D.C.: American Psychological Association, 1979.

Austen, Roger. *Playing the Game: The Homosexual Novel in America*. New York: Bobbs-Merrill, 1977.

Baldwin, James. *Another Country*. 1962. New York: Dell, 1988.

———. *Giovanni's Room*. 1956. New York: Dell, 1988.

———. *Go Tell It on the Mountain*. 1953. New York: Dell, 1985.

Barnes, Djuna. *Nightwood*. New York: Harcourt, Brace and Co., 1937.

Barr, James. *Quatrefoil: A Modern Novel*. New York: Greenberg, 1950.

Bell, Alan P., Martin S. Weinberg, and Sue Kiefer Hammersmith. *Sexual Preference: Its Development in Men and Women*. Bloomington, Ind.: Indiana University Press, 1981.

Bergman, David. *Gaiety Transfigured: Gay Self-Representation in American Literature*. Madison: University of Wisconsin Press, 1991.

The New English Bible. Oxford: Oxford University Press, 1970.

The Holy Bible: Revised Standard Version, Containing the Old and New Testaments with the Apocryphal/Deuterocanonical Books: An Ecumenical Edition. New York: World Bible Publishers, 1973.

Blair, Ralph. *Ex-Gay.* New York: Homosexual Community Counseling Center, 1982.

Blau, Herbert. *The Eye of Prey: Subversions of the Postmodern.* Theories of Contemporary Culture 9. Bloomington, Ind.: Indiana University Press, 1987.

Boone, Joseph Allen. "Mappings of Male Desire in Durrell's *Alexandria Quartet.*" *South Atlantic Quarterly* 88.1 (1989): 73–106.

———. *Tradition Counter Tradition: Love and the Form of Fiction.* Chicago: University of Chicago Press, 1987.

Borgman, C. F. *River Road.* New York: New American Library, 1988.

Boswell, John. *Christianity, Social Tolerance, and Homosexuality: Gay People in Western Europe from the Beginning of the Christian Era to the Fourteenth Century.* Chicago: University of Chicago Press, 1980.

Boyd, Malcolm. "Telling a Lie for Christ?" Gay Spirit: Myth and Meaning, ed. Mark Thompson. New York: St. Martin's Press, 1987, 78–87.

Brady, Stephen Michael. *The Relationship Between Differences in Stages of Homosexual Identity Formation and Background Characteristics, Psychological Well-Being and Homosexual Adjustment.* Unpublished doctoral dissertation, University of California, Santa Barbara. November 1983.

Brown, Howard. *Familiar Faces, Hidden Lives: The Story of Homosexual Men in America Today.* New York: Harcourt, Brace, Jovanovich, 1976.

Bruffee, Kenneth A. *Elegiac Romance: Cultural Change and Loss of the Hero in Modern Fiction.* Ithaca, N.Y.: Cornell University Press, 1983.

Buell, Lawrence. "Observer-Hero Narrative." *Texas Studies in Literature and Language* 21 (1979): 93–111.

Burroughs, William S. *Naked Lunch.* 1959. New York: Grove Press, 1966.

———. *Queer.* [Written in 1953]. New York: Viking, 1985.

Cameron, Ron. "Introduction to the *Secret Gospel of Mark.*" The Other Bible, ed. Willis Barnstone. San Francisco: Harper and Row, 1984, 339–40.

Campbell, Joseph. *The Hero with a Thousand Faces.* 1948. Princeton, N.J.: Princeton University Press, 1968.

Carpenter, Edward. *Selected Writings. Volume I: Sex.* London: G[ay] M[en's] P[ress] Publishers, 1984.

Caserio, Robert L. "Supreme Court Discourse vs. Homosexual Fiction." *South Atlantic Quarterly* 88.1 (1989): 267–99.

Cass, Vivienne C., M.Psych., M.A.Ps.S. "Homosexual Identity Formation: A Theoretical Model." *Journal of Homosexuality* 4.3 (1979): 219–35.

Cheever, Benjamin, ed. *The Letters of John Cheever.* New York: Simon and Schuster, 1988.

Cheever, John. *Falconer.* New York: Ballantine Books, 1977.

———. *The Stories of John Cheever.* New York: Alfred A. Knopf, 1978.

Chester, Alfred. "Fruit Salad." Review of *City of Night,* by John Rechy. *New York Review of Books* February 1963. Rpt. in *Selections from the first two issues of* The New York Review of Books, ed. Robert B. Silvers and Barbara Epstein. New York: New York Review of Books, 1988. 79–84.

Clayton, Jay. "Narrative and Theories of Desire." *Critical Inquiry* 16.1 (1989): 33–53.

Clemons, Walter, with Ray Sawhill, Sue Hutchinson, Nadine Joseph, Janet Huck, and bureau reports. "Out of the Closet Onto the Shelves: In the Era of AIDS, Gay Writers are Moving into the Mainstream of American Publishing." *Newsweek* 21 March 1988: 72–74.

Clum, John M. " 'Something Cloudy, Something Clear': Homophobic Discourse in Tennessee Williams." *South Atlantic Quarterly* 88.1 (1989): 161–79.

Coleman, Eli. "Bisexual and Gay Men in Heterosexual Marriage: Conflicts and Resolution in Therapy." *Homosexuality and Psychotherapy: A Practitioner's Handbook or Affirmative Models,* ed. John C. Gonsiorek. New York: Haworth Press, 1982, 93–104.

———. "Developmental Stages of the Coming Out Process." *Homosexuality and Psychotherapy: A Practitioner's Handbook of Affirmative Models,* ed. John C. Gonsiorek. New York: Haworth Press, 1982, 31–44.

Conrad, Joseph. *Heart of Darkness.* 1899. Ed. Robert Kimbrough. 3d ed. New York: W. W. Norton, 1988.

———. *Lord Jim.* 1917. Ed. Thomas C. Moser. New York: W. W. Norton, 1968.

Crompton, Louis. "Don Leon, Byron, and Homosexual Law Reform." *Essays on Gay Literature,* ed. Stuart Kellogg. 1983. New York: Harrington Press, 1985, 53–72.

Crowley, Mart. *The Boys in the Band.* New York: Farrar, Straus & Giroux, 1968.

De Rougemont, Dennis. *Love in the Western World.* Revised and Augmented Edition. Trans. Montgomery Belgion. Garden City, N.Y.: Harcourt, Brace, Jovanovich, 1957.

D'Emilio, John. *Sexual Politics, Sexual Communities: The Making of a Homosexual Minority in the United States, 1940–1970.* Chicago: University of Chicago Press, 1983.

D'Emilio, John, and Estelle B. Freedman. *Intimate Matters.* New York: Harper and Row, 1988.

Downing, Christine. *Myths and Mysteries of Same-Sex Love.* New York: Continuum, 1989.

Duberman, Martin. "Theater: The Season." Review of *The Boys in the Band,* by Mart Crowley, and other plays. *Partisan Review* 35 (1968): 415–29.

———. *About Time: Exploring the Gay Past.* New York: Gay Presses of New York City, 1986.

Durrell, Lawrence. *Balthazar.* 1958. New York: Pocket Books, 1961.

Edel, Leon. *Henry James: A Life.* New York: Harper and Row, 1985.

Edelman, Lee. "The Plague of Discourse: Politics, Literary Theory, and AIDS." *South Atlantic Quarterly* 88.1 (1989): 307–17.

Ellison, Ralph. *Invisible Man.* New York: New American Library, 1952.

England, Michael E. *The Bible and Homosexuality.* 2d ed. N.p.: Beulahland Press, 1979.

Epstein, Stephen. "Gay Politics, Ethnic Identity: The Limits of Social Constructionism." *Socialist Review* 17.3–4 (1987): 8–54.

Evans, Arthur. *The God of Ecstasy: Sex-Roles and the Madness of Dionysos.* New York: St. Martin's Press, 1988.

———. *Witchcraft and the Gay Counterculture: A Radical View of Western Civilization and Some of the People It Has Tried to Destroy.* Boston: Fag Rag Books, 1978.

Fenwick, Henry. "Living on the Edge of Time: Paul Monette Explores the World of AIDS Widowers in *Afterlife.*" *The Advocate: The National Gay Newsmagazine* 551 (22 May 1990): 58–60.

Ferro, Robert. *The Family of Max Desir.* 1983. New York: Plume/NAL Penguin, 1984.

———. *Second Son.* New York: Crown Publishers, 1988.

Fiedler, Leslie. *Love and Death in the American Novel.* 1960. New York: World Publishing, 1962.

Fisher, Peter. *The Gay Mystique: The Myth and Reality of Male Homosexuality.* New York: Stein and Day, 1972.

Fitzgerald, F. Scott. *The Great Gatsby.* 1925. New York: Charles Scribner's, n.d.

Forster, E. M. *Maurice.* 1971. New York: W. W. Norton, 1987.

Foucault, Michel. *The History of Sexuality. Volume I: An Introduction.* Trans. Robert Hurley. 1978. New York: Vintage Books, 1980.

———. *The Use of Pleasure: The History of Sexuality. Volume II.* Trans. Robert Hurley. 1985. New York: Vintage Books, 1986.

Frankel, Sara. "Gay, Lesbian Writers Find a Community Not Wholly United." Rpt. *San Francisco Examiner* 5 March 1990: n.p.

Frazer, Sir James George. *Adonis, Attis, and Osiris.* 2nd ed., rev. London: Macmillan, 1907.

———. *The Golden Bough: A Study in Magic and Religion.* 1922. New York: Macmillan, 1963.

Freiberg, Peter. "New Math: A Good Man is Hard to Find, Particularly If a New Report is Right." *The Advocate: The National Gay Newsmagazine* 519 (28 February 1989): 14–15.

Freud, Sigmund. Letter to Anonymous, 9 April 1935. *Letters of Sigmund Freud,* ed. Ernst L. Freud, trans. Tania Stern & James Stern. New York: Basic Books, 1960, 423–24.

Friedman, Sanford. *Totempole.* New York: E. P. Dutton, 1965.

Frontain, Raymond-Jean. Review of *Crystal Boys,* by Pai Hsien-Yung. *The James White Review: A Gay Men's Literary Quarterly* (Winter 1991): 15.

Gide, André. *The Immoralist.* 1902. Trans. Richard Howard. New York: Alfred A. Knopf, 1970.

Ginsberg, Allen. *Howl, and Other Poems.* San Francisco: City Lights Pocket Bookshop, 1956.

Goldstein, Richard. "The Art of Outing: When Is It Right to Name Gay Names?" *Voice* 1 May 1990: 33–37.

Goulden, Joseph C. *Fit to Print: A. M. Rosenthal and His Times.* Secaucus, N.J.: Lyle Stuart, 1988.

Grahn, Judy. "Some of the Roles of Gay People in Society." *Gay Spirit: Myth and Meaning,* ed. Mark Thompson. New York: St. Martin's Press, 1987, 3–9.

Greenberg, David F. *The Construction of Homosexuality.* Chicago: University of Chicago Press, 1988.

Griffin, Gail. "Homosexuals Twice as Likely to Abuse Drugs." *U: The National College Newspaper* 3 (December 1989): 2.

Hall, Richard. "Gay Fiction Comes Home." *New York Times Book Review* 19 June 1988: 1, 25–27.

Hansen, Joseph. *Gravedigger: A Dave Brandstetter Mystery/6.* 1982. New York: Holt, Rinehart and Winston, 1985.

Hardy, Robin. "Andy Warhol Goes Straight: How the Life of an Artist Who 'Liked the Swish' Is Being Whitewashed." *The Advocate: The National Gay Newsmagazine* 539 (5 December 1989): 58–60.

Holleran, Andrew. *Dancer from the Dance.* 1978. New York: New American Library, 1986.

———. *Ground Zero.* 1988. New York: New American Library, 1989.

———. *Nights in Aruba.* 1983. New York: New American Library, 1984.

Hopcke, Robert H. *Jung, Jungians, and Homosexuality.* Boston: Shambhala, 1989.

Indiana, Gary. *Horse Crazy.* New York: Grove Press, 1989.

Isherwood, Christopher. 1967. *A Meeting by the River.* New York: Avon Books, 1978.

Katz, Jonathan [Ned]. *Gay American History: Lesbians and Gay Men in the U.S.A.: A Documentary.* 1976. New York: Harper and Row, 1985.

Killian, Kevin. *Shy.* Freedom, Calif.: Crossing Press, 1989.

Kinsey, Alfred C., Wardell B. Pomeroy, and Clyde E. Martin. *Sexual Behavior in the Human Male.* Philadelphia: W. B. Saunders, 1948.

Koestenbaum, Wayne. *Double Talk: The Erotics of Male Literary Collaboration.* New York: Routledge, 1989.

Kramer, Larry. *Faggots.* 1978. New York: Plume/New American Library, 1987.

Kübler-Ross, Elisabeth. *On Death and Dying.* New York: Macmillan, 1969.

Labonte, Richard. "Shelf Life: Bad News, Good News for Gay Lit." *The Advocate: The National Gay Newsmagazine* 513 (6 December 1988): 72.

———. "Shelf Life: Giving Credit Where Credit is Due." *The Advocate: The National Gay Newsmagazine* 506 (30 August 1988): 60.

Lahr, John. *Prick Up Your Ears: The Biography of Joe Orton.* 1978. New York: Vintage Books/Random House, 1987.

Lassell, Michael. "Paul Monette: The Long Road to *Becoming a Man*." *The Advocate: The National Gay Newsmagazine* 604 (2 June 1992): 34–35.

Leavitt, David. *The Lost Language of Cranes.* New York: Alfred A. Knopf, 1986.

Leo, John R. "The Familialism of 'Man' in American Television Melodrama." *South Atlantic Quarterly* 88.1 (1989): 31–51.

Levinson, Daniel J., with Charlotte N. Darrow, Edward B. Klein, Maria H. Levinson, and Braxton McKee. *The Seasons of a Man's Life.* 1978. New York: Ballantine Books, 1979.

Mann, Thomas. "Death in Venice." 1911. *Stories of Three Decades,* trans. H. T. Lowe-Porter. New York: Alfred A. Knopf, 1955, 378–437.

Manvell, Roger. "Censorship of Film." *The International Encyclopedia of Film,* ed. Dr. Roger Manvell. New York: Crown Publishers, 1972, 123–24.

Mars-Jones, Adam. "Gay Fiction and the Reading Public." *Mae West is Dead: Recent Lesbian and Gay Fiction,* ed. Adam Mars-Jones. Boston: Faber and Faber, 1983, 13–43.

Melville, Herman. *Moby Dick, or The White Whale.* 1851. New York: New American Library, 1980.

Millen, Frederic. "Exodus Cofounders Tell Ex-Gay Movement to Get Real." *The Advocate: The National Gay Newsmagazine* 565 (4 December 1990): 39.

Monette, Paul. *Afterlife.* New York: Crown Publishers, 1990.

———. *Borrowed Time: An AIDS Memoir.* New York: Harcourt, Brace, Jovanovich, 1988.

————. *The Gold Diggers.* 1979. Boston: Alyson Publications, 1988.

————. *Taking Care of Mrs. Carroll.* 1978. New York: St. Martin's Press, 1987.

Moon, Michael. "Disseminating Whitman." *South Atlantic Quarterly* 88:1 (1989): 247–65.

Moritz, William. "Seven Glimpses of Walt Whitman." *Gay Spirit: Myth and Meaning,* ed. Mark Thompson. New York: St. Martin's Press, 1987, 131–51.

Murdoch, Iris. *The Bell.* 1958. Harmondsworth, Middlesex, England: Penguin Books, 1962.

Nelson, Charles. *The Boy Who Picked the Bullets Up.* New York: Morrow, 1981.

Nelson, James P. "Religious and Moral Issues in Working with Homosexual Clients." *Homosexuality and Psychotherapy: A Practitioner's Handbook of Affirmative Models,* ed. John C. Gonsiorek. New York: Haworth Press, 1982, 163–74.

Norton, Rictor. *The Homosexual Literary Tradition: An Interpretation.* New York: Revisionist Press, 1974.

Orton, Joe. *What the Butler Saw.* London: Methuen, 1969.

Pattison, E. Mansell, and Myrna Loy Pattison. " 'Ex-Gays': Religiously Mediated Change in Homosexuals." *American Journal of Psychiatry* 137:12 (December 1980): 1553–62.

Peterson, Robert W. "Frank Reassessment: Utah Cuts, then Restores Gay Material in Lessons about the Holocaust." *The Advocate: The National Gay Newsmagazine* 549 (24 April 1990): 14.

Plant, Richard. *The Pink Triangle: The Nazi War Against Homosexuals.* New York: Henry Holt and Company, 1986.

Plante, David. *The Catholic.* New York: Atheneum, 1986.

Proust, Marcel. *Remembrance of Things Past.* Trans. C. K. Scott Moncrieff and Terence Kilmartin. New York: Vintage Books/Random House, 1982.

Puig, Manuel. *Kiss of the Spider Woman.* Trans. Thomas Colchie. New York: Vintage Books/Random House, 1980.

Rechy, John. *City of Night.* 1963. New York: Grove Press, 1988.

————. *Numbers.* New York: Grove Press, 1967.

————. *The Sexual Outlaw: A Documentary. A Non-Fiction Account, with Commentaries, of Three Days and Nights in the Sexual Underground.* 1977. New York: Grove Press, 1984.

Sarotte, Georges-Michel. *Like a Brother, Like a Lover: Male Homosexuality in the American Novel and Theater from Herman Melville to James Baldwin.* 1976. Trans. Richard Miller. Garden City, N.Y.: Anchor Press/Doubleday, 1978.

Scanzoni, Letha, and Virginia Ramey Mollenkott. *Is the Homosexual My Neighbor?: Another Christian View.* San Francisco: Harper & Row, 1980.

Schrader, Scott. "Get Behind Me, Homosexuality: One Man's Experience with a 'Recovery' Program for Gays." *The Advocate: The National Gay Newsmagazine* 516 (17 January 1989): 33–41.

The Secret Gospel of Mark. In *The Other Bible,* ed. William Barnstone. San Francisco: Harper and Row, 1984, 339–42.

Sedgwick, Eve Kosofsky. *Between Men: English Literature and Male Homosocial Desire.* New York: Columbia University Press, 1985.

Sheehy, Gail. *Passages: Predictable Crises of Adult Life.* New York: E. P. Dutton, 1976.

Sheppard, R. Z. "Journals of the Plague Years: Three Books Reveal the Risks and Rewards of Writing about AIDS." *Time* 18 July 1988: 68, 70.

Summers, Claude J. *Gay Fictions: Wilde to Stonewall. Studies in a Male Literary Tradition.* New York: Continuum, 1990.

Suppe, Frederick. "The Bell and Weinberg Study: Future Priorities for Research on Homosexuality." *Journal of Homosexuality* 6:4 (1981): 69–97.

Thompson, Mark. "The Evolution of a Fairie: Notes Toward a New Definition of Gay." *Gay Spirit: Myth and Meaning,* ed. Mark Thompson. New York: St. Martin's Press, 1987, 292–302.

———. "Gay Soul Making: Coming Out Inside: A Group Interview." *Gay Spirit: Myth and Meaning,* ed. Mark Thompson. New York: St. Martin's Press, 1987, 237–54.

———. "Harry Hay: A Voice from the Past, A Vision for the Future." *Gay Spirit: Myth and Meaning,* ed. Mark Thompson. New York: St. Martin's Press, 1987, 182–99.

———. "This Gay Tribe: A Brief History of Fairies." *Gay Spirit: Myth and Meaning,* ed. Mark Thompson. New York: St. Martin's Press, 1987, 260–78.

———, ed. *Gay Spirit: Myth and Meaning.* New York: St. Martin's Press, 1987.

Torchia, Joseph. *As If After Sex.* New York: Holt, Rinehart, and Winston, 1984.

Troiden, Richard R. "Becoming Homosexual: A Model of Gay Identity Acquisition." *Psychiatry: Journal for the Study of Interpersonal Processes* 42 (1979): 362–73.

Twain, Mark. *Adventures of Huckleberry Finn.* 1884. New York: Harper and Row, 1987.

Vidal, Gore. *The City and the Pillar.* New York: E. P. Dutton, 1948.

———. *Myra Breckinridge.* Boston: Little, Brown & Co., 1968.

———. *Myron.* New York: Random House, 1974.

Walker, Mitch, and Friends. *Visionary Love: A Spirit Book of Gay Mythology.* Berkeley, Calif.: Treeroots Press, 1980.

Warren, Robert Penn. *All the King's Men.* New York: Harcourt, Brace, 1946.

Weatherby, W. J. *James Baldwin: Artist on Fire.* New York: Donald I. Fine, 1989.

Weinberg, Thomas S. *Gay Men, Gay Selves: The Social Construction of Homosexual Identities.* New York: Irvington Publishers, 1983.

White, Edmund. *The Beautiful Room Is Empty.* 1988. New York: Ballantine Books, 1989.

———. *A Boy's Own Story.* 1982. New York: New American Library, 1983.

———. *Caracole.* 1985. New York: New American Library, 1986.

———. *Forgetting Elena.* 1973. New York: Penguin Books, 1981.

———. *Nocturnes for the King of Naples.* New York: St. Martin's Press, 1978.

Wilde, Oscar. *The Picture of Dorian Gray and Other Writings.* Ed. Richard Ellman. New York: Bantam Books, 1982.

Williams, Walter L. *The Spirit and the Flesh: Sexual Diversity in American Indian Culture.* Boston: Beacon Press, 1988.

Wylen, Bert. "Can George Bush Read Gay Lips? One Gay Man's Very Odd Meeting with the President and First Lady." *The Advocate: The National Gay Newsmagazine* 546 (13 March 1990): 40–42.

Index

Bargaining: compared with other stages
of coming out, 20, 23, 74–75; in gay
writing, 20, 25, 74, 77, 85–87, 94,
146; in Kübler-Ross's model, 14–15,
74, 78; as stage in coming out, 14,
15–16, 25, 73–79, 85–87, 96–98, 100
Bars, gay, 12–13, 24, 43, 45, 50, 56–
57, 61–62, 67, 68, 73, 76, 95, 103,
105, 106, 117, 132, 133, 138, 149.
See also Discotheques
Bartmess, Ken, 126
Bathhouses, gay, 99, 103, 105, 107,
111, 112, 117
Beautiful Room Is Empty, The (White),
6, 14, 20, 24, 25, 43, 68, 73–74, 76–
79, 85–89, 92–95, 103, 110. Characters: Dale, 92, 94; Fred, 94; Maria,
73, 77, 87, 93; Mick, 93; Dr.
O'Reilly, 73, 79, 92–94; parents of
hero, 74, 88, 92; Sean, 73, 92, 94–
95; Simon, 94–95; Tex, 92; unnamed
hero, 73–74, 76–77, 85, 86–87, 88,
93
"Becoming Homosexual" (Troiden), 9,
17–19, 75, 90, 101, 120, 150
Behavior versus identity: coming out as
change in identity not behavior, 18,
49; conflict within men who have not
come out, 17, 20, 24, 29, 32, 37, 40,
42, 45, 49, 57, 89, 101; shift in debate from behavior to identity, 2, 39,
148–49. *See also* Denial
Benkert, Dr. Karoly Maria, 85
Berdache, 58, 79, 138–39, 140, 141,
150
Bereavement leave. *See* Gay rights
Bergman, David, 24, 103, 112, 138,
145
Bias, anti-gay. *See* Discrimination, anti-
gay; States with gay rights laws
Bible, 57, 78, 84, 138, 145. *See also*
Christianity; Church; *Secret Gospel
of Mark*
Bildungsroman, 6, 73, 124
Bisexuality: belief in all people's, 61; of
Beth Carroll (*Taking Care of Mrs.
Carroll*), 127; of John Cheever, 31;
of David (*Giovanni's Room*), 60, 62,

65; as Denial of homosexuality, 32–
33, 37, 44; and sexual ambiguity, 18
Blackmun, Harry A. (U.S. Supreme
Court Justice), 148
Blair, Ralph, 80–81
Boone, Joseph Allen, 3
Borrowed Time (Monette), 123, 148
Boy's Own Story, A (White), 43, 86,
124, 145
Brady, Stephen Michael, 22, 75
Brothers, 33, 38. *See also* Families of
gay men
Brown, Howard, 86, 91
Buckley, William F., Jr., 23
Buddhism, 76, 141
Burroughs, William, 23, 122, 146
Bush, President and Mrs. George, 124

Camp, 47, 100, 108, 112, 127, 129
Campbell, Joseph, 9–10
Carpenter, Edward, 120, 140, 141
Cass, Vivienne C., model of Homosexual Identity Formation, 19–22, 74–
75, 102. Stages: Identity Acceptance,
21; Identity Comparison, 20, 54, 57,
58, 75; Identity Confusion, 19–20,
28, 30, 54, 57; Identity Pride, 21;
Identity Synthesis, 21–22, 123; Identity Tolerance, 20–21, 75, 101
Causes of homosexuality (supposed),
41–42, 83, 90, 92, 121–22
Celibacy, 2, 79, 83
Cheever, John, 24, 30–34, 37; correspondence of, 32, 40; Denial of, 30–
32, 59; internalized homophobia of,
24, 31, 37, 40, 46, 77. *See also* Falconer
Chester, Alfred, 44, 88
Chicago Society for Human Rights, 143
Childhood, 9, 17, 41, 122, 124
Children, 8, 11, 28, 29, 58
Christianity, 66, 79, 80, 84–85, 98,
126. *See also* Bible; Church
*Christianity, Social Tolerance, and Ho-
mosexuality* (Boswell), 39, 66, 84–85,
144
Church, 63–64, 83–85, 144. Denomi-
nations and groups: Affirmation

Male bonding, 3, 66, 69

Mapplethorpe, Robert, 147, 148

Mark, Secret Gospel of, 57, 84

Marriage: of bisexuals, 36, 38, 125, 127; desire for, 66, 110–11; of heterosexuals, 106, 124; of homosexuals, 30, 86, 87; same-sex, 104; versus gay identity, 144

Masculinity: assertion or pose of, 45, 46, 48, 58; homosexuality thought to be unrelated to, 79, 130, 139; homosexuality thought to reinforce, 66; homosexuality thought to undermine, 54, 101, 112, 122, 129; linked with femininity, 125; reexamination of, by gays, 47, 139–40, 149; as social construction, 39, 134, 139

Mattachine Society, 67, 68, 141, 143

Metropolitan Community Church, 9, 85, 98

Middle age, 120, 128–29, 131

Mimesis, 137, 146

Misconceptions. *See* Homophobia; Stereotypes of gay men

Misogyny, 39, 66, 120

Models of coming out. *See* Coming out

Molly-houses, 103, 138

Monette, Paul, 120, 121, 123, 126, 134–35

Monogamy, 8, 105, 144

Monotheism versus polytheism, 78–79. *See also* Bible; Christianity; Church; God

Mothers: of gay men, 42, 103, 121–22; surrogate, 125

Mythology. *See* American myths and culture; Gay myths

Narcissism, 41, 48, 85, 89, 132, 151. *See also* Appearance

Narrative: first-person versus third-person, 41, 43, 53, 86, 108; theories of, 137, 142, 145–46

"Narrative and Theories of Desire" (Clayton), 142, 146–47

Native Americans, 58, 79, 138–39, 140, 150

Nazis and Nazi persecution of homosexuals. *See* Holocaust

New Testament. *See* Bible

Nights in Aruba (Holleran), 110

Nineteenth century, 3, 4, 64, 90, 95, 103, 138

Nineteenth-century novels, 3, 4

Nocturnes for the King of Naples (White), 23

Novels: allegorical, 23; American (*see* American literature); autobiographical, 43, 59, 60, 73, 86; British, 3, 86, 100, 122–23; coming-out, 137, 142, 144; detective, 23–24, 144; eighteenth-century, 23; epistolary, 22–23; gay (*see* Gay fiction); nineteenth-century, 3–4; science fiction, 23, 144. *See also* Publishing; Reviews of gay fiction; *titles of individual novels*

Numbers (Rechy), 55

O'Connor, John Cardinal, 8, 147

Old Testament. *See* Bible

Oppression. *See* Discrimination, anti-gay

Orientation. *See* Sexual orientation

Parents and Friends of Lesbians and Gays (P-FLAG), 88

Parents' expectations, 8, 10, 28, 29, 88, 123, 124. *See also* Families of gay men; Fathers; Mothers

Partners, domestic, 9

Passing as heterosexual. *See* Denial; Self-image of bisexual or homosexual men as heterosexual

Patriarchy, 4, 21, 54, 66, 140, 144, 146

Pattison, E. Mansell, and Myrna Loy Pattison, 80–81

Pattison study, 80–81, 82

Peers, 58, 76, 129. *See also* Friendship; Support groups/networks

Persons with AIDS (PWAs), 71, 100, 124, 147–48. *See also* AIDS

P-FLAG (Parents and Friends of Lesbians and Gays), 88

Pioneer archetype, 43. *See also* American myths and culture; Archetypes

About the Author

WILFRID R. KOPONEN is a lecturer in the English department at Stanford University. He has degrees from the University of California, Yale Divinity School, Columbia Business School and Brown University. He is a contributor to Greenwood's *Contemporary Gay American Novelists*, a recently released reference edited by Emmanuel Nelson.